D0209972

Introduction to Aesthetics

Introduction to Aesthetics
An Analytic Approach

George Dickie

New York   Oxford
OXFORD UNIVERSITY PRESS
1997

Oxford University Press

Oxford New York
Athens Auckland Bangkok Bogotá Bombay
Buenos Aires Calcutta Cape Town Dar es Salaam
Delhi Florence Hong Kong Istanbul Karachi
Kuala Lumpur Madras Madrid Melbourne
Mexico City Nairobi Paris Singapore
Taipei Tokyo Toronto

and associated companies in
Berlin Ibadan

Copyright © 1997 by Oxford University Press, Inc.

Published by Oxford University Press, Inc.
198 Madison Avenue, New York, NY 10016

Oxford is a registered trademark of Oxford University Press

All rights reserved. No part of this publication may be reproduced,
stored in a retrieval system, or transmitted, in any form or by any means,
electronic, mechanical, photocopying, recording, or otherwise,
without prior permission of Oxford University Press.

Library of Congress Cataloging-in-Publication Data

Dickie, George.
Introduction to aesthetics: an analytic approach / George Dickie.
p. cm. Includes bibliographical references and index.
ISBN 0-19-511303-9 (cloth).—ISBN 0-19-511304-7 (pbk).
1. Aesthetics. I. Title.
BH39.D494 1996 96-26825
111'.85—dc20 CIP

1 3 5 7 9 8 6 4 2

Printed in the United States of America
on acid-free paper

For Joyce

Contents

Preface

This book is intended to be an introduction to aesthetics. However, in addition to discussing the problems of aesthetics, I have not hesitated to put forward my own point of view. In doing so, I hope I have been fair to the theories criticized.

This book differs from most introductory aesthetics books in its historical introduction, whose purpose is to trace the central, organizing strains of the field and thereby set the stage for discussion of present-day problems in aesthetics.

The title of the first version of this book, published in 1971, was *Aesthetics: An Introduction*. Because of changes that have occurred in the field since that time, I have changed the title to *Introduction to Aesthetics: An Analytic Approach*. This narrower title more accurately describes the contents of this book in relation to the current state of aesthetics.

In this revised version, I have changed from a five-part organization to a four-part one. I have brought all the twentieth-century material from the original version on the concept of the aesthetic and twentieth-century philosophies of art before the 1950s into the historical introduction. This history now runs from ancient Greek times to the 1950s. The material on eighteenth-century theories of taste in this history has been extensively rewritten to bring it into accord with my 1996 book, *The Century of Taste: The Philosophical Odessey of Taste in the Eighteenth Century*. The sections on disinterested attention and Monroe Beardsley's metacriticism from the original version have been reorganized and rewritten.

The material on philosophies of art since the 1950s from the original version has been very substantially rewritten to conform with my 1974 book, *Art and the Aesthetic*, and my 1984 book, *The Art Circle*. The chapter on intentionalist criticism from the original version has been rewritten to bring it into accord with my article, "Defending Beardsley" (co-authored with W. Kent Wilson). The material on the evaluation of art from the original version has been reorganized and rewritten, and I have added a chapter on Nelson Goodman's account of the evaluation of art and a chapter on my own views of the evaluation of art to bring it into accord with my 1988 book, *Evaluating Art*.

I remain thankful to those persons who read all or parts of the manuscript of the original version of this book. My greatest debt is to the late Monroe Beardsley who read every chapter and gave me numerous helpful comments. The original version and many of my other projects would not have been possible without his help and encouragement. Both William Hayes and Elmer Duncan read the whole manuscript of the original version and each gave me much useful advice. The following persons read and commented helpfully on one or more chapters of the original version: Virgil Aldrich, Arthur Danto, Marcia Eaton, Göran Hermerén of Lund University, Sweden, Hilda Hein, Jerome Stolnitz, and Ben Tilghman. Bernadette McBrien and James Enright read the historical introduction of the original version and made many useful suggestions for its improvement. Timothy O'Donnell and Daniel Nathan also read the original version and made a number of very useful suggestions. My late wife, Joyce, provided a great deal of editorial assistance on the orginal version of this book.

I want to thank Anita Silvers, Carolyn Korsmeyer, and David Hoekema who read the revised manuscipt for Oxford University Press and made many useful comments.

G. D.

June 1996
Chicago, Illinois

Part I

An Historical Introduction to Analytic Aesthetics

Chapter 1

Introductory Remarks

The problems included in aesthetics are many and appear to be heterogeneous. This makes a study of the literature of aesthetics a perplexing matter. One of the major aims of Part I will be to outline the basic historical routes along which the problems of aesthetics have evolved from ancient Greek times to just past the middle of the twentieth century. Such an outline will serve to orient the reader and show how various problems are historically and logically related to each other. Without such a guide, the problems of aesthetics have the appearance of being a series of not very closely connected questions.

The questions included within the field of aesthetics have developed out of twin concerns in the history of thought: the theory of beauty and the theory of art. These two philosophical concerns were first discussed by Plato. Although philosophers have disagreed about the theory of art (roughly, disagreed about how art should be defined), they have until very recently continued to debate the theory of art pretty much on the same terms as Plato did. The theory of beauty, however, underwent a drastic change in the eighteenth century. Whereas earlier philosophers had discussed only the nature of beauty, eighteenth-century thinkers began to be interested in additional concepts: the sublime, the picturesque, and so on. This new activity may be thought of as either breaking up beauty into its parts or supplementing beauty with additional concepts.

At the same time that beauty was undergoing this change, a related development was taking place—the concept of taste was being worked out in the thought of such philosophers as Shaftesbury, Hutcheson, Burke, Alison, and Kant. In general, these philosophers were concerned about developing a theory of taste that would enable them to give an adequate analysis of the *experience* of the beautiful, the sublime, the picturesque, and related phenomena as they occur in nature and art. The notion of *disinterestedness* forms the center of these analyses and is the core of these philosophers' concept of taste. After the eighteenth century, theorizing in the taste mode was replaced by theorizing about the aesthetic. The word "beautiful" then came to be used either as a synonym of "having aesthetic value" or as one of the many aesthetic adjectives on the same level as "sublime" and "picturesque," which are used to describe art and nature. Since the end of the eighteenth century until the middle of the twentieth century, the twin concerns of aestheticians have been the theory of the aesthetic and the theory of art.

It may seem that the theory of the aesthetic became the prime concern of aestheticians and that the theory of art and the question of aesthetic qualities are simply subsumed under that theory. The concept of art is certainly related in important ways to the concept of the aesthetic, but the aesthetic cannot completely absorb the concept of art.

My discussions of beauty, eighteenth-century theories of taste, and the philosophy of art are, for the most part, developed by examining and summarizing the theories of historical figures. This arrangement permits the reader to glean some idea of the theories of, for example, Plato, Aristotle, Shaftesbury, and Kant and, at the same time, get a sense of how the problems and theories of aesthetics have developed through history.

The subject matter of twentieth-century analytic aesthetics will be presented here and divided into three areas: (1) the philosophy of the aesthetic, which in the nineteenth century replaced the philosophy of beauty, (2) the philosophy of art, and (3) the philosophy of criticism or metacriticism. Developments in twentieth-century philosophy and in the thought of twentieth-century art critics (mostly literary) have produced this third area in aesthetics. The philosophy of criticism or metacriticism is conceived of as a philosophical activity that analyzes and clarifies the basic concepts art critics use when they describe, interpret, or evaluate particular works of art. The development in philosophy that led to metacriticism in aesthetics was the widespread influence of analytic, linguistic philosophy, which conceives of philosophy as a second-order activity taking as its subject matter the language of some first-order activity. The relevant development in art criticism that led to metacriticism was the renewed emphasis by such critics as I. A. Richards and the school of critics known as the New Critics[1] on the importance of focusing critical attention on the works themselves rather than on the biography of the artist and the like. The rise of the New Criticism was important to the development of metacriticism because the concepts used by the New Critics in describing, interpreting, and evaluating works of art were taken by the metacritics (the philosophers) as their subject matter. Examples of the concepts an art critic might use are representation ("The painting is a representation of London

Bridge"), the intention of the artist ("The poem is a good one because the poet succeeded in realizing his intention"), or form ("This music has a sonata form").

The twentieth-century representatives of the theory of the aesthetic are the philosophers who use and defend a notion they call "the aesthetic attitude." Such philosophers maintain that there is an identifiable aesthetic attitude and that any object, artifactual or natural, toward which a person takes the aesthetic attitude can become an aesthetic object. An aesthetic object is the focus or cause of aesthetic experience and therefore the proper object of attention, appreciation, and criticism. There is nothing in metacriticism, that is, the analysis of the concepts of criticism, that actually contradicts the theory of the aesthetic attitude. In fact, Jerome Stolnitz, who has been one of the most prominent attitude theorists, conceives of aesthetics and presents it in his book[2] as the theory of the aesthetic attitude plus metacriticism. However, Monroe Beardsley, who was the foremost defender of metacriticism, developed his complete theory without using the notion of the aesthetic attitude.[3] Others have explicitly argued that the notion of the aesthetic attitude is untenable.[4] I will examine the aesthetic-attitude theory in detail in Chapter 3.

As noted, I will present twentieth-century analytic aesthetics as divided into three areas: the philosophy of the aesthetic, the philosophy of art, and the philosophy of criticism. Art and its subconcepts, however, are concepts that critics use, and for that reason it might be thought that they are simply concepts of criticism and that the philosophy of art is subsumable under the philosophy of criticism. But philosophers have had a *direct* interest in the concept of art since the time of Plato, long before the rise of the idea of the philosophy of criticism. If this argument is unconvincing, the independence of the philosophy of criticism and the philosophy of art is demonstrated by the fact that some of the essential aspects of works of art are not things of the sort to which criticism can be addressed. This point will be argued in later chapters.

I have been greatly helped in understanding all phases of the history of aesthetics by Monroe Beardsley's *Aesthetics from Classical Greece to the Present*.[5] My discussion of the development of aesthetic theory in eighteenth-century British philosophy relies heavily on a series of incisive studies by Jerome Stolnitz: "On the Significance of Lord Shaftesbury in Modern Aesthetic Theory,"[6] "Beauty: Some Stages in the History of an Idea,"[7] and "On the Origins of 'Aesthetic Disinterestedness.'"[8] On many points I have been helped by W. J. Hipple's *The Beautiful, The Sublime, and the Picturesque in Eighteenth-Century British Aesthetic Theory*.[9] In the years since the first version of this book was published, I have worked from time to time on eighteenth-century theories of taste; this has culminated in my book, *The Century of Taste: The Philosophical Odessey of Taste in the Eighteenth Century*.[10]

Chapter 2

The Theory of Beauty

Plato to the Nineteenth Century

Plato

Consider first the theory of beauty presented by Plato (428–348 B.C.) in the *Symposium*.[1] The general theme of the *Symposium* is love. Each of the characters in the dialogue gives a speech about love, and the question of beauty arises because it is concluded that beauty is the object of love. Socrates sets forth his view indirectly in his speech by relating a conversation with a woman named Diotima of Mantineia in which Diotima outlines the proper way to learn to love beauty. Instruction should begin at an early age and the young should first be taught to love one beautiful body (a human body). When this has occurred, it can be noticed that the first body shares beauty with other beautiful bodies. This provides a basis for loving all beautiful bodies, not just one. The learner ought then to come to realize that the beauty of souls is superior to the beauty of bodies. Once the physical has been transcended, the second spiritual stage is to learn to love beautiful practices and customs and to recognize that these activities share a common beauty. The next step is to recognize the beauty in the various kinds of knowledge. The final step is to experience beauty itself not embodied in anything physical or spiritual.

Notice that this process rises through increasingly abstract levels until it reaches the ultimate in abstraction—the Form of Beauty. Plato's treatment of beauty here is an example of his theory of the Forms. General terms have as their meanings abstract entities called "Forms." For example, the terms "beauty," "goodness," "justice," and "triangularity" have as their meanings the abstract entities or Forms *Beauty, Goodness, Justice,* and *Triangularity.* A particular, observed physical object or action is beautiful (or good or just or triangular) by virtue of its "participation" in the abstract Form of Beauty (or Goodness or Justice or Triangularity). Plato therefore draws a sharp line between (1) beautiful things that are included within the class of objects that we see, hear, or touch in "the world of sense" and (2) *Beauty* itself (and the other Forms), which exists apart from the world of sights and sounds in what Plato calls "the intelligible world." The nontemporal, nonspatial Forms are the eternal and unchanging objects of knowledge. The Platonic philosophy does not have much use for or interest in the world of sense, and considers it from a philosophical point of view to be a kind of illusion. Plato's philosophy as he presents it does not provide a very hospitable basis for either a theory of beauty or a theory of art as conceived today. For him beauty transcends the world of sense experience, which means that the experience of beauty (not beautiful things) is unlike what we would today describe as aesthetic experience. A philosophical theory that dismisses sights and sounds as illusory is not likely to have a sympathetic view of art.

Plato, however, does take an interest in the beautiful things of the world of sense, even though this interest is tinged with ambivalence. For example, he tries to discover the properties that all beautiful *things* have in common.[2] There are beautiful things that are simple (e.g., pure tones and single colors), and beautiful things that are complex. The simple things have unity in common and the complex things have measure and proportion of parts in common, which are also a form of unity. But Plato does not mean to identify beauty and unity; that is, he does not think that the word "beauty" and the word "unity" are identical in meaning. Something is beautiful by virtue of its participation in the Form of Beauty, and it is simply a discoverable fact (allegedly) that all beautiful things are unified. Unity is an *always accompanying* characteristic rather than a *defining* characteristic of beauty. In fact, Plato's view seems to be that beauty is a simple, unanalyzable property, which means that the term cannot be defined at all and is logically similar to such "primitive" terms as "red." It is frequently maintained that color terms such as "red" are logically primitive (cannot be defined) and that we can learn the meaning of such terms or how to use them properly only by direct experience—by someone pointing to the color and uttering the appropriate color word. So beauty is considered a simple property that a thing may possess in some degree; if a thing possesses beauty, it also always has *another* property, unity.

Plato's emphasis on measure and proportion set an important precedent for all subsequent philosophers. Some of the philosophers also followed him in adopting some version of his theory of the Forms and thought of beauty as an object that does not exist in the world of sense. Other philosophers simply identified beauty with measure and proportion as we find it in our sensuous experience.

Perhaps the most pervasive and important result of the theory of Plato was the establishment of the notion of contemplation as a central idea in the theory of beauty and, consequently, in the theory of aesthetic experience. Almost all subsequent theories have maintained in one way or another that the experience of beauty or, more generally, aesthetic experience involves contemplation. When philosophers such as Plato spoke of contemplation, they meant a kind of meditation in which a person has as the object of his awareness some nonsensuous entity, for example, the Form of Beauty or the Form of Triangularity. There is, of course, another sense of "contemplation" that is something like steadfast attention to some object, which may, of course, be an object of the world of sense. Most modern theories of aesthetics no doubt vaguely intend the latter sense of contemplation, but I think that some of the aura of the Platonic sense infects the use of "contemplation" in modern aesthetic theories. It is not so much the nonsensuous-object aspect as the aspect of reverent meditation that haunts modern theories. This spiritualistic holdover is probably at least partially responsible for the solemn and pompous attitude toward art and beauty that some persons display. "Contemplation" is one of those highly abstract words that sometimes masks important distinctions. Some experiences of art and nature are properly contemplative—for example, listening to religious music or looking at a statue of Buddha. But a great many of our experiences of art and nature are not contemplative—they are gay, spirited (not spiritual), titillating, humorous, uproariously funny, and so on. It would seem then that if a word is desired that will correctly characterize all our aesthetic experiences, "contemplation" is not appropriate because it is too narrow. Such narrowness is not surprising when we consider that the notion has its source in the views of unworldly philosophers.

St. Thomas Aquinas

The philosophy of Plato was influential for many centuries. For example, St. Augustine (A.D. 354–430), who was an important philosopher and theologian, perpetuated the Platonic theory of beauty as well as other Platonic doctrines. Almost nine hundred years after Augustine's time, the influence of Aristotle (384–322 B.C.), a student and contemporary of Plato, replaced Plato's influence on Christian thinkers. Aristotle had rejected the Platonic view that the Forms transcend the world of experience and exist in their own distinct realm. Aristotle's philosophy retains the concept of the Forms but maintains that they are embodied in nature as we experience it and have no independent existence. For Aristotle there are not two worlds—as Plato held—but only one, and it is perfectly intelligible. For Aristotle the world as we sensuously experience it is in no basic way illusory, and his philosophy provides a basis for an interest in the phenomena of both nature and art.

Within the sphere of Christian thought, Aristotelian philosophy received its most powerful and influential expression in the works of St. Thomas Aquinas

(A.D. 1225–1274). Aquinas's conception of beauty is not an unworldly one; he defines "beauty" as "that which pleases when seen."[3] Beauty is also related to desire in that "the beautiful is that which calms the desire, by being seen or known." Aquinas attempts to isolate the properties of the objects that do please and calm desire. He concludes that the conditions of beauty are three: perfection or unimpairedness, proportion or harmony, and brightness or clarity.

Aquinas's theory has both objective and subjective aspects. The stated conditions of beauty are objective features of the world of experience. But the idea of pleasing as part of the meaning of "beauty" introduces into the theory of beauty a subjective element. Being pleased is a property of a subject (a person) who has an experience, not a property of an object a person experiences. Aquinas's introduction of pleasing is a significant step away from the objective Platonic conception of beauty toward a subjective conception.

Aquinas stresses the cognitive (knowing) aspect of the experience of beauty. This means that in the experiences of beauty the mind grasps a Form that is embodied in the object of the experience. Aquinas seems to suggest that there is no single Form or property of beauty that is common to all beautiful things, but rather that the mind grasps or abstracts the Form that causes an object to be what it is. For example, the mind grasps the Form of Horseness when the object experienced is a horse. Of course, as any object whatsoever embodies a Form, the grasping of a Form is not the only thing involved in the experience of beauty. In addition, there are the three objective conditions of beauty that must be met and there is the subjective factor of being pleased by what is seen or known. The experience of beauty is a cognitive one but there is more to it than that, and the object of such a cognitive experience is not the Form of Beauty.

The Eighteenth Century: Taste and the Decline of Beauty

The eighteenth century was a critical time in the history of aesthetics. During this period a number of British and continental thinkers worked intensively on "the philosophy of taste" and provided the basis for aesthetics in its modern form. About the middle of the century, the minor German philosopher Alexander Baumgarten (1714–1762) coined the term "aesthetics," which in time became the name of the field.[4] Baumgarten's view, however, had very little influence on the subsequent development of aesthetics.

The philosophical tradition of explaining behavior and mental phenomena by attributing each kind of phenomenon to a distinct faculty of the mind had a strong influence on both the rationalists such as Baumgarten and the empiricist British philosophers. The doctrine of mental faculties had been worked out in great detail during the medieval period. According to this medieval doctrine, there are the vegetative faculty (which explains nutrition and procreation), the locomotive faculty (which explains movement), the rational faculty (which explains mental behavior), and the sensory faculties (which explain perception, imagination, and the like). Baumgarten tries to work aesthetics into a scheme of this type by conceiving of it as the science of sensory cognition. He thinks of art as a low-level means of cognition, that is, as a low-level means of gaining knowledge. In short, Baumgarten conceives of art as falling under the domain of both the sensory faculty and the intellectual faculty as a mode of inferior cognition. By contrast, the main tendency of the British philosophers is to subsume the experience of beauty under the sensory faculty alone, conceiving of it as a phenomenon of taste. The external, cognitive senses such as seeing or hearing are not the focus of their theorizing. By analogy with the theory of the internal senses (memory, imagination, and so on) developed by medieval philosophers, the British philosophers of the early eighteenth century focused on the notion of an internal, reactive sense of beauty (or something similar) that supposedly produces pleasure in response to the perception by the external senses of certain features of the external world.

Prior to the eighteenth century it was generally assumed by philosophers that "beauty" named an objective property of things, either a transcendental or an empirical property, depending on the theory. These earlier philosophers concluded that objective judgments of beauty could be made, just as we can make objective judgments about red things. But the analysis of beauty furnished by the eighteenth-century philosophers of taste shifts the focus of theorizing. They try to furnish a basis for objective judgments of beauty, but they do so by focusing their attention on the alleged faculty or faculties with which individuals react to certain features of the objective world. The apparatus of taste is conceived of by some of them to be a special single faculty (the sense of beauty), by some to be composed of several special faculties (the sense of beauty, the sense of the sublime, and so on), and by some as simply the ordinary cognitive and affective faculties functioning in an unusual way. When only the ordinary faculties are involved in a theory of taste, the mechanism of the association of ideas is sometimes seen as operating in an essential way with these faculties in the experience of beauty. These taste theorists are interested in human nature and its relationship to the objective world. This movement in aesthetics was not an isolated phenomenon but part of a larger philosophical movement that began with the interest of seventeenth-century philosophers in human nature and the limits of human knowledge. In the hands of these thinkers, philosophy became *subjectivized* in that they turned their attention in on the subject (the human being) and analyzed the states of the subject's mind and the subject's mental faculties. For all their interest in the nature of a subject experiencing beauty, the theorists of taste also attempted to specify the features external to the subject that evoke the experience of beauty.

Another important eighteenth-century development was the bringing in of notions other than that of beauty—for example, the notions of the sublime and the picturesque. This development gave a richer and more adequate theory, but it also made the theory more complicated and less unified. The traditional theory of beauty is highly unified, if for no other reason than that it is about one thing—

beauty. The disunity caused in the eighteenth century by the fragmentation of beauty with the introduction of notions such as sublimity, novelty, and the like, set up a tension that was resolved first by subsuming all such notions under the central concept of taste. Later, in the nineteenth century, all these various notions were subsumed under the central concept of the aesthetic, and aesthetic theory became the dominant mode of theorizing. By "aesthetic theory" I mean a theory that makes the concept of the aesthetic basic and defines other concepts of the theory in terms of the aesthetic. Both the concept of taste and the concept of the aesthetic—each in its time—furnished a unified theory and reestablished equilibrium.

In addition to the appearance of competing concepts, another reason for the decline of the theory of beauty was that a satisfactory definition of beauty (in terms of proportion, unity in variety, fitness, or whatever) could not be worked out. The alternative view that beauty is indefinable and transcendental was unacceptable to the British philosophers, who were committed to empiricism. Still another reason for the decline of the theory of beauty was a drift away from theories that conceive of the apparatus of taste as a single sense or a set of special senses specifically related to certain kinds of objects. From about the middle of the eighteenth century, associationist theories began to appear in which the ordinary cognitive and affective faculties plus the mental mechanism of the association of ideas constitute the apparatus of taste. These associationist theories propose that it is possible for almost anything to be beautiful, given the appropriate associations of ideas. Thus the mechanism of the association of the ideas provides a means for indefinitely extending the range of things that can be judged beautiful and also renders the traditional way of defining (i.e., by finding something common to all the things denoted by the term to be defined) impossible in the case of beauty. In associationist theories, beauty becomes an exceedingly diffuse concept that does not serve to distinguish one thing from another. This situation is similar to that of the present-day aesthetic-attitude theories that maintain that anything can be aesthetic if only it is experienced while in the aesthetic attitude.

Shaftesbury

It is appropriate to begin the discussion of eighteenth-century philosophers by outlining the main features of the thought of the third Earl of Shaftesbury (1671–1713) whose views, although transitional, are of great importance. His diffuse and unsystematic views are transitional because he holds a Platonic theory of beauty. He also, however, propounds and is the main source of the influential theory of the faculty of taste. These two theories are not logically inconsistent. Nevertheless, although a large number of eighteenth-century British philosophers adopted some version of the faculty-of-taste theory, few if any of these empirically inclined thinkers accepted the Platonic doctrine of the Forms. There is, Shaftesbury thinks, a single faculty of taste that can function either as a moral sense for making judgments about behavior or as a sense of beauty for making judgments about whether or not something possesses that quality. The object of a judgment of beauty is the platonic Form of Beauty. Thus, the sense of beauty for Shaftesbury has a cognitive function, that is, it is a mode of coming to *know* something. For Francis Hutcheson and other later theorists of taste, the sense of beauty is a noncognitive, reactive faculty that produces the feeling of pleasure. Shaftesbury of course does not deny that feeling plays a role in matters of taste.

Shaftesbury was one of the first eighteenth-century thinkers to focus attention on the sublime, and this is his second influential contribution to the theory of taste. His interest in the sublime is probably related to his conception of the world as the creation of God; the vastness and incomprehensibility of that creation could only be described as sublime. Even though Shaftesbury distinguished a new taste category, he maintained a unified theory by classifying the sublime as one kind of beauty. Both the noting of the sublime and the doctrine of taste were important for later theory.

Shaftesbury made another important contribution when he introduced the notion of *disinterestedness,* which was to become integral first to the concept of taste and later to the concept of the aesthetic. Shaftesbury begins by insisting on the significance of disinterestedness for morality. That is, in order for an action to have moral merit (not simply good consequences), the person acting must be disinterested, that is, must not be motivated solely by selfish motives. Shaftesbury was reacting to the views of the seventeenth-century philosopher Thomas Hobbes who had maintained that all behavior is driven by selfish motives. Shaftesbury introduced disinterestedness into the theory of beauty in an almost incidental way. The example which is frequently cited as Shaftesbury's demonstration of the necessity of disinterestedness for the appreciation of beauty occurs in a passage in which his main concern is to defend the Platonic thesis that "whatever in nature is beautiful or charming is only a faint shadow of that first beauty."[5] ("That first beauty" is the Platonic Form of Beauty.) Shaftesbury tries to defend his Platonic thesis by constructing an analogy that contrasts the contemplation of beautiful things in the world of sense with the desire to possess them. The analogy is supposed to illuminate the relation between the Form of Beauty and beautiful things (its "faint shadow") and show the superiority of the Form. In the analogy, the Form of Beauty is likened to beautiful things and beautiful things are likened to the desire to possess beautiful things. It is debatable whether Shaftesbury's remarks can be called an argument, but it is the examples in his analogy that turned out to be important for the theory of taste and aesthetic theory, not his argument.

Shaftesbury actually gives several examples, all of which contrast the contemplation of beautiful things with the desire to possess them. The general point he is making with his examples is that the contemplation of beautiful things and the desire to possess them are *distinct*. One example contrasts the contemplation of a tract of land with the desire to possess the land, another example contrasts the contemplation of a grove of trees with the desire to eat the fruit of the trees, and another contrasts the contemplation of human beauty with the desire for sexual possession. This last example most clearly contains the elements that later become important.

> . . . certain powerful forms in human kind . . . draw after them a set of eager desires, wishes, and hopes; no way suitable, I must confess, to your rational and refined contemplation of beauty. The proportions of this living architecture [human bodies], as wonderful as they are, inspire nothing of a studious or contemplative kind.[6]

This last example also illustrates the distinctness of the comtemplation of beautiful things and the desire to possess them, but Shaftesbury here also claims that the contemplation of beautiful things and the desire to possess them are in conflict. Following Shaftesbury, some theories of taste and all aesthetic theories have held that selfish or interested desires, of which the desire for possession is the paradigm, are destructive of the appreciation of beauty. Some theorists have even concluded that selfish or practical desires are wholly incompatible with such appreciation.

That the contemplation of the beauty of an object is quite distinct from the desire to possess the object must be granted, but Shafteshury's suggestion that such desires are "no way suitable" when contemplating beauty is both hasty and unfortunate. It is true that the desire for possession might be so compelling that it would be incompatible with the appreciation of beauty. It is, however, a mistake to generalize from an extreme case. From the obvious fact that ungovernable desire is incompatible with the appreciation of beauty, it does not follow that all desires are in "no way suitable" to appreciation. Shaftesbury's failure to appreciate the importance of degrees of desire is probably rooted in two related conceptions: (1) a puritanism that treats all desire alike and (2) a Platonism that views both the senses and desire as suspect. The fact that for thousands of years people have appreciated the beauty of art that frequently displays "the proportions of this living architecture" and invites desire does not seem to have occurred to Shaftesbury.

Given his philosophical orientation, it is not surprising that Shaftesbury fails to make the appropriate distinction. Unfortunately, a whole tradition in aesthetics has followed him on this point. The philosophers most influenced in this regard are the aesthetic-attitude theorists of the nineteenth and twentieth centuries, although not every such philosopher follows the extreme disinterestedness line. It should also be noted that Shaftesbury's theory of the disinterested appreciation of beauty is developed in terms of motives: interested or selfish motives (and activity) are thought to undercut appreciation. But many aesthetic-attitude theorists, especially in the present day, have extended the scope of disinterestedness and developed the view that there is a special kind of *perception*—disinterested perception—that is the foundation of aesthetic experience. I will discuss disinterested perception at some length in Chapter 3.

Hutcheson

Francis Hutcheson (1694–1746) is perhaps the single best representative of the eighteenth-century British theorists of taste. In him the transition to doctrines that characterize this group is complete. There is no trace of Platonism; his theory focuses squarely on the phenomena of sense; his theory contains an account of the faculty of taste and the pleasure of taste; and disinterestedness is worked smoothly into his conception of sense.

In Hutcheson's view, not only does the word "beauty" not name a platonic Form, it does not name any object that is seen, heard, or touched. "Beauty," he says, names an "idea rais'd in us";[7] that is, it denotes an object in the private consciousness of a subject (a person). The idea that is aroused is pleasure and it is aroused by the perception of certain kinds of external objects. Beauty, in being tied necessarily to a subject, has become subjectivized. Hutcheson, however, still connects it to certain kinds of perceptual objects in the world.

Once the experience of beauty is recognizable, an inquiry can be made as to whether there are any features of the objects of perception that regularly trigger the experience of beauty. Hutcheson's answer is *uniformity in variety*. He sometimes refers to uniformity in variety as beauty, but this must be taken as a kind of shorthand because in his theory, strictly speaking, it is the cause of beauty. What Hutcheson meant by "the idea of beauty" might best be rendered as the beauty feeling, that is, pleasure.

Shaftesbury holds that there is a single sense with several functions and that it is cognitive in nature, that is, that it enables the mind to know of something external to the mind. Hutcheson believes there are a number of distinct internal senses (the moral sense, the sense of beauty, the sense of grandeur, and so on) with single functions and that they are affective and reactive (noncognitive) in nature, that is, that they function to produce pleasure. These senses are *internal* senses, which means that their objects are internal to the mind, as constrasted with the external senses such a sight and hearing, whose objects are external to the mind. When Hutcheson speaks of the internal *sense* of beauty, he means a power or ability to have pleasure aroused in a mind.

Hutcheson's formalistic view that the beauty pleasure is caused by the perception of the complex idea *uniformity in variety* excludes from the cause of beauty pleasant, simple ideas such as single colors and single sounds. Simple ideas are ruled out because he believes that the pleasure from them derives from the external senses and that beauty is tied to an internal sense. Thus, Hutcheson cannot account for what we would call "sheer beauty of color" because single colors are simple ideas. His theory also can not account for any other kind of nonformal beauty.

Following Shaftesbury, Hutcheson tries to refute Thomas Hobbes's psychological theory that all behavior is selfish. One reason for calling the faculty of beauty a sense, according to Hutcheson, is that awareness of beauty (the beauty feeling) is immediate, that is, unmediated by thought. The experience of beauty is like the taste of salt or sugar in this respect. Hutcheson thinks that if the experience of beauty is free of thought and calculation, then such appreciations cannot be selfish. If I open my eyes and see a red pencil, my awareness of redness is not influenced by any selfish desires, and even if it is greatly in my selfish interest to see green at that moment, there is nothing I can do about it. Hutcheson's theory is designed to make the experience of beauty and judgments about beauty objective by tying them to fundamental, inborn faculties of the human constitution and render them disinterested by maintaining that these faculties are senses and hence impervious to influence. As Hutcheson puts it, the sense of beauty is passive; that is, it simply reacts in an automatic fashion, and the beauty feeling does not derive from "any knowledge of principles, proportions, causes, or of the usefulness of the object."[8]

Hutcheson claims that taste is an objective aspect of human nature and is thus objective. He is, nevertheless, aware that disagreements over taste occur. He tries to explain these disagreements as the result of either physical defect or the association of ideas. In the first kind of case, for example, a person with poor eyesight or one who is deaf will not be able to appreciate certain objects of taste. In the other case, a person who has experienced pain in the presence of a beautiful object may not be able to appreciate its beauty because of the associated pain. For Hutcheson, the association of ideas is a psychological mechanism that can pervert taste from its natural objects.

Burke

Edmund Burke (1728–1797) published his book on the sublime and the beautiful[9] shortly after the middle of the eighteenth century in 1757. The book's most important contribution to the historical line being traced here is his full-scale theory of the sublime. In contrast to Shaftesbury, he treats the sublime as a category separate from beauty—in fact, he regards the sublime as opposed to beauty. This splitting put an additional strain on the unity in the eighteenth-century theory of taste.

Burke rejects the theory of special internal senses, perhaps because he saw that it would be very difficult or even impossible to prove the metaphysical thesis that there are internal senses. He tries to make the ordinary affective phenomena of pleasure and pain the basis for beauty and the sublime. He distinguishes between positive pleasure and relative pleasure, which he calls "delight." Delight results from the removal of pain or the removal of the anticipation of pain. The pleasure taken in beauty is love (positive pleasure), and this pleasure is generally related to the passions useful for the preservation of society. The pleasure taken in the sublime is delight (relative pleasure), and this being pleased by the removal of pain or threat of pain is generally related to the passions useful for the individual's preservation. Burke says, "By beauty I mean, that quality, or those qualities in bodies, by which they cause love, or some passion similar to it."[10] Unfortunately, he then defines "love" a few lines further on as "that satisfaction which arises to the mind upon contemplating any thing beautiful."[11] These two passages form a circle and

Burke has been criticized for his reasoning. A few lines later, however, he specifies those qualities of bodies—smallness, smoothness, being polished, lines deviating insensibly from "the right line" (right angle), and so on—that trigger love, and perhaps this specification is enough to remove the viciousness from the circle. The sublime is whatever excites delight. The experience of the sublime is induced, for example, by obscure objects and objects of great size. Such objects ordinarily threaten and terrorize us, but if we can contemplate these objects and still be secure, then they are experienced as sublime.

Whereas Hutcheson claims the there is only one beauty-making property—uniformity in variety, Burke claims that there are a number of beauty-making properties and sublimity-making properties. His is a "short-list" theory rather a single-formula one like Hutcheson's. Thus, Burke pursues a different strategy in trying to account for beauty.

Disinterestedness plays a role in Burke's theory of beauty, and its function is more accurately described by Burke than it is by either Shaftesbury or the later aesthetic-attitude theorists of the nineteenth and twentieth century. He illustrates his view with an example of male love and desire:

> We shall have a strong desire for a woman of no remarkable beauty; whilst the greatest beauty in men, or in other animals, though it causes love, yet excites nothing at all of desire. Which shews that beauty, and the passion caused by beauty, which I call love, is different from desire, though desire may some-times operate along with it. [12]

Burke distinguishes between love (the appreciation of beauty) and desire for possession, which is to say that love is disinterested. But he finds no necessary incompatibility between love and the desire for possession—they may sometimes "operate" along with one another.

Hume

David Hume's "Of the Standard of Taste" [13] was published shortly after the middle of the eighteenth century in 1757, the same year that Burke's book appeared. Hume's account of the nature of taste is basically Hutchesonian in flavor—but Hume has a much deeper understanding of the philosophical issues involved in theorizing about taste than do the theorists discussed thus far. For example, Hume makes explicit that he assumes, as did other British theorists, that the inquiry into the nature of taste is an empirical investigation of certain aspects of human nature. Hume's theory is, I believe, the best of the eighteenth-century theories of taste.

"Of the Standard of Taste," which is a short essay, is Hume's mature work on the problem of taste. He begins the essay by admitting that there is a great variation and disagreement among individuals on questions of taste. The task of the essay is to show that these disagreements are due to the accidental features of the circumstances in which people find themselves. Hume first states the skeptical view that it is impossible to dispute taste and then claims that such a view entails the absurd consequent that we cannot rate any work above any other. He then writes:

> Whoever would assert an equality of genius and elegance between Ogilby and Milton, or Bunyan and Addison, would be thought to defend no less an extravagance, than if he had maintained a mole-hill to be as high as Teneriffe, or a pond as extensive as the ocean.[14]

Hume's argument might be called "a disproportionate pairs" argument. He selects pairs of works of art in which the works are of greatly different values—a great work and a very poor one. Hume thinks that when one is faced with such a pair that even a skeptic will have to agree that the one work is better than the other. He thus concluldes that the skeptical view is false.

Hume rejects reasoning *a priori* as the source of what he calls "the rules of composition" (the standard of taste). This view he shares with the other British aestheticians we have discussed, except Shaftesbury. He is denying that we rationally intuit beauty or the rules that govern it. He affirms that the foundation of the rules of composition is *experience*. The rules of composition are "but general observations, concerning what has been universally found to please in all countries and in all ages."[15] His claim is then that the normative question of what it is correct to call beautiful can be solved by a comprehensive empirical survey of the taste of individuals.

But even if Hume conceives of himself as sketching the outlines of an empirical investigation, he states that not every case of a person being pleased is to count as evidence for the generalizations that are the rules of composition. Certain kinds of cases must be discounted, and Hume makes a careful attempt to spell out the conditions under which a proper inquiry can be made.

> When we would make an experiment of this nature, and would try the force of any beauty or deformity, we must choose with care a proper time and place, and bring the fancy to a suitable situation and disposition. A perfect serenity of mind, a recollection of thought, a due attention to the object; if any of these circumstances be wanting, our experiment will be fallacious, and we shall be unable to judge of the catholic and universal beauty.[16]

These conditions must be met in order to rule out cases of being pleased that are the result of the caprices of fashion and the mistakes of ignorance and envy. In addition to these considerations, there is the alleged fact that what Hume here calls "mental taste" is more acute in some individuals than in others. Just as some people can discriminate more accurately in the case of "bodily taste"—for example, in distinguishing the subtle qualities of wine—some are better in discriminating those qualities that trigger the faculty of taste. Only those who possess what Hume calls "delicacy of taste" are fit subjects for his *experiment*.

Hume's methodological considerations have now been spelled out. His substantive, although very abstract, conclusion is well stated in the following quotation:

> Though it be certain, that beauty and deformity, more than sweet and bitter, are not qualities in objects, but belong entirely to the sentiment, internal or external; it must be allowed, that there are certain qualities in objects, which are fitted by nature to produce those particular feelings.[17]

Notice that beauty and its opposite, deformity, are not *in objects* but are *feelings*. The feelings, however, are not just feelings but are feelings linked by the nature of our human constitution to "certain qualities in objects." Thus, it is possible to have objective judgments about beauty and deformity in the sense that universal agreement among normal subjects is possible. Notice also that Hume mentions "certain qualities in objects" that cause pleasure. Unlike Hutcheson, he does not try to reduce them to a formula (uniformity in variety). On the other hand, unlike Burke, he does not try to specify a complete, *short* list of beauty-making qualities. Hume mentions in passing some twenty or so beauty-making qualities such as uniformity, variety, luster of color, clearness of expression, exactness of imitation. He gives the impression that his rather long list is by no means complete or can be completed.

After having developed an objective theory of taste based on certain alleged stabilities in human nuture, at the end of his essay Hume allows for certain acceptable variations of taste due to age and temperament. Young men prefer "amorous and tender images," but older men prefer "wise philosophical reflections." "Mirth or passion, sentiment or reflection; which ever of these most predominates in our temper, it gives us a peculiar sympathy with the writer who resembles us."[18] In such cases no standard of taste is available to rate one preference better than the other. Is Hume consistent in allowing such variation? Probably so, for the diversity has its origin in the factors of age and temperament, factors that cannot be ruled out by the conditions of Hume's experiment and are not due to the inability to discriminate.

Alison

Archibald Alison (1757–1839) published his book on the theory of taste near the end of the century in 1790.[19] His central concern is to map the terrain of the faculty of taste, but he abandons the idea of special internal senses of beauty and the sublime in favor of a theory involving the ordinary cognitive and affective faculties and the psychological mechanism of the association of ideas. Whereas Hutcheson thought that the association of ideas can pervert taste, Alison claims that the association of ideas is an essential aspect of the faculty of taste.

The faculty of taste for Alison is "that . . . by which we perceive and enjoy whatever is Beautiful or Sublime in the works of Nature or Art."[20] By "perceive" here Alison means not simply the perception of the external world but something broader, namely, awareness; thus, he could speak of perceiving (feeling) pain. For Alison, the faculty of taste is composed of sensibility (emotional response) and the imagination (the locus of the association of ideas). He maintains that human beings are so constituted that certain features of the material world, either objects of nature or of art, cause them to experience what he calls the "emotion of taste." In order for an object of the material world to evoke the emotion of taste, it must be a sign of or expressive of a quality of mind. For works of art, the mind is the artist's, and for natural objects, the mind is that of the "Divine Artist." A curious aspect of his theory is that it seems to presuppose the existence of God; what is essentially a psychological theory suddenly presupposes a theological commitment. But this commitment could be avoided by saying that the emotion of taste is evoked when a natural object is *taken to be* sign of the Divine Artist.

Alison's description of the functioning of the faculty of taste is bewilderingly complex, involving a host of distinct items. First, when an object of taste is perceived, a simple emotion, say, cheerfulness, is produced in the mind. The simple emotion produces a thought (typically an image) in the imagination. This first thought produces a second thought in the imagination and it a third, so that by the association of ideas a whole *unified* train of images is produced. Each image in the train of associated thoughts also produces a simple emotion, so that in addition to the original simple emotion that started the train of thought, there is a set of simple emotions, whose members are unified by their relation to the coherent train of thought. This set of simple emotions produces the emotion of taste, which is a complex emotion. In addition, each simple emotion is accompanied by a simple pleasure, and the functioning of the imagination also produces a simple pleasure. This set of simple pleasures constitutes the complex pleasure that accompanies the emotion of taste and which Alison calls "delight." Probably the only way to get a clear idea of this scheme would be for the reader to draw a diagram of it.

The association of ideas is also involved, according to this view, in an aspect of the material world being expressive of or a sign of a quality of mind. According to Alison, an aspect of the material world is expressive of or a sign of a quality of mind because it has become associated in some way with that quality. So, the association of ideas plays a role both in the building up of the emotion of taste and supplying the basis for the expressiveness of aspects of the material world.

According to Alison, any aspect of the material world may become associated with a quality of mind and thereby evoke the simple emotion required to initiate the emotion of taste. Thus, in this view, it is possible for *any* aspect of the material world to become beautiful, no matter what it looks like! It is not objects' perceptible qualities that cause them to be beautiful but their associations! Alison concludes that a blind person can have the same experience of beauty of color that a sighted person can because both a blind person and a sighted person can form all the associations that color can acquire.

Alison's theory appears to be superior in some respects to many earlier theories—Hutcheson's, for example—in that it appears to provide a basis for explaining the richness and complexity of the experience of art and nature. It is difficult to explain a great deal of beauty wholly in terms of uniformity in variety, and thus Hutcheson's view is too limited. Alison's theory, however, goes to the opposite extreme, claiming that anything in the material world can be beautiful if it has the right associations.

Alison's use of the notion of disinterestedness is evident when he considers the state of mind "most favorable to the emotion of taste." This occurs, he says, when

> attention is so little occupied by any private or particular object of thought, as to leave us open to all the impressions which the objects that are before us can produce. It is upon the vacant and the unemployed, accordingly, that the objects of taste make the strongest impression.[21]

"The husbandman" and "the man of business" are oblivious to the beauty of, say, some aspect of nature because they are interested in profiting from it, and "the philosopher" is oblivious because he is lost in thought. Because Alison here speaks of the conditions "*most* favorable to the emotion of taste," it does not follow that interest is incompatible with the emotion of taste. Still, the drift of his remarks gives aid and comfort to those who wish to claim that the experience of beauty is incompatible with interest in the useful, the personal, and so on. Alison himself is inclined in this direction when he concludes that criticism destroys appreciation because it considers art in relation to rules or compares it to other art. That criticism is incompatible with appreciation is an unfortunate and persistent prejudice that results from pressing the significance of disinterestedness too far.

Kant

The famous work on the theory of taste, *Critique of Judgment*, by the German philosopher Immanuel Kant (1724–1804) was published in 1790—the same year Alison's book appeared.[22] The major roadblock to understanding Kant's theory of taste is that it is part of a formidable philosophical system. His statement of the theory bristles with technical terms and is organized according to a complex scheme worked out earlier for his theory of knowledge. Insofar as it is possible, the technical aspects of his system are avoided here. I will discuss only his theory of beauty; his theory of the sublime is omitted. Kant consciously uses the work of many of the thinkers already discussed and is clearly within the tradition of the philosophy of taste.

To understand Kant's theory of beauty, it is necessary to have some idea of his philosophical system, which differs radically from that of the British empiricist philosophers. These philosophers held that knowledge derives wholly from experience, and Hume held that we cannot be certain of anything. Kant tried to develop a system that would show how it is possible for us to have some knowledge that is certain, that is, *a priori* knowledge that does not derive from experience.[23] In brief, Kant maintains that the mind itself contributes the general structure that our experience has and that for this reason we can have certain *a priori* knowledge of a very general sort. For example, we know, independently of any experience, that every event will have a cause because the mind structures the events of our experience into a causal network. Kant held that our knowledge is limited to the domain of experience and that, for example, we cannot *know* that God exists.

In his moral philosophy, however, Kant argued that we have a justified belief in the existence of God because God's existence is a necessary prerequisite for our morality. Although Kant claimed that a theoretical proof of God's existence cannot be given, he claimed that we are nevertheless assured that God exists and that the universe is his creation.

Thus, Kant comes to his theory of taste with the assurance that nature is God's teleological (purposive) system. This system's organisms (humans, animals, plants, etc.), which Kant calls "the purposes of nature," are, Kant says, God's "unfathomably great art."[24] Since he believed that the goal of art is beauty, Kant apparently concluded that organisms (or rather their form), which are God's art, must be beautiful because if anyone could achieve the goal of art, God could. This appears to be the reasoning behind Kant conclusion that natural beauty is "the form of purpose," that is, the form of the purposes of nature.

Kant accepts as given, as did Hutcheson and others, that there are judgments of taste (beauty) and that "beauty" is not a concept, that is, refers in some way to pleasure and not to something in the objective world. There are, Kant thinks, only two kinds of judgments: (1) ordinary judgments that apply a known concept to something in the world—for example, apply the concept *red* and get "This apple is red" and (2) reflective judgments that try by reflecting to find a concept to apply to something(s) when no such concept yet is known—for example, when someone tries to think up a more generic concept that will cover two or more species of animals. Since Kant thinks that beauty does not refer to anything in the world, that is, that beauty is not a concept, he concludes that a judgment of beauty cannot be an ordinary judgment that applies a known concept to something in the world. Since the only other kind of judgment is reflective judgment, Kant concludes that a judgment of beauty must be a reflective judgment, that is, one that seeks a new concept. Since beauty is not a concept, a judgment of beauty is a reflective judgment looking for a nonexistent concept.

Kant's theory of taste has its place within his account of the aesthetic. Kant uses the term "aesthetic" in a very broad sense to include not only judgments of beauty and the sublime but also judgments about pleasure in general. For Kant, all aesthetic judgments focus on pleasure, which is a property of the experiencing subject rather than of the objective world. Such judgments are *subjective* because pleasure does not play a role in the cognition of the objective world external to the subject. But if judgments of beauty are subjective, Kant also thinks that they are stable and universal in a way that other pleasures are not. That is, he seeks a theory that will show that although the pleasure felt in the taste of, say, chocolate or anchovies is merely personal, the pleasure felt with beauty is universal and necessary.

Kant divides the discussion of his theory of beauty into four parts, each of which treats a major concept. These concepts are (1) disinterestedness, (2) universality, (3) necessity, and (4) the form of purpose. The theory may be summarized in a sentence: A judgment of beauty is a disinterested, universal, and necessary judgment concerning the pleasure that everyone *ought* to derive from the experience of a form of purpose.

Disinterestedness. Kant argues, following the British philosophers, that judgments of beauty are disinterested. He characterizes interest and disinterest (in a way that is unique to him) in terms of desire and real existence; that is, to view something with an interest is to have a desire that that thing actually exist but to view something with disinterest is to be indifferent to its existence. Care should be taken to note that Kant does not say that a person who makes a judgment of beauty is indifferent to the existence of the object of the judgment, but simply that the judgment of beauty is independent of the interest in real existence. Once a person correctly makes a judgment of beauty, then no doubt he will typically assume an interest in the existence of the object responsible for his experience, but this is a second and different judgment. One of Shaftesbury's examples can be used to illustrate the point. If I appreciate the qualities of fruit in the way that involves a judgment of beauty, my appreciation and my judgment are directed toward the visual qualities of the object I am aware of and not toward the existence of the object that makes that awareness possible.

Universality. Kant asserts that the universality of judgments of beauty is deducible from their disinterested nature. If a person is pleased with something in a disinterested way, then the pleasure cannot derive from anything personal and peculiar to the person. Interest springs from individual inclinations, but this is just what disinterestedness rules out. Consequently, if disinterested pleasure is possible, then it must derive from what is common to all humanity and not from interests peculiar to only some people. When we utter judgments of taste, we speak, Kant says, "with a universal voice." But he maintains that judgments of taste ("This rose in beautiful") are subjective, which means that *beautiful* is not a concept as, for example, *red* is. When one says that a rose is red, the concept *red* is being applied to a rose and the concept refers to an objective feature of the world. Any normal person can look at the rose and see that it is red, and this confers universality on the statement, "This rose is red." But how can this be done when "beautiful" does not refer to something objective? Kant falls back on the familiar notion of the faculty of taste, not the special-sense version but the version in which ordinary cognitive faculties function in an unusual way. First, the cognitive faculties are common to all people and in their ordinary employment produce universally valid judgments about the objective world. In judgments of taste, which are reflective judgments, rather than doing their usual *work* of applying concepts, the cognitive faculties of the understanding (the faculty of concepts) and the imagination engage in *free play*—an interaction in which no concept is *or can be* applied. This free play exhibits the harmonious relation of the cognitive faculties and results in the pleasure felt in judgments of taste. The pleasure is universally valid because it depends solely on universal faculties.

Necessity. Judgments of beauty, an addition to their universality, are also necessary. This necessity is justified by Kant in a way similar to that used to justify the universality of judgments of taste. When we say that something is beautiful, we are, Kant thinks, making a demand that everyone agree with *us*. He states that of course not everyone *will* agree with *us*. The reason that we make such a demand is that we are talking about something causing a pleasure that derives from faculties common to all people. Thus, if something gives one person pleasure as the result of the free play of the cognitive faculties (which all persons share), it ought to give any person pleasure. In other words, the thing ought *necessarily* to give pleasure to every person. Kant, however, denies that we can derive general rules of beauty. Every judgment of taste is a *singular* judgment, and no general rule can be formulated from the whole set of judgments. If Kant's view is correct, it is easy enough to see why all people ought to agree, but it does not tell us how we can get such agreement.

Form of purpose. Disinterestedness, universality, and necessity are primarily involved with the experiencing subject. The fourth concept that Kant discusses—the form of purpose—focuses on the object of the appreciation. Kant is raising the point that Hutcheson tried to make by talking about uniformity in variety. Philosophers of taste generally tried, in addition to giving a description of the faculty of taste, to specify exactly what feature or features of the objective world it is that triggers that faculty. Like Hutcheson, Kant focuses on formal relations as the stimulus of the beauty experience. As noted earlier, Kant thinks that organisms ("purposes of nature") are God's unfathomably great art and that they are therefore beautiful, or rather that their forms are. It is in this way that Kant works the notion of purpose into his theory. He must be careful in doing this, however, because the recognition that something has a purpose involves applying a concept, which would make the judgment of taste objective rather than subjective and would take that judgment past immediately experienced qualities. Consequently, he asserts that it is recognition of the *form* of purpose, not recognition of the purpose itself, that evokes the beauty experience. The form of a work of art—for example, the design of a painting or the compositional structure of a musical piece—is the result of purposive activity of a human agent. The forms of nature are the result of the purposive activity of God. Judgments of taste focus on these forms themselves without considering them in relation to the purpose they realize.

Kant denies that color as such is beautiful; he says it is agreeable. The agreeable pleasure of color may be enjoyed along with pleasure taken in form, but the two are distinct. Only form, which is universal and necessary because of its *a priori* source, is beautiful. Color, according to Kant, is part of the *content* rather than the form or structure of experience and, consequently, is not *a priori*. People may disagree about what colors they find pleasant without raising any problem, but they ought to agree about form because it is *a priori*. Of course, forms may be built up out of colored elements, but the forms are distinguishable from their elements. Similar considerations hold for nonvisual forms and their elements.

It is widely held that Kant's theory of taste is the culmination and the best of the eighteenth-century theories. As I indicated earlier, I believe that this distinction should go to Hume's theory. There are a number of very serious difficulties in Kant's theory.

First, Kant's concludes that "Beauty is an object's form of *purposiveness* insofar as it is perceived in the object *without the presentation of a purpose.*" The identification of beauty with the form of purposiveness is entirely implausible. To illustrate his thesis, Kant gives lists of forms of purpose that are beautiful; for example, he lists as natural beauties parrots, hummingbirds, and birds of paradise. Granted that the birds he lists are beautiful and are forms of purposiveness as understood in Kant's theory, but his list is too short. It should include starlings, vultures, and the like, since they are just as much forms of purposiveness as are the listed birds. Kant's formula is, thus, implausible because it captures many nonbeautiful things.

Second, beautiful things fall within a range of more and less beautiful, that is, they admit of degrees. For purposes of the argument, let it be said that a bird of paradise is more beautiful than a parrot. Kant's theory has no way of taking account of this because the one bird is just as much a form of purpose as the other. Another degree problem is that beauty is a threshold notion. For example, there are many beautiful people, but most people are ordinary looking—that is, most people fall below the beauty threshold. Kant's theory has no way of taking account of this because being a form of purposiveness does not admit of degrees. A beautiful person and an ugly person are equally forms of purposiveness as Kant's theory pictures things.

Finally, many experiences of beauty—sunsets, for example—depend largely on color independently of any formal aspects. Kant's theory (and Hutcheson's) cannot take account of this because he makes form the whole story. Any theory that rules out color as a source of beauty has got to be defective.

Summary of Eighteenth-Century Theories of Taste

By the end of the eighteenth century, the theory of the faculty of taste in its various versions had pretty well run its course. By this time, philosophers had largely lost their taste for faculties as a way of solving philosophical problems. When faculties were no longer available to furnish a kind of minimal unity to the fragmented elements of the field, the concept of the aesthetic seized the imagination of philosophers and they began to organize their theories around it instead. Each of the philosophies of taste discussed here subjectivized beauty, but only partially; for each claimed that some specific feature of the *objective* world triggered the faculty of taste. Thus, each theory made an attempt to anchor itself to some objective aspect of the world. The following list summarizes this feature of each theory.

Shaftesbury	the Form of Beauty
Hutcheson	uniformity in variety
Burke	a short list of qualities—smallness, smoothness, etc.
Hume	a long list of qualities—uniformity, variety, luster of color, etc.
Alison	a sign of a quality of mind
Kant	the form of purpose

In the case of Alison's theory, the association of ideas virtually negates "a sign of a quality of mind" as the objective feature of the world that triggers the faculty of taste, since the theory allows that almost anything can by association become a sign of a quality of mind.

The significance of the eighteenth century for aesthetics may be roughly summarized as follows. Before the eighteenth century, *beauty* was a central concept; during the century, it was replaced by the concept of *taste*; by the end of the century, the concept of taste had been exhausted and the way was open for the concept of *the aesthetic.*

The Nineteenth Century: The Birth of the Aesthetic—Schopenhauer

As the philosophy-of-taste approach was abandoned, "aesthetic" theories began to take hold. The following is a quotation from the work of the nineteenth-century German philosopher Arthur Schopenhauer who is largely responsible for the introduction of aesthetic theory.

> When we say that a thing is beautiful, we thereby assert that it is an object of our aesthetic contemplation . . . it means that the sight of the thing makes us objective, that is to say, that in contemplating it we are no longer conscious of ourselves as individuals, but as pure will-less subjects of knowledge. [25]

This theory is almost totally subjectivized in that a thing is said to be beautiful because it is an object of a person's (a *subject's*) aesthetic contemplation. No specific objective character is required for something to be beautiful; an object's beauty is acquired as the result of being the object of some person's aesthetic consciousness. Almost anything can become beautiful if aesthetic consciousness is turned on it, but there are limits. Schopenhauer held that the obscene and the nauseating cannot become objects of aesthetic consciousness.

Whereas Kant's view has all the features of a theory of taste—a faculty of taste, a specific kind of object of taste, and the like—Schopenhauer retains from Kant only the notion of cognitive faculties functioning in a nonordinary way. Schopenhauer imports Platonic and other speculative metaphysical ideas into the theory. One result of these importations is that Schopenhauer maintains that aesthetic consciousness must have as its object some Platonic Idea. The other important metaphysical importation is the idea that everything that happens in the world is the expression of an underlying cosmic Will. Each person's will is an expression of this Will. Each animal action is an expression of this Will. Even inorganic matters are a function of this underlying cosmic Will; for example, a stone's *supporting* of another stone on top of it is an expression of the cosmic Will.

Schopehauer maintains that ordinary consciousness is the intellect (the cognitive faculties) totally in the service of a person's will and, hence, in the service of the cosmic Will. In ordinary consciousness the objects of perception are simply the intersections of sets of temporal, spatial, and causal relations because it is through knowledge of these relations that the Will is served. Aesthetic consciousness is very different and rare. The infrequent transition to aesthetic consciousness "can happen only by a change taking place in the subject."[26] This change occurs when a person is "raised up by the power of the mind . . . [to] . . . relinquish the ordinary ways of considering things."[27] The change "takes place suddenly . . . [when] ... knowledge tears itself free from the service of the will."[28] When aesthetic consciousness is achieved, what before was perceived as the intersection of relations is then perceived as a perceptually relationless Platonic Idea. It is a Platonic Idea that becomes the object of aesthetic contemplation. Aesthetic consciousness is also precarious. He writes, "What makes this state difficult and therefore rare is that in it the . . . intellect . . . subdues and eliminates the . . . will, although only for a short time."[29] The aesthetic state can be maintained ". . . only when we ourselves have no interest in ... [the objects of perception, i. e.,] . . . they stand in no relation to our will."[30] "[T]he absolute silence of the will . . .[is]. . . required for the purely objective apprehension of the true nature of things . . . [Platonic Ideas]"[31] Finally, the aesthetic "state is conditioned from the outside by our remaining wholly foreign to, and detached from, the scene to be contemplated, and not being at all actively involved in it."[32]

First, Schopenhauer's account of aesthetic consciousness does not involve any sort of faculty of taste as do theories of taste; the whole account is in terms of the intellect and its objects. Second, aesthetic consciousness depends on or is conditioned by the intellect's ability to act in such a way as to detach the object of its perception from its relations and make it perceptually relationless. Third, for Schopenhauer, once the detaching and isolating act occurs, disinterested contemplation of an object of perception becomes possible. Fourth, if any trace of the will manages to breach the isolating action of the intellect, aesthetic consciousness is destroyed; there is an absolute antagonism between aesthetic consciousness and interest. How, in Schopenhauer's view, does artistic representation work into his conception of aesthetic experience?

Consider a portrait of Churchill. A Schopenhauerian aesthetic experience of the portrait would be an experience of a detached, and relationless object, such that the relation of the portrait to Churchill is nullified. An aesthetic experience of the portrait, according to Schopenhauer, has no role for representation. In an aesthetic experience of the work, the object of the experience would be a Platonic Idea—presumably the Platonic Idea of Man.

For Kant, the experience of a beautiful object is not just an experience of that object separable from whatever relations it has to other things, it is an experience of that object in that whatever relations that it has to other things have been experientially nullified. Schopenhauer has perpetuated this Kantian doctrine which eliminates from the experience of beauty not only desire of future benefit but imitation and any other relation the object of beauty has to anything outside the experience. This Schopenhauerian doctrine of the nature of what the experience of art ought to be is very different from our actual experiences of art and has, consequently, distorted our conception of what the nature of art experiences ought to be.

Chapter 3

The Aesthetic Attitude in the Twentieth Century

Thus far I have been concerned with the history of the organizing strain of aesthetics that began with Plato's theory of beauty. The discussion of this organizing strain ended with the introduction of the concept of the aesthetic in the nineteenth century. While the second organizing strain, the philosophy of art, has enjoyed a renewed interest in the twentieth century, the concept of the aesthetic has also claimed considerable attention from twentieth-century philosophers. Out of the tradition of Schopenhauer and others has developed a collection of theories that are called "aesthetic-attitude theories." The attitude theories have been challenged by the view called "metacriticism." The dispute between these two types of theory ultimately revolves around the issue of which view gives the correct account of the nature of the object of criticism and appreciation that both the aesthetic-attitude theorists and the advocates of metacriticism call "the aesthetic object."

This chapter is devoted to a discussion of three versions of the aesthetic-attitude theory. The first of the attitude views is the psychical-distance theory of Edward Bullough, which was published early in the present century.[1] Bullough's article is reprinted in most anthologies of aesthetics, and it has had enormous influence. The second attitude view is the *theory of disinterested attention*, which is a descendent of Bullough's theory and has many adherents. I will discuss this view as it is defended by Jerome Stolnitz[2] and Eliseo Vivas.[3] The third attitude theory is Virgil Aldrich's account,[4] which makes the notion of *seeing as* the central notion.[5]

Chapter 4 is devoted to a discussion and criticism of Monroe Beardsley's metacritical version of aesthetic object.[6] In connection with this discussion I will make some positive suggestions of my own toward a way of conceiving objects of criticism.

It is not completely clear what "attitude" means in the expression "aesthetic attitude," except that the acts and psychological states (attitudes?) of persons are essentially involved in the theories. Each of the three versions discussed here claims that a person can *do* something (achieve distance, perceive disinterestedly, or see as) that will change any object perceived into an aesthetic object. The reader can easily note the influence of Schopenhauer on the attitude theorists.

The Aesthetic State: Psychical Distance

Edward Bullough introduces the concept of psychical distance by using as an example the appreciation of a natural phenomenon rather than a work of art. Consider, he says, how enjoyable various aspects of a fog at sea can be, even though to be in such a situation is dangerous. Bullough writes,

> Distance is produced in the first instance by putting the phenomenon, so to speak, out of gear with our practical, actual self; by allowing it to stand outside the context of our personal needs and ends—in short, by looking at it "objectively," as it has often been called, by permitting only such reactions on our part as emphasize the "objective" features of the experience.[7]

Distance has an inhibitory aspect, a "putting" [of phenomenon] out of gear with our practical, actual self." The psychological state of inhibition may be induced by an action of the perceiver or it may be a psychological state into which the perceiver is induced; once the state has occurred, an object can be aesthetically appreciated. "Distance" for Bullough is the name of a psychological state that can be achieved and can be lost. He describes two ways in which distance can be lost, calling them cases of "over-distancing" and "under-distancing." His example of under-distancing is the case of a jealous husband at a performance of *Othello* who keeps thinking of his own wife's suspicious behavior. Sheila Dawson, a follower of Bullough, gives as an example of over-distancing the case in which a person is primarily interested in the technical details of a performance.

It is significant that Bullough uses the appreciation of a natural entity that threatens the safety of the observer (a fog at sea) to introduce his theory of psychical distance. It seems natural to assume that there must be some psychological phenomenon that in some way removes the threat of harm to an observer so that he or she may appreciate the qualities of a threatening entity like a fog at sea. Bullough's account here is reminiscent of Schopenhauer's theory of the sublime. Schopenhauer speaks of the forcible detachment of the will (roughly the self) required for the appreciation of a sublime and threatening object. But do we need to postulate a special kind of action called "to distance" and a special kind of psychological state called "being distanced" to account for the fact that we can sometimes appreciate the characteristics of threatening things? Wouldn't it be simpler and more economical to explain this phenomenon in terms of *attention*, that is, as a case of focusing attention on some of the characteristics of, say, a fog at sea and ignoring others? In fact, one may be fully and painfully aware of the danger of the situation and still appreciate some of the characteristics of something like a fog at sea. Of course, there is no virtue in being theoretically economical if one ignores actual fact. The issue presumably has to be settled introspectively. Do we, in order to appreciate some object, commit a special act of distancing? Or, if in a given case it is not a question of doing something, are we ever induced into a state of being distanced when faced with a work of art or a natural object? It does not seem that either of these two states occurs.

Although the theory of psychical distance seems to have some initial plausibility when invoked to deal with threatening natural objects, it has very little when it is used to explain our relation to works of art. The jealous husband at *Othello* is not someone who has lost or failed to achieve something (psychical distance), he is simply someone who, for reasons peculiar to him, is having difficulty attending to the action of the play. A hypothetical case frequently used to illustrate the theory is that of a spectator who mounts the stage to save a threatened heroine. It is claimed that such a person would have lost psychical distance, but a better explanation would be that he has lost his mind and is no longer mindful of the rules and conventions that govern theater situations, in this case the rule that forbids spectators from interfering with the actions of the actors. There are similar conventions and rules for each established art form. Of course, in the case of some present-day theater productions, the participation of the audience is invited. One of the nonhypothetical examples used by some defenders of psychical distance to illustrate how the psychological state works actually throws suspicion on the theory. Both Sheila Dawson,[8] a follower of Bullough, and Susanne Langer,[9] whose view that art is illusion is in some ways similar to Bullough's theory, make use of the scene in *Peter Pan* in which Peter Pan turns to the audience and asks them to clap their hands in order to save Tinkerbelle's life. These theorists claim that Peter Pan's action destroys psychical distance (or the necessary illusion) and is a moment "when most children would like to slink out of the theater and not a few cry—not because Tinkerbelle may die, but because the magic is gone."[10] The claim is, in effect, that a theatrical device destroys or gravely impairs the status of *Peter Pan* as an aesthetic object, that is, as an object of aesthetic appreciation and experience. But before any theoretical conclusions are drawn from this alleged fact it should be determined if children actually are made "acutely miserable"[11] by Peter Pan's action and want to slink out of the theater. In fact, children respond enthusiastically to the appeal to participate in the play. Langer remembers that as a child the appeal caused her acute misery, but she also reports that all the other children clapped and enjoyed themselves! If we are to take account of actual responses in drawing theoretical conclusions, it seems most plausible to develop the theory along the lines of the response of the overwhelming majority of the children. In addition, a little reflection reveals that many highly rated plays and movies employ devices similar to the one in *Peter Pan*—for example, *Our Town, A Taste of Honey,* and *Tom Jones.*

If Bullough had begun by thinking about what may be called "nonthreatening cases" such as looking at a painting of a vase of flowers rather than such threatening cases as a fog at sea and a jealous husband at *Othello,* he would not have been induced into feeling the need for a mental mechanism to block thoughts (e.g., of a suspected wife) and actions (e.g., to avoid the dangers of a fog at sea).

If the theory of psychical distance were simply a complicated and somewhat misleading way of talking about attending or not attending to things, there would be little reason to be concerned about it. Its defenders, however, see it as the first and key step of an aesthetic theory, and it is held to have far-reaching implications. The *Peter Pan* case shows that it is thought that the theory can provide some basis for evaluating works of art. It is also thought that being in a state of psychical distance can reveal the properties of a work of art that properly belong to the aesthetic object, that is, those properties to which we ought to direct our attention and from which our aesthetic experience ought to derive. In short, it is thought that substantive guidelines for art criticism and appreciation can be derived from the nature of a certain kind of psychological state. If there is no such psychological state, this approach is in serious difficulty.

Aesthetic Awareness: Disinterested Attention

The view that the concept of the aesthetic can be defined in terms of disinterested attention is an outgrowth of both the theory of psychical distance and the notion of disinterestedness in the eighteenth-century theories of taste. But whereas "psychical distance" is supposed to name a special action or psychological state, "disinterested attention" is held to name the ordinary action of attending done in a special way. The persuasiveness of this version of the aesthetic attitude depends entirely on the clarity and validity of the descriptions of the alleged disinterested attention to art and nature.

Before proceeding to a discussion of disinterested attention, it will be useful to discuss the two pairs of concepts: interested/disinterested and interested/uninterested. The meanings of the interested/disinterested pair involves such notions as financial interest, partiality and impartiality, and/or selfishness and unselfishness. Thus, someone is an interested party with regard to a particular company when he owns shares in a company and thus has a selfish reason for the company's doing well or someone is an interested party when as a prospective juror he is a friend of, a relative of, or stands in some such relation to the accused. A disinterested person would be the opposite of an interested person. The meaning of the interested/uninterested pair involves the notions of concern and attentiveness. Thus, some one is interested in something, say, a book, if he or she is concerned with or attentive to the book, for example, persists in reading the book. A person would be uninterested in a book if he or she is indifferent to or not attentive to it, for example, fails to continue reading it after starting. People sometimes use "disinterested" to mean what "uninterested" means, that is, to say that there is indifference in a particular situation, but this usage blurs an important distinction. If the distinction between the two pairs of notions is preserved, it can be seen how a person can be both *interested* in something and be *disinterested* concerning that something at the same time. For example, a juror might be very interested in the case being tried, that is, attentive to and concerned about it, and at the same time be disinterested concerning the case, that is, impartial about the case or have no selfish motive connected to the case. In any event, it is disinterestedness in the interested/disinterested sense that is important for the discussion of aesthetic-attitude theories.

Jerome Stolnitz's definition of aesthetic attitude may be taken as a standard one. He defines it as the "disinterested (with no ulterior purpose) and sympathetic attention to and contemplation of any object of awareness whatever, for its own sake alone."[12] Eliseo Vivas's conception of aesthetic attitude is similar to Stolnitz's. Vivas uses the term "intransitive" rather than "disinterested" to refer to the crucial mode of attention, but the two terms have essentially the same meaning.

Consider some cases of the kind used to illustrate the disinterested-attention theory of the aesthetic. Suppose that Ann is listening to some music in order to write an analysis of it for an examination. Since Ann has an ulterior purpose, she is supposedly not attending to the music disinterestedly. Ann's attention to the music must therefore supposedly be interested, as contrasted with disinterested. Suppose that Bob is looking at a painting and a figure depicted in the painting suddenly reminds him of someone he knows. Bob then proceeds to muse about his acquaintance or perhaps to tell stories about the acquaintance, all the while standing before the painting. Bob is now using the painting as a vehicle for his associations and would, thereby, supposedly be attending to the painting in an interested fashion.

The disinterested attention/interested attention distinction is applied by its adherents quite generally to the experience of all the arts, but perhaps one more example will suffice for present purposes. Eliseo Vivas cites a number of ways in which literature may be attended to transitively, or interestedly: when it is read as history, social criticism, diagnostic evidence of an author's neurosis, or a springboard for free associations uncontrolled by the literary work. Remember that these are supposed to be nonaesthetic ways of attending to literature, and hence the objects of such attention are not supposed to be aesthetic objects. According to this theory, a work of art or a natural object may or may not be an aesthetic object, depending on whether or not it is attended to disinterestedly. The same object may be an aesthetic object on one occasion and not on another.

The theory of disinterested, or intransitive, attention entails that there are at least two distinguishable kinds of attention and that the concept of the aesthetic can be defined in terms of one of them. The adherents of this theory explain disinterested attention in a negative way, describing and giving cases of what it is *not*, that is, cases of interested attention. Presumably, if the nature of interested attention can be made clear, we will have at least some idea of what disinterested attention is. The crucial question is, then, are the kinds of cases cited as instances of interested attention to works of art genuine cases of a species of attention? Perhaps there is only one kind of attention.

Consider the case of Bob, who fell to musing or telling stories while looking at a painting. Now although Bob is standing in front of the painting with his eyes turned toward it, he is not attending to the painting at all. He is attending to the objects of his musing or to the story he is telling. So this case of alleged nondisinterested attention to the painting turns out to be a case of *in*attention to the painting, not a special kind of attention at all. In another case, Bob might, say, be telling a story and still have his attention on the painting. Even in this case, however, there is no reason to think that there is more than one kind of attention involved. Consider the case of Ann, who was listening to music in preparation for an examination. She would have motives for what she is doing that are different from those of someone listening to the music with no such ulterior motives, but would this mean that the two are *attending* in a different way? They could both enjoy or be bored by the music, no matter what their motives are. In either case, attention might lapse, reawaken, drift, and so on. So although it is easy enough to see what it means to have different motives, it is not so easy to see how having different motives affects the nature of attention. Different motives may direct attention to different objects, but the activity of attention itself remains the same.

Finally, consider Vivas's contentions about literature as aesthetic object. One startling clue that something is wrong with the disinterested–attention theory is Vivas's claim that his conception of the aesthetic posits "that *The Brothers Karamazov* can hardly be read as art,"[13] that is, it can hardly be experienced as an aesthetic object. Since *The Brothers Karamazov* is a great novel, it must surely be a paradigm case of an aesthetic object, and any theory that denies this must be suspect. Why, according to Vivas, isn't it an aesthetic object? Perhaps because he thinks its complexity and size prevent intransitive attention, but most probably because one can hardly avoid reading it to some extent as social criticism, which is one of the ways that Vivas mentions literature is attended to nonaesthetically. But are the kinds of cases mentioned by Vivas actually cases of transitive, or interested, attention to literary works? Two of the alleged cases of attending interestedly to a literary work are really ways of *not attending* to the work. To use the work as a springboard for free associations uncontrolled by the literary work is simply a case of losing touch with the work and ceasing to attend to it. Similarly, to use the work to diagnose the author's neurosis is a way of being distracted from the work, rather than a special way of attending to it. In some cases, one might still be attending in the usual way to some aspects of the work and at the same time be attending to (thinking about) the author's neurosis. These would be cases of partial distraction. In other cases, the distraction might be complete, with the author's neurosis becoming the sole object of attention.

The two other cases of alleged interested attending—reading literature as history or as social criticism—are quite different and are not cases of distraction. Works of literature sometimes contain historical references and social criticism. Assume that reading a work as, say, history means being aware that a historical reference is made by the work and perhaps even that it is correct or incorrect. How does one's attention differ in this case from the attention given when one is unaware that an actual historical reference is made or when the work is wholly fictional? Assume that reading a work as history means reading it simply or solely as history. Even this way of reading does not mark out a special kind of attention; it means only that a single aspect of a work is being attended to and that the many other aspects of the work are being ignored or missed. The historical or socially critical content, if any, of a literary work is a part of the work (although only a part), and any attempt to say that it is somehow not a part of the aesthetic object when other aspects of the work are, seems strange. Why should, say, an aspect as important as social criticism be segregated out of the aesthetic object? The disinterested-attention theorist argues that such a segregation is effected simply by a perceptual distinction—a certain kind of attention can take as its objects only certain kinds of objects. There is, however, a serious doubt that such a species of attention exists.

The alleged cases of interested attention may be summarized as follows: Ann's attention to the music turned out to be just like that of any other listener; Bob's "interested attention" to the painting turned out to be a case of not attending; free associating and diagnosing the author's neurosis turned out also to be cases of not attending; attending to historical or socially critical content turned out to be simply attending to one aspect of literature. Many other examples of allegedly interested attention could be discussed, but if the ones analyzed are typical, the theory of disinterested attention cannot be a correct account of the aesthetic attitude and cannot be used as a basis for the description of the concept of aesthetic object.

Aesthetic Perception: "Seeing As"

Virgil Aldrich developed an aesthetic theory out of one of the central notions of the philosophy of Ludwig Wittgenstein. Aldrich's view is an aesthetic-attitude theory because he claims it is something that a subject *does* or has happen to the subject that determines whether an object is an aesthetic object or not. Whereas the previously discussed theories make use of the notion of a special psychological state or a special kind of attention, Aldrich's view concludes that there is an *aesthetic mode of perception*.

Although he did not make use of them for aesthetic theory, Wittgenstein called attention to ambiguous figures. A line drawing that sometimes looks like steps seen from above and sometimes like steps seen from below is an example of an ambiguous figure. The one made famous by Wittgenstein is "the duck-rabbit": a drawing sometimes seen as a duck's head and at other times as a rabbit's head. Aldrich leads into his theory by way of a discussion of ambiguous figures, noting that three things can be distinguished in the case of such figures. These are (1) the design the lines make on paper, (2) the representation of, say, a duck, and (3) the other representation of, say, a rabbit. Nothing that Aldrich says about ambiguous figures and the notion of "seeing as," which is used in describing such figures, is controversial.

Aldrich develops his aesthetic theory as a parallel of the perceptual phenomenon of ambiguous figures. He asserts that earlier theorists were mistaken in thinking that there is only one mode of perception. He claims there are two: the aesthetic mode of perception and the nonaesthetic mode of perception. The nonaesthetic mode he calls "observation" and the aesthetic mode he calls "prehension." *Observation* and its object, which Aldrich terms "*physical object*," parallel the seeing of one of the representations, say, the duck. *Prehension* and its object, which Aldrich calls "*aesthetic object*," parallel the seeing of the other representation, say, the rabbit. The parallel of the ambiguous design itself Aldrich calls a "*material object*." A material object is seen as a physical object when observed and as an aesthetic object when prehended.

Aldrich's theory provides a neat solution to the problem of aesthetic object and from this point of view is admirable. It also avoids any commitment to disinterested attention or psychical distance, which were seen to involve difficulties. Finally, it purports to be a development out of one of the most powerful and influential philosophical movements of the twentieth century, the philosophy of Wittgenstein. Is there, however, any reason to think that Aldrich's theory is true? Does he present good evidence for his contention that there really are two modes of perception?

Aldrich explicitly states that his remarks about ambiguous figures are not supposed to be evidence for his aesthetic theory: they simply served to suggest the theory to him. The lack of an evidential relation between the two, however, must be made clear. The fact that a single design can function alternatively as two representations gives no evidence for two modes of perception. For example, the seeing of the duck representation is exactly like the seeing of the rabbit representation so far as the seeing is concerned. Only one kind of perception is involved, although the perception has two objects (representations). The notion of *seeing as* may be useful in providing an analysis of the concept of representation but that is clearly another matter. The phenomenon of ambiguous figures is supposed to be a kind of model for Aldrich's theory. However, it is not even a complete model, for there are not two kinds of perception involved in the seeing of ambiguous figures.

The only evidence that Aldrich gives for his theory in the book in which he sets forth his view is the following alleged example of aesthetic perception.

> Take for example a dark city and a pale western sky at dusk, meeting at the sky line. In the purely . . . aesthetic view of this, the light sky area just above the jagged sky line protrudes toward the point of view. The sky is closer to the viewer than are the dark areas of buildings. This is the disposition of these material things in aesthetic space.[14]

Almost everyone would agree that the experience described in this passage is an aesthetic experience and that it has aesthetic value. Doubtless, also, the sky could appear to be closer to the viewer than the actually closer buildings. The fact, however, that things look different and that visual relations appear to alter under varying conditions of lighting is no reason for thinking that there are two modes of perceiving that a person can switch off or on. At the end of the city-at-dusk example, Aldrich gives a general characterization of aesthetic perception that suggests that something is radically wrong with his whole approach. He writes that aesthetic perception "is, if you like, an 'impressionistic' way of looking, but still a mode of perception."[15] Independently of whether or not it makes sense to speak of an impressionistic way of looking, it is surely not the case that all the experiences we call aesthetic are impressionistic, although perhaps some are. What is impressionistic about watching *Hamlet*, looking at a Ming vase, or looking at a painting by Rembrandt? What, for that matter, is impressionistic about *looking* at an impressionistic painting or listening to impressionistic music?

Several years after the publication of his book, Aldrich offered another example to exemplify aesthetic perception and thereby serve as evidence for his theory.[16] He recalls watching illuminated snowflakes falling at night. If he focused his eyes at a point in the dark behind the snowflakes, the snowflakes appeared comet-shaped, tails up. Aldrich calls this an "impressionistic" way of looking at the snowflakes and contrasts it with the ordinary way of looking at them. The snowflakes case is different from the city-at-sunset case in that the observer actually does something—the trick of focusing one's eyes. Nevertheless, the snowflake case does not serve as evidence for the theory that there are two ways of perceiving. While it is no doubt true that snowflakes perceived when one's eyes are focused behind them are aesthetically pleasing, it is also true that snowflakes are aesthetically pleasing when looked at in the ordinary way. There are many tricks one can do that will produce new and unusual perceptual qualities. One may squint at snowflakes (or at a painting), watch them with a telescope or a microscope, look at them while under the influence of drugs, and so on. None of these tricks will serve to pick out just those perceptual qualities that are called "aesthetically pleasing." We may find some of these tricks useful on some occasions—as when we squint at a painting to screen out details in order to see its composition or structure. We do not, however, always or even frequently use such tricks when we look at paintings, watch plays, and so on. The "impressionistic" way of looking at snowflakes is no more a uniquely aesthetic way of looking than is the "impressionistic" way of looking at the city at sunset. One must conclude that Aldrich has given us no reasonable evidence for the truth of his theory.

Concluding Remarks

Twentieth-century aesthetic-attitude theories grew out of such nineteenth-century theories as that of Schopenhauer with its insistence on the aesthetic as a will-less, nonpractical state of contemplation. These theories have roots even further back in the eighteenth-century notion of disinterestedness. The aesthetic-attitude theories share with the eighteenth-century taste theories the view that a psychological analysis is the key to a correct theory. But they reject the eighteenth-century assumption that some particular feature of the world such as uniformity in variety triggers the aesthetic, or taste, response. The aesthetic-attitude theories share with the nineteenth-century aesthetic theories the view that any object (with certain reservations about the obscene and the disgusting) can become an object of aesthetic appreciation. But they reject the nineteenth-century assumption that aesthetic theory must be embedded in a comprehensive metaphysical system, e.g., Schopenhauer's philosophical system.

Theories of aesthetic attitude have three main goals. First and most basic, they attempt to isolate and describe the psychological factors constituting the aesthetic attitude. Second, they attempt to develop a conception of aesthetic object as that which is the object of the aesthetic attitude. Third, they attempt to account for aesthetic experience by conceiving of it as the experience derived from an aesthetic object. For these theories, an aesthetic object has the function of being the proper locus of appreciation and criticism (with criticism understood as including description, interpretation, and evaluation). For these theories, the concepts of aesthetic-attitude and aesthetic object have a normative function. That is, they are supposed somehow to guide our attention to the qualities of art and nature that are "aesthetically relevant" and thereby serve as a foundation for criticism. Recall how it was thought that the concept of psychical distance had evaluative implications for *Peter Pan* and that the concept of disinterested perception had evaluative implications for *The Brothers Karamazov*. Aesthetic-attitude theories held that these works of art contain elements that are not only aesthetically irrelevant but positively destructive to aesthetic values. It seems that each of these three influential versions of aesthetic attitude involves some fundamental difficulty. If this is so, then it seems reasonable to conclude that the aesthetic-attitude concept of aesthetic object with its attendant theory of criticism and aesthetic experience is also probably in difficulty. Is there a viable alternative that will provide a concept of aesthetic object and a basis for a theory of criticism? Metacriticism is thought by some to be such an alternative.

Chapter 4

Metacriticism

Alternative to Aesthetic Attitude

To repeat what was said earlier, metacriticism is the philosophical activity that takes as its task the analysis and clarification of the basic concepts that art critics use when they describe, interpret, or evaluate particular works of art. Monroe Beardsley's theory of aesthetic object will be discussed and criticized in this chapter. This is not to suggest that Beardsley's view is the only possible metacritical theory of aesthetic object. Beardsley's version is, however, the only one that is fairly completely worked out. The summary of Beardsley's theory presented here differs in two respects from his original presentation. First, he does not formulate in an explicit way the *criteria* implicit in his argument, as is done here. Second, the theory as set forth here concerns only works of art and does not discuss natural objects. Neither of these two differences violates the spirit or intent of his theory.

Beardsley shares with the aesthetic-attitude theorists the assumption that there is a clear-cut way to distinguish aesthetic objects from all other things, but he does not try to use the notion of the aesthetic attitude to make this distinction. Although he does not formulate explicit criteria in developing his theory of aesthetic object, Beardsley implicitly uses three criteria: distinctness, perceptibility, and what he calls the consideration of the basic properties of perceptual fields.

Although he no doubt has it in mind throughout, the criterion of distinctness is most clearly used in connection with Beardsley's argument that the intention of the artist (what the artist has in mind to do) is not part of his aesthetic object.

His argument very briefly is that although an artist's intention is causally related to the work of art the artist produces, an intention is *distinct from* (not part of) an actual work. His view is that if something is not part of a work of art, it cannot be part of the aesthetic object of that work. Beardsley has many other things to say about this topic, but this is the core of his argument.

The *criterion of distinctness* as a necessary condition for aesthetic objects may be formulated in the following way:

> If something is part of an aesthetic object, then it must be (is) part of (not distinct from) a work of art.

This criterion functions to *exclude* things—artist's intentions, for example—from aesthetic objects. (An analysis of the concept "work of art" will not be given until later, but the expression "work of art" is being used here in the classificatory, nonevaluative sense, and it is not being used as a synonym for "aesthetic object.") Please remember that the current discussion of aesthetic objects is limited to the domain of art. Natural objects may, of course, be aesthetic objects, but they are not under discussion here. A brief remark about natural objects as aesthetic objects is made at the end of this chapter.

Assuming that the criterion of distinctness is acceptable and that its application in the case concerning intention is correct, more is obviously needed to sort out the widely differing aspects of works of art. It is clear that it would be silly to take many of the aspects of works of art to be parts of their aesthetic objects. For example, the color of the back of a painting or the actions of stagehands backstage at the performance of a play are surely not properly objects of appreciation and criticism.

Drawing on a long tradition that emphasizes the importance of sensory elements in aesthetics, Beardsley attempts to use the distinction between the perceptible and the nonperceptible and make perceptibility a necessary condition of aesthetic objects. His *criterion of perceptibility* may be formulated in the following way:

> If something is part of an aesthetic object, then it must be (is) perceptible under the normal conditions of experiencing the kind of art in question.

The qualification about normal conditions must be added because, for example, the color of the back of a painting is perceptible, but not under the normal conditions of viewing paintings. This second criterion also functions to *exclude* things from aesthetic objects.

I will now consider some cases to illustrate how the criterion of perceptibility is supposed to work and how difficulties arise in certain cases.

First, consider the case of the stagehands in traditional theater productions. Although this work is necessary for a performance of the actors, the performance of the stagehands is clearly not part of the aesthetic objects of the plays to which they are connected. The performance of the stagehands is part of a work of art in a broad sense, that is, is not *distinct* from a work of art, so it is not excluded by the criterion of distinctness. The performance of the stagehands, however, is not *perceptible* to the audience under normal conditions. It deductively follows from Beardsley's criterion of perceptibility that the performance of the stagehands is not part of an aesthetic object as is shown by the following valid argument.

1. If something is part of an aesthetic object, then it is perceptible under normal conditions.
2. A stagehand is not perceptible under normal conditions.

Therefore,

3. A stagehand is not part of an aesthetic object.

In this case, our intuition that stagehands are not part of aesthetic objects and the results of the application of Beardsley's criterion of perceptibility yield the same result. This first case does not raise any problems for Beardsley.

Second, consider the case of the onstage performance of an actor in *Hamlet*. Clearly the performance is recognizable as part of an aesthetic object, that is, part of that which is properly appreciated and criticized. The performance is perceptible under normal conditions. The performance satisfies Beardsley's criterion of perceptibility, so it is not ruled out by the criterion. On the other hand, the performance is not *ruled in* as part of the aesthetic object of the play because Beardsley's criterion of perceptibility does not connect logically with the relevant statement about the performance. The following premises show this.

1. If something is part of an aesthetic object, then it is perceptible under normal conditions.
2. The performance is perceptible under normal conditions.

Nothing follows from these two premises. Beardsley's criterion does not rule out the performance as part of an aesthetic object, but this is not surprising because the performance satisfies the criterion, that is, it is perceptible. The criterion does not *rule in* the performance as part of an aesthetic object either, but this is not surprising because both of the first two criteria function to exclude things from aesthetic objects. This case reveals that Beardsley's criterion of perceptibility cannot complete a clear-cut account of aesthetic object.

There is, however, a third criterion that presumably can complete the task of ruling in and ruling out those things that need to be ruled in and ruled out, namely, the criterion of the consideration of the basic properties of perceptual fields. Beardsley's discussion of this criterion amounts to his characterizing aesthetic objects disjunctively as either a visual design or a musical composition or a literary work and so forth. Thus, Beardsley's third criterion may be formulated in the following way.

> An aesthetic object is either a visual design or a musical composition
> or a literary work or. . . .

I will discuss only visual design, which will sufficiently illustrate how the criterion is supposed to work. Beardsley defines "visual design" as "a bounded visual area that exhibits heterogeneity." Presumably, this definition is supposed to complete the process of isolating the elements of purely visual aesthetic objects.

I return now the case of the performance of the actor in *Hamlet*, focusing only on its visual aspects as seen from a seat in a theater. Beardsley's notion of visual design certainly applies here. The outline of the stage furnishes a boundary and the various elements within that boundary exhibit a heterogeneity. Thus, since a visual design is by definition an aesthetic object, any element of visual design, which includes the actor's performance, is ruled in as an element of a visual design.

Consider now a third case—the case of the property man in traditional Chinese theater, who appears on stage while the action of the play is in progress and moves props around, shifts scenery, and so on. (In this case also I am concerned only with the visual aspects of plays.) The Chinese property man is not, however, part of an aesthetic object as are the actors in the play to which the property man is connected. The Chinese property man is in a broad way a part of the play to which he is connected and he is perceptible under normal conditions, so the first two criteria do not exclude him from the aesthetic object of the play. Will the notion of visual design rule him out? Since the Chinese property man is visible on stage just as the actors are, if the notion of visual design rules the actors in, it also rules in the property man. The notion of visual design is not discriminating enough in what it rules in.

Consider now a fourth case, not in connection with the third criterion, but in connection with the criterion of perceptibility. This is the hypothetical case of a ballet dancer who uses imperceptible wires in order to make incredible leaps. These imperceptible wires are part of the aesthetic object because it would be necessary to know if such wires were being used in order to appreciate and evaluate the performance correctly. A given leap might be magnificent if wires were not being used but mediocre if wires were being used. The wires would be an integral part of the performance.[1] However, it deductively follows from the criterion of perceptibility that the wires are not part of an aesthetic object as is shown by the following valid argument.

1. If something is part of an aesthetic object, then it is perceptible under normal conditions.
2. The invisible wires are not perceptible.

Therefore,

3. The invisible wires are not part of an aesthetic object.

The criterion of perceptibility is thus shown to be defective because it entails the false conclusion that the imperceptible wires are not part of an aesthetic object. In this case, our intuitions and the results of the applications of Beardsley criteria yield different results.

The criterion of the consideration of the basic properties of perceptual fields is defective because it rules in things —the Chinese property man, for example—that ought not to be ruled in. The criterion of perceptibility is defective because it rules out things—the invisible wires, for example—that ought not to be ruled out.

Concluding Remarks

Unlike the attitude theorists who seem to be wrong in a very basic way, Beardsley's difficulty seems more a matter of detail. Perhaps, then, an adequate metacritical theory of aesthetic object may be worked out by following the trail Beardsley has blazed.[2]

Perhaps the criterion of distinctness can be applied a second time to yield the desired results. In its first use, this principle was used to distinguish art from nonart—specifically, the work of art from the artist's intention. Perhaps the criterion can be applied *within* the category of art to distinguish those aspects of a work of art that belong to an aesthetic object from those that do not. This second application would come off if, on inspection and reflection, the various aspects of works of art fall into two distinct classes, one of which contains all and only those aspects it is proper to appreciate and criticize. These aspects would constitute aesthetic objects.

However, by this time it may already be evident that the criterion of distinctness in its first use cannot actually be applied in a simple, straightforward way. Knowing whether something is distinct from a work of art presupposes that one already knows what kinds of things are and are not parts of works of art and their aesthetic objects. Determining whether or not something is part of a work of art is actually a case of *realizing*, on the basis of what one knows about works of the type in question, that a given thing is or is not a part. There will no doubt be cases of artistic innovation concerning which very little information is available and for which conventions have not been established. Time will take care of these cases in one way or another. Even if the determination of distinctness between things that are and are not parts of a work of art cannot be made in an easy way, it does seem that it can be made. And, if this is so, it encourages one to think that a second and similar kind of determination of distinctions can be made *within* the category of art. That is, on the basis of what one knows about the various types of art and the conventions and rules that govern their presentation, one can come to realize which aspects are the proper aspects for appreciation and criticism. The realization at either of the two levels will not always or even typically be easy. In many cases, a great deal of thought will be necessary and controversy will certainly not be easily settled. The controversy, for example, over whether or not the intention of the artist is part of a work of art is still hotly debated. It is worth noting that the abandoned criterion of perceptibility cannot be applied in a simple, straightforward way either; perceptibility is qualified by "under the normal conditions of experiencing the kind of art in question," which indicates that perceptibility is not established independently of the concept of a particular type of art.

To sum up, it seems that a conception of aesthetic object can be arrived at but not in the clean-cut way that either the attitude theorists or Beardsley had hoped. What it makes sense to appreciate and criticize in the case of a given work of art cannot be known *antecedent to* a rich experience of and full understanding of works of art of the type in question. Thus, the method of arriving at a concept of aesthetic object will have to be piecemeal reflection on one type of art at a time. The concept produced by this procedure will be complicated and variegated, but this simply reflects the complexity of the arts.

There are two matters that it seems appropriate to mention at this point. First, Beardsley's view of aesthetic object as it is formulated here and that of the aesthetic-attitude theorists are different in scope. According to the latter, anything—work of art or natural thing—may become an aesthetic object, whereas Beardsley's view does not include an account of natural objects as aesthetic objects. This is not surprising because metacriticism takes art criticism as its subject matter and art criticism takes as its subject matter art, not natural objects. For metacriticism to be a complete aesthetic theory, some account that deals with natural objects must be added to it. There is not space to pursue this topic here, but perhaps the account might be developed along these lines: a natural object is an aesthetic object when it functions in someone's experience in a manner similar to the way a work of art functions when it is taken as an object of appreciation and/or criticism.

Second, it may seem appropriate at this point to have a discussion of the nature of aesthetic experience. However, insofar as the aesthetic attitude theorists are concerned, aesthetic experience seems to mean "that experience that is had when in the aesthetic attitude." Thus, for the attitude theories, the concept of aesthetic experience has, in effect, already been discussed. Beardsley, however, has an explicit theory of aesthetic experience, arguing that it has certain specific characteristics that differentiate it from ordinary experience. Since Beardsley's theory of aesthetic experience is so closely related to his account of evaluation, it seems best to leave a discussion of it until Part IV.

Chapter 5

The Theory of Art
Plato to the Nineteenth Century

The first part of this chapter will consist of a discussion of the imitation theory of art. From ancient Greek times until the nineteenth century, the imitation theory of art was more or less "in the air" and assumed to be a correct theory of art without ever having been subjected to close scrutiny. Plato does not so much advance and defend the imitation theory as to use it in order to attack art. Aristotle endorses the imitation theory at least by implication. I will also discuss Plato's and Aristotle's theories of the origin of art and of the effect of art on people. I will then discuss expressionism, a nineteenth-century view that was the first theory to challenge the dominance of the imitation theory. In the period between Plato and the nineteenth century, what debate there was over the theory of art took place within the imitation theory and was concerned with the proper objects to be imitated. Twentieth-century theories of art will be discussed in Chapter 6.

The imitation theory focuses attention on the objective properties of the work of art. It may be said that this theory of art is *object centered*. Plato also held an emotionalistic theory about the origin and effect of art. The development of the expressionist theory of art in the nineteenth century can be thought of as a conversion of the emotionalistic theory of the origin and effect of art into a theory of art itself. What Plato had kept separate as two theories—a theory of art and a theory of the origin of art—was collapsed by the expressionists into one. Expressionism shifts attention away from the work of art toward the artist; this theory is *artist centered*.

Although Plato uses and Aristotle holds the imitation theory of art, they have radically different views about how art affects people. It should also be noted that whereas Plato's account of the imitation theory is hostile to art, Aristotle's version is friendly.

Plato

That art is imitation was no doubt a popularly held view of Plato's time. What Plato does is to make use of this conception in connection with his philosophical theory of the Forms, an adaptation that produces a two-level theory of imitation. In the *Republic,*[1] Plato says that an artisan who makes furniture, say, a chair, imitates the Form of Chairness and an artist who paints a picture of the chair imitates the chair. There are, then, two levels of imitation. Of course, when an artist paints a picture of a natural object, that is, a nonartifact, there are still two levels of imitation. Plato's contention is that there are the Forms, the objects in the world of sense that imitate the Forms, and representations made by artists that imitate the objects of the world of sense. Plato compares paintings with mirror images, suggesting that paintings are only appearances and thereby "untrue." (Actually, paintings should be called appearances of appearances in Platonic theory, since objects of the world of sense are appearances of the Forms.) Plato's characterization of paintings as untrue appearances may be the origin of the view that art is illusion, a view held by some recent theorists.

Plato's first quarrel with art, and the one that flows directly from his conception of art, is that since it is a twice-removed imitation of reality (the Forms), it cannot be a good source of knowledge. Plato thus places art in competition with such disciplines as mathematics and science as a source of knowledge. He is especially concerned to press this contention in connection with the art of poetry, and with some point. The poetry of Homer and other poets was considered by many Greeks to be authoritative not only as a source of knowledge concerning horsemanship, the making of war, and other such technical matters, but also as a source of moral knowledge. Plato maintains that only a philosopher can be the source of moral knowledge and that only specialists in such areas as horsemanship are accurate guides in such technical matters. When poets speak of chariot driving, making war, or noble action, they only pretend to know and hence are false guides. Plato's first quarrel with art is that art is doubly unreal and hence is an especially inferior product and a poor guide for conduct.

Plato's second quarrel with art concerns its alleged bad effect on people, both because it sometimes presents unsuitable examples of conduct and because of its emotional nature. The first problem can be dealt with by censorship, and Plato advocates a very severe censorship in the ideal state. But the emotional nature of art, which derives from its irrational source, is more difficult to deal with and perhaps impossible to eradicate. In the dialogue entitled *Ion* in a discussion with the rhapsode Ion,[2] Socrates sets forth a theory that purports to explain how poetry is created and how it affects spectators. The main point is that the process is an irrational one and that all the human beings involved with poetry are "out of their minds." The poet creates a poem not by a rational procedure but by being inspired by a god. When a rhapsode such as Ion performs, he is inspired by the poem and the spectator is inspired by the rhapsode. Socrates uses the analogy of a magnet and a set of iron rings: an iron ring will cling to a magnet, a second iron ring will cling to the first iron ring, and so on until there is a chain of rings. Only the first ring touches the magnet, but the magnet's power passes through the whole chain and sustains it. Analogously, the god through his inspiration sustains the chain of poet, rhapsode, and spectator. None of the human beings in the chain *knows* what he or she is doing, each is being manipulated by forces outside themselves. A spectator may weep or appear panic-stricken when listening to a rhapsode or watching a play. Poetry "waters the passions" rather than instructs reason, and Plato has great fear of its effects on spectators. He believes that this feeding of the passions will produce bad citizens. In a dialogue entitled *Phaedrus*,[3] he seems to take a more sympathetic view of inspiration when he says that a poet possessed by the muses and in a frenzy will produce better poetry than a sane man who tries to write poetry with the help of technical skill, that is, rationally. Thus, Plato's second quarrel with art is somewhat ambivalent. It should be noted that when Plato talks about inspiration, he speaks only of poetry, and he may have wished to restrict the theory to the creation of poetry. That is, he may not have been setting forth a general theory about the creation of all art.

Aristotle

Plato's interest in art is derivative and arises within the context of an attempt to deal with problems such as the place of the artist in the ideal state. Aristotle, however, takes a direct interest in art or rather in the various species of art such as tragedy and comedy. Either Aristotle did not devote a work to the general topic of art or it has not survived. There are a number of remarks about art in his various works, but his main contribution to aesthetics is his *Poetics*, which is concerned with three species of art: tragedy, comedy, and epic poetry. Aristotle believes that art is imitation. However, since Aristotle holds that the Forms are not separate from the world of sense, he has no hostility toward the world of sense as such and consequently no hostility toward art that imitates the world of sense. In fact, Aristotle's general philosophical position intrudes very little on his poetic theory, or perhaps it should be said that his general philosophic position allows him to base his poetic theory on an analysis of actual tragedies, comedies, and epics. One of the impressive things about the *Poetics*[4] is the wealth of information it contains about the history of the art forms being discussed, about technical aspects of plays and of the theater.

The *Poetics* is a theory of literature, or more specifically of literature as it existed in Greek times. Given that literature is imitation, Aristotle's first problem is to distinguish the various species of literature from one another and ultimately give definitions for these species. To do this, he distinguishes three aspects of imitation: medium of imitation, object of imitation, and manner of imitation. As the media of imitation, he cites rhythm, language, and tone. But media alone are not sufficient to sort out poetry from prose; for example, both Homer who was a poet and Empedocles who was a philosopher wrote in verse. The object of imitation is *man acting*, and this aspect will distinguish, for example, comedy (which imitates the action of base men) from tragedy (which imitates the action of noble men). Manner of imitation involves the question of whether the story is told by narration or direct discourse or both, or by having actors act it out. Aristotle thinks that these distinctions will be useful in distinguishing and defining the various literary genre.

Having made these initial distinctions, Aristotle discusses the origin and history of tragedy, comedy, and epic poetry. He then gives his famous definition of tragedy and specifies the six elements of tragedy—plot, character, language, thought, spectacle, and music. The remaining four-fifths of the *Poetics* is devoted to a detailed analysis of the elements of tragedy with a little space given to the epic and comedy. The great bulk of this analysis is a discussion of plot: the size and unity of plot, the relation of plot to history and legend, types of plot, plot reversals, the best kinds of plots and defective plots, and so on. Aristotle's definition of tragedy is as follows:

> Tragedy, then, is the imitation of a good action, which is complete and of a certain length, by means of language made pleasing for each part separately; it relies in its various elements not on narrative but on acting; through pity and fear it achieves the purgation (catharsis) of such emotions.[5]

Notice that Aristotle builds into his definition his general theory of art (imitation) and his three initial distinctions: object of imitation (good action), medium of imitation (language made pleasing), and manner of imitation (acting). But also notice that he places in his definition his doctrine of *catharsis*. This means that he builds into his definition a subjective element involving the emotions of spectators along with the large number of objective elements that refer to aspects of tragedies themselves. His theory of tragedy, therefore, has a kinship to later expressionist theories of art.

The theory of catharsis is probably Aristotle's attempt to combat Plato's suspicions that art, or at least tragedy, leaves the spectator in an emotionally agitated and dangerous frame of mind. According to Aristotle, tragedy purges the spectator of pity and fear, and he leaves the theater free of such emotions. Aristotle apparently takes seriously Plato's contention that poetry, of which tragedy is a species, is inherently bound up with emotion, but he develops a theory that tragedy does not have bad effects. Unfortunately, Aristotle has very little to say about emotion in the *Poetics*. There is not even a discussion of catharsis in the *Poetics* as it has come down to us, and the interpretation of catharsis as a therapeutic effect on spectators is based on a passage in Aristotle's *Politics*.[6]

The last clause of the definition of tragedy stipulates that the action imitated must be pitiful and fearful, and this condition dictates the conclusions that Aristotle draws much later in the *Poetics* about the nature of the tragic hero. The tragic hero has two essential characteristics: (1) he must be a person like us, with regard to virtue, who goes from good to bad fortune, and (2) his bad fortune must result from an error (the tragic flaw). For the events of the play to be *fearful* to us, bad fortune must befall someone like us, that is, someone with whom we can identify. In order for the events of the play to be *pitiful*, bad fortune must not befall a good person (that would be repulsive) or a bad person(she would deserve what she got); through an error, it must befall a person who is neither good nor bad. There are perhaps some problems of consistency or at least of interpretation to be worked out among the definition of tragedy, the characterization of the tragic hero, and other of Aristotle's remarks about the characters in tragedy, but that cannot be attempted here.

The Nineteenth Century: New Directions—The Expression Theory of Art

It was not until shortly before the beginning of the nineteenth century that the imitation theory of art was called into question. During the nineteenth century, the theory that art, and especially literature, is the expression of the emotion of the artist came to be the dominant view, and the imitation theory went into an extended period of withering away. A theory of art does not spring up in an intellectual vacuum. The fact that art in Greece typically had a representative function was converted into a *theory* of art by attaching it to the theory of the Forms. The rise of the expression theory of art is related to Romanticism, an important intellectual and philosophical development of the eighteenth and nineteenth centuries.

The philosophical doctrines that underlie Romanticism are mainly those of Fichte, Schelling, Schopenhauer, and Nietzsche, although these four made other contributions to the thought about art. These philosophers developed notions that have their origins in Kant's theory of knowledge. Kant distinguishes between the empirical world of nature, which is the object of scientific knowledge, and the noumenal world, which in some sense lies behind the world of sense and of which we cannot know anything (knowledge being restricted to the empirical world). In part, the world of experience has the nature it has because of the structure that is impressed on it by the structure of the mind. The world of noumena, or things-in-themselves, undistorted by the structures of the human mind and lying mysteriously behind the sensuous world, fascinated many philosophers and men of letters in the nineteenth century. As far as philosophical theory is concerned, Romanticism may be thought of as a reaction against empiricist philosophy and the scientific mentality and as an attempt to reach behind the sensuous screen of ordinary knowledge to something thought to be vital and important. A strong aura of religion and mysticism hovers around Romanticism.

When philosophical Romanticism was applied to the world of art, it generated a new role for the artist and a new interest in artistic creation. The artist was conceived to be a means of getting in touch with vital sources and of attaining a kind of knowledge that science could not give, and artistic creation was identified or at least associated with the release of emotion. In this context, emotion assumes an importance it had not previously had; it is somehow involved in attaining a superior kind of knowledge. And art becomes the vehicle of this knowledge and a competitor of science. This new role for the artist is pointed up by the following passage from Nietzsche's *Will to Power.*

> Our aesthetics have hitherto been women's aesthetics, inasmuch as they have only formulated the experiences of what is beautiful, from the point of view of the receivers in art. In the whole of philosophy hitherto the artist has been lacking.[7]

In addition to its male chauvinist language, Nietzsche's statement is also something of an exaggeration because Plato's theory of artistic creation resembles in certain respects the Romantic conception.

Besides these philosophical developments, there seems to have been at the time a heightened appreciation of Dionysian qualities in art (vigor, intensity, elation) and a decreased interest in Apollonian qualities (calmness, order). Out of this intellectual milieu emerged the expression theory of art: art is the expression of the emotion of its creator (the artist). Most versions of the expression theory follow this two-term formula: one term is the expression of emotion, the other term is the artist who expresses the emotion. For example, Eugène Véron writes late in the nineteenth century,

> Art is the manifestation of emotion, obtaining external interpretation, now by expressive arrangement of line, form or color, now by a series of gestures, sounds, or words governed by particular rhythmic cadence.[8]

Alexander Smith (?–1851), writing in 1835, defines poetry by contrasting it with prose.

> The essential distinction between poetry and prose is this:—prose is the language of *intelligence,* poetry of *emotion.* In prose, we communicate our *knowledge* of the objects of sense or thought—in poetry, we express how these objects affect us.[9]

Leo Tolstoy (1828–1910) holds a three-term version of the expression theory that brings reference to spectators, readers, and the like into the definition of art.

Art is a human activity consisting in this, that one man consciously, by means of certain external signs, hands on to others feelings he has lived through, and that other people are infected by these feelings and also experience them.[10]

The expression theory of art can be seen as an attempt to accomplish a number of things. First, it is an attempt to reestablish for art a central place in Western culture. By the nineteenth century the increasing role of science and the consequent expansion of technology and industrialization had greatly reduced the relative role and status of art in the life of the culture. The expression theory tries to show that art can also do something important for people. And if this is so, the role of the artist takes on a significance it did not previously have. Second, the expression theory is an attempt to relate art to the lives of people. Emotion is something everyone is capable of experiencing, and that it is important is clear to everyone. Third, the theory is an attempt to account for the emotional qualities of art and the way in which art moves people. The imitation theory seems adequate to explain why a work that represents (imitates) an emotional event, say, the Crucifixion, has an emotional impact on people. However, art that is not representative in any apparent way, say, instrumental music or nonobjective painting, can also be very moving. Music, by the way, plays a large role in the thought of the romantic philosophers, and the great development of music in the centuries just prior to the nineteenth century provided a strong motive for rejecting the imitation theory and thereby paved the way for the expression theory. The expressive power of music seemed to be positive support for the theory.

What Is a Theory of Art?

What is a philosopher supposed to be doing when he or she works out a theory or definition of art? According to the traditional approach to definition, a philosopher would have to specify the necessary and sufficient conditions needed for something to be a work of art. A necessary condition for being an X is a characteristic that any object must have in order to be an X. A sufficient condition of an X is a characteristic that, if an object has that characteristic, it is an X. For example, consider the Greek definition of man as a rational animal. According to this definition, rationality and animality are each *individually* necessary for something to be a man and rationality and animality are jointly sufficient for something to be a man.

Both the imitation and the expression theories of art are so simple that it is perhaps not surprising that both appear to fall when judged as traditional definitions. At the level of necessary condition, it is impossible to show that every work of art imitates; for example, much music and, by definition, nonobjective painting do not imitate. Similarly, not every work of art seems to express emotion; for example, some works consist wholly of formal designs.

The heroic way to defend either of these theories as at least necessary conditions is to say that each theory specifies a characteristic that is an essence of art and that any object failing to have that characteristic just is not art. The embarrassing consequence of this defense is that one is left with a large class of objects, the members of which everyone (except the defender) calls "art" and treats as if they were art, but which the defender insists are not art. This raises the general philosophical question of how disputes about the adequacy of definition are to be settled, but I do not have space to discuss that problem here.

It may be that a definition of art cannot be given; the concept of art may be too rich and complicated to be captured in the traditional manner. This problem will be discussed in the next three chapters. But if the imitation and expression definitions are inadequate as theories of art, they clearly do say something important about some aspects of some works of art. That a certain work of art is imitative is sometimes the most important feature of that work, and if the imitative aspect of a work is not its *most* important feature, it may still be an important one. Similarly, the emotional content of art is frequently of great significance. (Whether or not it is significant that the emotional content is *someone's expression* is a question that requires a detailed inquiry.) Because of the obvious pertinence of both theories to certain elements in works of art, neither the imitation nor the expression theory should simply be dismissed. Perhaps both may be thought of as theories of *aspects* of art, that is, theories that have a limited application within the class of art and that point to significant and widely pervasive features in art.

While on the subject of the theory of art, I should point out that the term "art" or "work of art" is used in at least two senses: a classificatory sense and an evaluative sense. The first sense concerns the question of whether or not a given object is to be classified as a work of art. The classification of something as a work of art, however, does not determine that the thing is a *good* work of art. The fact that an animal is correctly classified as a horse does not mean that it is a good horse. However, the expression "work of art" is sometimes used to make a positive evaluation of something. A painting or waterfall may be praised by saying that it is a work of art. It is easy to see that "This painting is a work of art" is an evaluation and not a classification because the first two words in the sentence ("This painting") alone presuppose that the object being referred to must be classified as a work of art. It is important not to confuse these two senses.

Chapter 6

Twentieth-Century Theories of Art

1914 to the 1950s

Earlier I outlined two theories, or philosophies, of art: the imitation theory, which dates from ancient times, and the expression theory, which came into prominence in the nineteenth century. Four theories of art of the first half of the twentieth century will be discussed in this chapter. Of these four, two—Susanne Langer's and R. G. Collingwood's—are descendants of the two earlier philosophies, Clive Bell's is closely related to the traditional theory of beauty, and Morris Weitz's view of defining "art" is of more recent origin. Each of these four theories has played a prominent part in the development of aesthetics during the first half of the twentieth century.

Bell's theory of significant form, which is discussed first, may be thought of as a theory that developed out of the Platonic theory of beauty. Although it now has few, if any, adherents, the concept of significant form was very influential in the early years of this century. Langer's theory of expressive symbolism may be thought of as a modern version of the imitation theory, although she probably would not wish it to be understood that way. Her conception of the arts as symbolic forms has been a very popular theory of art as far as the general public is concerned. However, her views have been severely criticized by many philosophers. Collingwood's theory of imaginative expression is a sophisticated version of the expression theory, which continues to be a powerful tradition. Weitz's analysis of the concept of art is an attempt to adapt some of the insights of the philosophy of Ludwig Wittgenstein to the theory of art.

Clive Bell: A Twentieth-Century Beauty Theory of Art

Clive Bell's book, entitled simply *Art*,[1] which appeared in 1914, has achieved the status of a modern classic, and the simplicity and lucidity of its argument gained it a wide audience and for a time great influence. The book is the origin of the expression "significant form," which once achieved wide currency and is still invoked by some. Bell's theory is, then, a good one with which to begin a discussion of the philosophy of art. However, it should be borne in mind that Bell qualifies his remarks by stating that he is talking only about *visual* art, although at one point he suggests that his theory might also hold for music.

Bell's theory in many respects, especially in a basic underlying assumption, resembles that of Plato, but the most immediate influence on Bell was the English philosopher G. E. Moore, who was himself something of a Platonist. Moore, in working out his *ethical* theory, developed what has been called "the open-question argument," which had great influence in ethics.[2] Bell attempted to adapt the conclusion of Moore's argument to aesthetics. Moore examined several traditional definitions of "good," arguing in each case that the open-question argument proved the definitions defective. Consider, for example, the hedonistic definition that "good" means "pleasure." Moore agrees that many pleasures are good but denies that "good" is *identical in meaning* with "pleasure" because he claims one can significantly ask of some given pleasure, "Is this pleasure good?" Moore's point is that if "good" and "pleasure" had the same meaning, it would be as silly to ask such a question as, "Is this bachelor married?" When we carefully consider the question of whether a given pleasure is good, it will become clear to us, Moore contends, that it is not a silly question. It is simply an *open question* whether some pleasure is good or not. It can be seen from this example that Moore is concerned with the *meanings* of ethical terms, or concepts, and that he is assuming that the criterion of the correctness of definition of such moral concepts is our intuitive understanding of them.

Moore actually applied his analysis to only a few definitions of "good," but he thought that it undermined *all* such definitions, and he concludes that "good" cannot be defined. In addition, Moore concludes that "good" designates a simple, unanalyzable, nonnatural quality that characterizes some actions and states of affairs. The alleged fact that good is simple and unanalyzable means that it cannot be broken down into parts and hence cannot be defined. By way of contrast, the Greek concept of "man" can be broken down into *rationality* and *animality* yielding the definition, "Man" means "rational animal." When Moore says that good is a nonnatural quality, he means that it is not an empirical quality perceived by the senses, like a color or a tone. The mind *intuits* rather than sees, hears, and so on, that an action or state of affairs is good. Moore's notion of intuition is similar to

Plato's concept of the knowing of nonempirical Forms. Also, like Plato, Moore makes an *essentialistic* assumption in developing his conception of goodness. He writes, "we must discover what is both common and peculiar to all undoubted ethical judgements."[3] His view is essentialistic because he assumes that a *single essence* characterizes the objects of all judgments of goodness, namely, the quality of goodness itself. (Later in this chapter, I will discuss the attack of Morris Weitz on essentialism in the theory of art.)

The three basic components of Bell's theory are: (1) his phenomenological starting-point, (2) his methodological assumption, and (3) his main conclusion. The first component is something he calls "the aesthetic emotion" and the third is "significant form," which he claims every work of art has. The second component is the assumption of essentialism, which relates the other two components, allowing significant form to be derived from the aesthetic emotion. Two quotations from the first chapter of Bell's book reveal the structure of his argument.

> The starting-point of all systems of aesthetics must be the personal experience of a peculiar emotion. The objects that provoke this emotion we call works of art. All sensitive people agree that there is a peculiar emotion provoked by works of art. . . . This emotion is called the aesthetic emotion.[4]

> . . . if we can discover some quality common and peculiar to all the objects that provoke [the aesthetic emotion], we shall have solved what I take to be the central problem of aesthetics. We shall have discovered the essential quality of a work of art . . . For either all works of visual art have some common quality, or when we speak of "works of art" we gibber. . . . What is this quality? . . . Only one answer seems possible—significant form.[5]

Bell begins by turning inward and claims to be able to distinguish a peculiarly aesthetic emotion that is not to be confused with the ordinary emotions of life such as fear, joy, anger, and such. He then turns outward and claims to discover that the objects that stimulate the aesthetic emotion are works of art. Finally, he attempts to discover what is common and peculiar to works of art by virtue of which they stimulate the aesthetic emotion, and he claims that this characteristic is significant form.

Bell is frequently criticized for arguing in a circle, that is, of saying when asked what the aesthetic emotion is that it is the emotion provoked by significant form and of saying when asked what significant form is that it is the object that provokes the aesthetic emotion. Perhaps Bell's way of expressing himself does leave him open to this charge, but he clearly intends to claim that the aesthetic emotion can be distinguished and isolated from all other emotions and can serve as a foundation for his philosophy of art. The most telling criticism that could be brought against Bell would be to show that there is no aesthetic emotion. However, it is perhaps impossible to show this because of the way in which he states his claim. If Jones maintains that he cannot discover the aesthetic emotion in his experience, Bell can answer that Jones must be insensitive (or has not had sufficient experience), because "All sensitive people agree that there is a peculiar emotion . . . the aesthetic emotion." The problem is that if one cannot discover the aesthetic emotion in one's own experience, then there must be the nagging suspicion that one is perhaps not sensitive enough and that one's experience is therefore not really a counterinstance to Bell's theory. Sheer numbers will not help either; there may simply be large numbers of insensitive people. Perhaps the best one could do by way of a test would be to see if persons who enjoy, are knowledgeable about, and frequently experience art and who are philosophically sophisticated enough to understand the issue claim to have the aesthetic emotion. At the present time, such persons do not seem to make such a claim, and it therefore seems that there is good reason to think that Bell is wrong in believing there is a peculiarly aesthetic emotion. Still, such a test would be difficult to set up and interpret definitively, and perhaps we must remain in some doubt.

At this point, it might seem that Bell's essentialistic assumption should be discussed. However, essentialism will be examined in detail later in this chapter and is omitted here. Before getting into a discussion of significant form, it will he helpful to give a general characterization of the term "form." By the form of a work of art is meant the total set of relations that obtain among its elements. (Homogeneous areas of color, for example, are elements of a work of art.) Consider a design that is made up of thirteen dots as elements.

The form of the design is the total set of relations among the thirteen dots. Some of these relations assume more importance in the design than others: the ten dots around the edge of the design tend to form themselves into four straight lines making a rectangle that encloses the three dots in the center, and these dots constitute themselves into three straight lines forming a triangle. Note that although all thirteen elements of the design are mentioned in the previous sentence, not all the relations were specified. For example, the straight-line relation between the upper left-hand dot and the dot at the apex of the triangle was not mentioned because it has no significance in this design. The relations that assume importance or the greatest importance in a design are called its "composition," or "structure," or even its "form." This last use of "form" is clearly not identical with the one under discussion, but the two notions are related.

Bell maintained that all works of art must have some quality in common, but what is it?

> Only one answer seems possible—significant form. In each [of the works of art he has just mentioned], lines and colours combined in a particular way,

certain forms and relations of forms, stir our aesthetic emotions. These relations and combinations of lines and colours, these aesthetically moving forms,
I call "Significant Form"; and "Significant Form" is the one quality common
to all works of visual art.[6]

On first reading, it appears that Bell is setting forth a view that may be called
Hutchesonian because of its resemblance to the view of the eighteenth-century
philosopher. Hutcheson maintained that uniformity in variety (significant form)
triggered the sense of beauty (the aesthetic emotion). In this Hutchesonian reading, "significant form" becomes the name of a certain set of relations, which
means that only two components are involved in the interpretation: a set of relations and the aesthetic emotion. However, because of the great influence of
Moore on Bell and because of the nuances of the way in which he states his view,
there is a possibility that Bell's theory should be given an intuitionist interpretation that is a bit more complicated than the Hutchesonian. In the passage quoted,
Bell says that "significant form" is the name of certain sets of relations, but he also
says that significant form is a *quality*. Philosophers have traditionally used the
terms "relation" and "quality" to refer to distinct and contrasting things. There
seem, then, to be two possible versions of Bell's theory: the Hutchesonian one,
which holds that "significant form" is the name of certain sets of relations, and
the intuitionist version, which holds that "significant form" is the name of a nonnatural *quality* that certain sets of relations have. The intuitionist version involves
three components: (1) the aesthetic emotion, (2) certain sets of relations, and (3)
the nonnatural quality that certain sets of relations have and which is named by
the expression "significant form." Which of these two versions did Bell hold? The
drift of most of his remarks seems to support the Hutchesonian interpretation.
Nevertheless, he also continues to speak of significant form as a quality. Late in his
book, when he is discussing changes that art has undergone throughout history,
he says, "So, though the essential quality—significance—is constant, in the choice
of forms there is perpetual change."[7] Here "significance" is used alone, not cou-
pled with "form," as the name of a quality, and this provides some evidence for
the intuitionist version that significant form, or significance, is a nonnatural quality that *accompanies* certain forms on certain occasions. Perhaps, however, the best
explanation of this situation is that Bell is not philosophically sophisticated
enough to realize all the implications of his remarks and vocabulary, much of
which was borrowed from G. E. Moore, one of the most acute analytic philosophers of the twentieth century.

Bell does not get around to providing a specific definition of "art" or "work of
art," but he clearly implies the following formulation: a work of art is an object
that possesses significant form, significant form being the name of whatever stim-
ulates the aesthetic emotion. A question that arises immediately is whether or not
a natural object can have significant form and thereby be a work of art. Bell
remarks that occasionally people "see in nature what we see in art,"[8] but he

thinks this exceedingly rare. With this qualification in mind, perhaps it is accurate to say that for Bell a work of art is an *artifact* that possesses significant form.

But now a paradox seems to arise from the definition. It is clear from what Bell says throughout his book that not every object ordinarily called a "work of art" is a work of art by this definition. The paradox is that there seem to be works of art that are not works of art. However, the paradox is resolved when it is remembered that there are at least two senses of "work of art." There is the classificatory sense, in which all paintings, statues, vases, buildings, and such are works of art; but clearly Bell is not explicating this sense. There is also the evaluative sense, in which the expression "work of art" is used to praise artifacts and sometimes even natural objects. Bell's definition must be seen as an attempt to isolate the meaning of this second sense of "work of art," and this is the reason his theory is called a beauty theory of art in the title of this section. Beauty in either of its traditional meanings—as the name of some empirical characteristics or the Platonic Form of Beauty—carries with it an evaluative aspect. To say of something that it is beautiful is to praise it.

Is Bell's definition an adequate one? Since it is based on the notion of the aesthetic emotion, the definition inherits all the obscurities involved in that slippery notion. Also, it seems plausible to demand that an adequate theory of art furnish explications of all the basic senses of "work of art," and Bell's theory does not deal at all with the classificatory sense. The two senses of "work of art" will be dealt with at some length in Chapters 7 and 8.

No discussion of Bell's view should omit at least mention of his famous conclusion concerning the value of representation in visual art. From what has been said thus far it should be clear that Bell thought that the formal relations within works of visual art are the source of great value, and surely he is correct in this matter. However, Bell drew a much stronger conclusion than this, namely, that representation in visual art has no aesthetic value at all and is often an aesthetic disvalue. He writes,

> Let no one imagine that representation is bad in itself; a realistic form may be as significant, in its place as part of the design, as an abstract. But if a representative form has value, it is as form, not as representation. The representative element in a work of art may or may not be harmful; always it is irrelevant.[9]

As Bell makes clear elsewhere, his claim is that representation is irrelevant to aesthetic value, although he readily admits that representation may have value of a nonaesthetic kind. His justification for distinguishing between two kinds of value is based on the notion of the aesthetic emotion. He thinks that only formal relations can evoke the aesthetic emotion and that representation cannot. Representations may depict, suggest, and evoke the ordinary emotions of life such as fear, joy, and so on, but never the aesthetic emotion.

As vague and unconvincing as Bell's theoretical justification is for denying the significance of representation, his conclusion played an important role in art criticism and in the shaping of taste in the period after his book, *Art*, appeared. Bell's theory of art served as a basis for the critical attack on the sentimental, illustrative art that so dominated English taste of the time. Popular representative art largely neglected the formal aspects of painting, and Bell and others sought to change people's minds about such art. Bell was one of those who was responsible for introducing the English public to the paintings of Cezanne and other French Post-Impressionist painters of the time. A dubious theory of art was, then, responsible in part for an important development in the history of art and taste.

Susanne Langer: A Twentieth-Century Imitation Theory of Art

Between 1948 and 1957, Susanne Langer set forth her philosophy of art in a series of books, *Philosophy in a New Key*,[10] *Feeling and Form*,[11] and *Problems of Art*.[12] Although she presents her theory as the view that art is an *expressive symbolism*, it is misleading to so describe it, and close inspection reveals that it is a version of the imitation theory adapted to accommodate emotion and feeling. Briefly put, Langer's theory of art consists of a definition of art and a thesis about how art functions. The theory rests on seven basic and variously interrelated technical notions: symbol, abstraction, expressiveness, feeling, form, illusion, and virtual image. The first five of these are involved in the definition and the last two (they are really one) in the thesis about art's function.

Langer is convinced that "art is essentially one," which means that she thinks a definition of art in terms of necessary and sufficient conditions can be given. The definition she gives is, "Art is the creation of forms symbolic of human feeling."[13] The two of the five technical notions that do not explicitly appear in this definition are abstraction and expressiveness, but they are implicit in her notion of symbol. A symbol is expressive of human feeling by means of abstraction. What this seems to mean is that a work of art is by definition an *iconic* symbol of human feeling, although Langer does not explicitly use the words "iconic" or "iconic symbol." An iconic symbol is a symbol that resembles in some way what it signifies; for example, a highway sign with two crossed lines is an iconic symbol because the sign resembles the crossroads it signifies. Most symbols are not iconic. It should be made clear at the outset that Langer explicitly distinguishes art as symbol—what she calls the "art symbol"—from symbols in art.[14] Symbols in art are elements in works of art, such as depictions of halos, lambs, and so on, that symbolize qualities such as holiness and love. For Langer, an art symbol is the work of art as a whole, and an art symbol may or may not contain symbols of the-symbol-in-art type.

Each of the arts symbolizes "human feeling" in its own way. "Music is a tonal analogue of emotive life."[15] "As *scene* is the basic abstraction of pictorial art, and *kinetic volume* of sculpture, that of architecture is an *ethnic* domain."[16] Similar statements are made about the other species of art. Presumably it is meant that music symbolizes emotional feelings, pictorial art symbolizes scenes of various kinds, and so on. At this point the theory is vague. For example, in what sense does *scene* necessarily involve human feeling? Langer's definition raises two basic questions: (1) is art a symbol? and (2) is the subject matter of art always human feeling?

What does she mean by "symbol"? "A symbol," she says, "is any device whereby we are enabled to make an abstraction."[17] But what, then, does "abstraction" mean? A form is abstract when it is *abstracted* or "removed" from its usual context.[18] Thus, a form becomes a symbol when it is abstracted from its usual context; at least, this seems to be what is meant in the case of the art symbol. A drawing of a woman would be an abstraction because the form of the drawing is less than the form of the whole context in which the woman who was the model exists. This drawing would be, in Langer's sense, a symbol, and since every work of art is like the drawing in this sense, every work of art is, therefore, an art symbol. Incidentally, this example should not be taken as indicating that every work of art must have some actual thing as a model.

Even though representation (depiction of objects in space) seems to satisfy Langer's definition of symbol, it turns out that she is not interested in representation. As she states, buildings, pots, and tunes are not representational, and her theory demands that all works of art have some single feature in common.

> Representational works, if they are good art, are so for the same reason as non-representational ones. They have more than one symbolic function— representation . . . and also artistic expression, which is presentation of ideas of feeling.[19]

All works of art are then also art symbols in this second sense. All works abstract and thereby symbolize human feeling, but feeling is not symbolized by means of representation. It is extremely difficult to understand Langer on this point, but presumably all works resemble the forms of human feeling but not to such a degree that the resemblance would constitute representation. A work of art symbolizes in this sense of "artistic expression" when

> It formulates the appearance of feeling, of objective experience, the character of so-called "inner life," which . . . the normal use of words . . . is peculiarly unable to articulate, and which therefore we can only refer to in a general and quite superficial way.[20]

Langer's use of the term "symbol" has been strongly criticized by a number of philosophers.[21] The nub of the criticism is that by definition a symbol is something that signifies something else by virtue of either an explicit or a tacit convention, and that Langer's notion of art symbol does not have the required conventional aspect. Remember that an art symbol is the work as a whole and that every work is a unique art symbol. Thus, there is the paradox of a unique, one-shot symbol. Contrast an art symbol with a symbol in art, say, a halo. The halo is a highly conventionalized entity and has appeared repeatedly throughout a long tradition. The characteristic of Langer's art symbol that is supposed to enable its symbolic function is its iconicity of human feelings. However, iconicity without convention is not enough to make something a symbol; if it were, almost everything would be a symbol of something, since almost everything is to some degree iconic of something else. For example, one table resembles another table, but we would not therefore conclude that either table is a symbol of the other. Even iconic symbols are established by convention—the crossroads highway sign, for example. It is thus difficult to see how a work of art as a whole can be symbolic, since it lacks the necessary conventional aspect.

Langer came to feel the weight of such criticisms and declared that a work of art is not a "genuine symbol" and said that henceforth she would use the expression "expressive form" rather than "art symbol." However, even in the essay in which she accepts the criticism, she continues to use "art symbol" interchangeably with "expressive form." And, as a kind of parting shot, she adds, "Yet the function of what I called 'the art symbol' . . . is more *like* a symbolic function than like anything else."[22] Why does she cling so to the notion of symbolism? Because not only is it the central idea of her philosophy of art, it is the only thing that makes her theory novel and significant. Semantic notions like "symbol" have assumed a very important place in philosophy, and it would be a significant philosophical contribution to show that these ideas have an application in defining "work of art."

Without the notion of symbol, Langer's theory turns out to be simply a version of the imitation theory of art. Works of art in some not very clear way are iconic of or imitate human feelings. Note that it is an imitation theory with a limited subject matter. In the imitation theory, the representation of a woman in a painting would count as an imitation, but in Langer's view, only human feeling is the universal subject matter of art. Even what is generally thought of as the most original feature of this theory—namely, the contention that music is symbolic (imitative) of human feeling—was in part anticipated by Aristotle, who maintained that the music of the flute, lyre, and pipes is imitation.

We come now to the second aspect of Langer's definition of art, the claim that all art has as its subject matter feeling or, as she puts it, that art "formulates the appearance of feeling." Is it true that all art does this? The great difficulty with evaluating the claim is its vagueness. There do seem to be some cases in which art is iconic of feeling. Beardsley suggests that Ravel's "Bolero" may be iconic of some psychological process or other,[23] and some music is expressive of longing, sadness, and so on. But is it true that all music is iconic? And of what human feeling is a Mondrian painting iconic? It is difficult to say more on this point and the reader may simply personally evaluate the claim that art is the appearance of feeling.

Langer's thesis about how art functions is that art is an *illusion*. Or to use another of her technical terms, every work of art is a *virtual image*. Although it cannot be asserted with complete assurance, "illusion" and "virtual image" seem to have essentially the same meaning in her theory. In discussing pictorial art, she explains one in terms of the other.

> This purely visual space is an illusion, for our sensory experiences do not agree on it in their report. . . . Like the space "behind" the surface of a mirror, it is what the physicists call "virtual space"—an intangible image.[24]

"Our sensory experiences do not agree" means that there is an appearance of objects in space but that they cannot be touched or felt. Perhaps it can also be said that in all but a very few cases of pictorial art the appearance of objects in space is recognizably different from that of our ordinary experience. Calling a work of art an "illusion" or a "virtual image" makes the point that there is a sense in which it is somehow different from objects encountered in our ordinary experience: a painting and its space are not the same as a window and its view; a stage murder is not the same as an actual one; and so on. No one can take exception to this obviously true point.

However, if Langer's claim is not disputable, her term "illusion" is subject to criticism as misleading. It suggests that art fools or deceives people, and although on rare occasions people are deceived, this is not typical. She recognizes the problem and explicitly declares that she is not claiming that people are deluded by art. Still, it is perverse to use the term, since its ordinary meaning involves deception as its dictionary definition reveals: "1. An unreal or misleading image. . . . 2. State or fact of being deceived. . . . 3. A perception which fails to give the true character of an object perceived."[25] She has taken a term with an established meaning, altered its meaning, and turned it into a technical term. It is not surprising that her readers have been confused. Other terms she uses in this connection—"semblance" and "virtual image"—better convey her meaning. To call the space in a painting a "virtual space" or a "semblance of space" conveys that it is not a real space but does not suggest that deception is involved.

How important is the claim that art creates an illusion? No one thinks that he can stick his hand through a painting as through a window or that a dancer's gesture exists in the same context as the usher's gesture. To insist on this point seems somewhat odd. This insistence is perhaps due to the tradition in aesthetics that spectators are always or at least sometimes in danger of confusing art with reality—stage murders with real ones, for example. I noted in Chapter 3, Langer's theory of illusion is similar to the theory of psychical distance. However, not only is talk about illusion not really informative, there is also some danger in it. For as the *Peter Pan* case showed us, to talk about art as illusion suggests that there is some illusion that may be shattered and therefore that certain limitations must be placed on the techniques of art.

Finally, Langer's view of art also illustrates another common difficulty—confusing the definition of art with a statement of what makes art good. This comes out clearly when she tries to justify calling art a symbol. She says that art may be called a symbol because it fulfills a certain function, namely, it formulates the appearance of feeling, and "this function every good work of art does perform."[26] This remark about good art is pointless, because if Langer's theory is correct, *all art*—

good and bad—formulates the appearance of feeling. The main point at issue here is that the conception of art must be independent of the criterion of good art, otherwise we would be unable to speak of bad art and we do in fact frequently speak of bad art. Langer blurs this distinction.

R. G. Collingwood: A Twentieth-Century Expressionist Theory of Art

R. G. Collingwood in 1938 in *The Principles of Art* [27] develops a comprehensive and influential expressionist theory of art. He attempts to work out systematically and on a large philosophical scale the widely held view that there is an essential connection between art and the expression of emotion. His book is a sustained and complex argument in support of his conclusion that *art is imaginative expression*.

The basis for Collingwood's theory of art is his analysis of the concept of craft, in which he argues that art and craft are completely distinct. What he calls "the technical theory of art," which, he says, begins with Plato and persists to the present day, maintains that art and craft are species of a single genus. Collingwood denies that art and craft share a common essential feature and combats the technical theory of art in whatever form he detects it. The *relation of means to ends* is for Collingwood the central characteristic of craft, and the following sums up his conception of craft: a craft is an activity in which some raw material is transformed by a learnable skill into a preconceived product. A work of craft is the product of this kind of activity. Shoemaking is a good example of craft; the shoemaker's skill and the leather are *means* to producing a specifiable and preconceived end (shoes).

Collingwood allows that craft and art can overlap so that the same thing can be a work of craft in one respect and a work of art in another. He also makes clear that an artist must master certain crafts as a prerequisite to communicating his or her art: a painter must know how to handle paints and the poet words so that their art (which is expression) can be made public. However, to have mastered such crafts does not make one an artist, and it is a mistake for the holder of the technical theory of art, according to Collingwood, not to realize this. What is the basis for Collingwood's claim that art (what he calls "art proper") and craft are completely different? He believes that he is simply making explicit how the word "art" is used in English. Collingwood's method in 1938 anticipates the "ordinary language" method popular later among one wing of analytic philosophy. He maintains that "art" has a number of senses in English and that when he describes "art proper" and distinguishes it from "art falsely so called," all users of English will recognize that his description marks out a usage of "art." He also assumes that it is this usage that underlies serious talk about art. His theory of art is, as he says, merely an attempt to tell us what we already know—because it is embedded in our language habits. We may not be able to formulate explicitly what we know in this sense, and Collingwood's aim is to help us formulate it. He does not give arguments to support his view that art proper and craft are completely distinct; he assumes the distinction is correct and that all he has to do is to describe it and readers will recognize its correctness. One can, however, think of the description as a kind of argument. The arguments he does give are subsequent to the art–craft distinction and presuppose that distinction.

Collingwood's first attempt to give a precise description of art proper involves trying to show that many of the things called "art" are *not* art proper. The two kinds of art falsely so called that he discusses are "amusement art" and "magical art." He characterizes amusement art as follows:

> If an artifact is designed to stimulate a certain emotion, and if this emotion is intended not for discharge into the occupations of ordinary life but for enjoy-ment as something of value in itself, the function of the artifact is to amuse and entertain.[28]

He thinks "that most of what generally goes by the name of art nowadays is not art at all, but amusement."[29] In preparing the way for his discussion of magical art, Collingwood, drawing on anthropological studies, presents a novel analysis of the concept of magic, whose value is by no means limited to the theory of art. Although it is not the only kind of magical art, religious art is alleged to be a good example of it.

> Obviously its [religious art's] function is to evoke, and constantly re-evoke, certain emotions whose discharge is to be effected in the activities of everyday life. In calling it magical I am not denying its claim to the title religious.[30]

Patriotic monuments are also good examples of magical art; they evoke emotions that are useful for everyday life. Collingwood is careful to point out that amuse-ment art is not necessarily bad if it is used sparingly and is not mistaken for art proper. He also points out that magical art has an important role to play, as it is part of the ritual important to organized social life.

Amusement art and magical art have in common that they both are intended to *evoke* emotion. They differ in the role that the evoked emotions play. The emo-tions evoked by magical art are interwoven with the rest of life and act as motives for our everyday actions; for example, patriotic emotions motivate one to defend one's country. The emotions evoked by amusement art are "intended to be earthed [grounded] instead of overflowing into the situations represented."[31] The situations represented by amusement art are "make-believe" and "unreal," and the emotions evoked are dissipated. Collingwood associates Aristotle's notion of catharsis with amusement art rather than with art proper. He argues that amuse-ment and magic are not art proper because they are forms of craft; it is taken for granted that art proper and craft are distinct. Amusement and magic are crafts because they are designed to evoke specific emotions that the maker of the arti-fact conceives of in advance. Collingwood thinks of the evoked emotions as prod-ucts in the same way that shoes are the product of the craft of shoemaking. The amuser, the magician, and the shoemaker all have in mind a product they want to produce, and each has a technique for doing so.

Having analyzed amusement and magic in terms of evoked emotion, Collingwood assumes without argument that there is a necessary connection between art proper and emotion, although it is not a matter of evoking. (His assumption is perhaps explained by the fact that E. F. Carritt, a well-known expressionist, was Collingwood's tutor at Oxford. Collingwood may, for all his subtlety, be perpetuating without question a tradition he learned at school. Collingwood's theory is also strongly influenced by the Italian philosopher Croce.) The connection between art and emotion seems so obvious to Collingwood that he simply asserts it to be the case.

> Art has something to do with emotion; what it does with it has a certain resemblance to arousing it, but is not arousing it.[32]

> Since the artist proper has something to do with emotion, and what he does with it is not to arouse it, what is it that he does?[33]

His answer is that art *expresses* emotion rather than evokes it. Collingwood's argument may be reconstructed in the following way.

1. Art has something to do with emotion.   Assumption

2. Art must either evoke emotion or express emotion; there are only two possibilities.   From 1 plus assumption about possibilities

3. Art is not craft.   Previously proved

4. Art cannot arouse emotion because if it did it would be craft.   From 2 and 3

5. Art is the expression of emotion.   From 2 and 4

The argument clearly depends on assumptions, and I will examine their acceptability later. The next task is to see what Collingwood means by "expresses emotion."

It is important to know what Collingwood means by "expresses emotion" because at this point he thinks that he has proved that art is identical with the expression of emotion and hence that an adequate description of the expression of emotion would also be an adequate theory of art. Emotion may be expressed in a number of ways—for example, by speech or by gesture. However, not every bodily movement involved with emotion is an expression of that emotion. A person may express his anger by saying, "You are an evil man." However, if a person says, "I am angry," he is not expressing his anger, he is describing it. It is even more important for Collingwood not to confuse *betraying* emotion with express-ing it. Care is required here, because we sometimes say, for example, that distor-tions of the face express pain and that turning pale and stammering express fear. These bodily phenomena are significantly different from other activities that are said to be expressions, and Collingwood marks the differences by saying that these are *betrayals* of emotion. Betrayals are uncontrolled reactions, and Collingwood presumably thinks that such reactions cannot be identified with art. The kinds of occurrences we call "expressions" and which Collingwood wants to identify with art are those that are "under our control and are conceived by us, in our awareness of controlling them, as our way of expressing these emotions."[34] The important differences between betraying and expressing emotion are *control* and *awareness of control*: distortion of the face when in pain is not controlled, nor need one be aware that one's face is distorted. The same may be said of stammering, turning pale, and so on. Late in his book, Collingwood says that betrayals are a primitive form of expression and designates them "psychical expressions,"[35] but this is done to distinguish them from what might be called "expression proper." Consciously controlled expression of emotion is, Collingwood says, *language*—language in a broad sense that "includes any activity of any organ which is expressive in the same way in which speech is expressive."[36] "Art must be language."[37] Colling-wood concludes that "the expressing of emotion," "art proper," and "language" all refer to the same thing: expression = art = language.

It is perhaps implicit in what has already been said, but there is a feature of Collingwood's conception of expressing emotion that needs to be made com-pletely explicit because it has such far-reaching consequences for his conception of art. He makes his point in this frequently quoted passage in which he describes what happens when someone expresses emotion.

> At first, he is conscious of having an emotion, but not conscious of what this emotion is. All he is conscious of is a perturbation or excitement, which he feels going on within him, but of whose nature he is ignorant. While in this state, all he can say about his emotion is: 'I feel . . . I don't know what I feel.' From this helpless and oppressed condition he extricates himself by doing something which we call expressing himself. . . . he expresses himself by speaking. . . . the emotion expressed is an emotion of whose nature the person who feels it is no longer unconscious.[38]

This passage makes it clear that expressing emotion involves the expresser's explicit knowledge of the *specific* emotion that is expressed. When Collingwood speaks of specific emotion, he does not mean simply fear, anger, and so on, but the specific *kind* of anger, fear, and so on. It follows from this analysis of expressing emotion that it cannot be known ahead of time that a specific emotion will he expressed or what, if any, emotion will be expressed. The nature of an expressed emotion cannot be known until it has been expressed. Since art has been identi-fied with expressing emotion, this means that an artist cannot know ahead of time what he or she will create. Collingwood presses this point very hard. He does not simply mean that an artist cannot know in complete detail what he will do. "No artist . . . can set out to write a comedy, a tragedy, an elegy or the like. So far as he is an artist proper, he is just as likely to write any one of these as any other."[39] Collingwood is not simply claiming the obvious, namely, that an artist might start out to write, say, a comedy and end up with a tragedy, for he says an artist proper is "just as likely to write any of these as any other." Readers may assume there must be many counterexamples to this statement, but Collingwood tries to neutralize these examples by classifying them as amusement or magic art. The amusement and magic artists know ahead of time what they want to produce and have the means to do so, and this is why their works are not art, but craft. Collingwood is very bold about what he classifies as craft: at one point, he suggests that the plays of Shakespeare are not art because they were designed to please (evoke emotion in) Elizabethan audiences.[40]

This is a startling conclusion, for most people would consider Shakespeare's plays to be paradigms of works of art. And there is a further question: how can someone other than the artist himself know that his work expresses emotion? Collingwood's answer is that "we know that he [the artist] is expressing his emotions by the fact that he is enabling us to express ours."[41] This answer suffices for some cases, but what of the cases in which, say, a poet has in fact expressed his or her emotion but the reader for some reason is unable to realize this fact? In such cases, the reader will not be able to tell whether the work is craft or art. Collingwood's reading of Shakespeare may be a case in point. Perhaps Shakespeare's words do not "work" for Collingwood and he has therefore concluded that they must have been designed to evoke emotion and are craft. This point brings out that Collingwood's criterion of art proper is difficult to apply.

Thus far, only the expressive aspect of Collingwood's theory of art has been discussed, but he thinks the definition of art also involves another aspect—imagination. In order for something to be art, it must be *both* expressive and imaginative.[42] Collingwood's use of imagination has come in for a great deal of adverse criticism. Alan Donagan, in an otherwise sympathetic treatment of Collingwood's theory of art, claims that Collingwood confuses two distinct senses of "to imagine" and as a result draws a false conclusion.[43] The two senses are the act of forming mental images and the act of bringing something into consciousness or awareness. Collingwood is correct when he concludes that a work of art *may* be imaginary in the first sense; for example, a poet might create a poem by saying some words to himself, and the poem would be only, to use Collingwood's phrase, "in his head." Let it be assumed that Collingwood is also right in thinking that *all* works of art are imaginary in the second sense, namely that they are the result of bringing something into consciousness. Nothing about bringing something into consciousness requires that the thing so brought is necessarily "in the head" only. For example, when an artist paints on a canvas, he brings something, say, the representation of a woman, into consciousness, but the representation is a public object and not in the head only. The second sense of "to imagine" appears to be identical with what Collingwood means by "to express," so that to say that works of art are expressions *and* imaginary in the second sense is redundant. Collingwood appears to have confused his two senses of "to imagine" and drawn the conclusion that *all* works of art are imaginary in the sense of being "in the head" only. Consequently, he denies that such public objects as statues, paintings, and the like are works of art. He claims that the only real works of art are the mental images formed in the mind of the artist before or as the artist creates a public object or the mental images formed in the spectator's mind as the result of experiencing a public object. This conclusion is especially strange for a philosopher who purports to be following ordinary usage.

There is a conflict involved in Collingwood's maintaining that art is identical with the *expression* of emotion and his maintaining that art is in the mind only. The problem is that the *expression* that occurs when emotion is expressed is always a public object—a smile, a scowl, the shaking of a fist, the uttering of exclamation, and the like. That is, the *expression* of emotion is never in the mind only.[44]

Collingwood tries to deduce criteria of good and bad art from his definition of art. He begins his discussion of the evaluation of art with the remark that "The definition of any given kind of thing is also the definition of a good thing of that kind."[45] But surely this is not true. Consider a dictionary definition of "goat" that reads, "Any of certain hollow-horned ruminant mammals allied to the sheep, but of lighter build, with backwardly arching horns, a short tail, and (usually) straight hair."[46] An animal might satisfy all of the criteria mentioned in this definition and still be a very poor goat. For example, he might have backwardly arching horns but they might be very short, or he might be chronically ill, and so on. Collingwood confuses the classification of a thing as a thing of a certain kind with the question of whether a thing is a good thing of its kind. If he were right, every goat would be a good goat, every man a good man, and every work of art a good work of art. We do, however, frequently speak of bad works of art. Collingwood tries to account for this by saying that "A bad work of art is an activity in which the agent tries to express a given emotion, but fails."[47] In other words, a bad work of art is something that tried to be a work of art but failed. The most obvious difficulty is the paradox that a bad work of art turns out not to be a work of art! One would think that for something to be a bad thing of a certain type, it would have to be of that type—a bad horse would have to be a horse to begin with. Also, Collingwood's evaluational scheme is so simple that it cannot account for some cases of bad art. For example, someone might write a poem that in fact expresses one's emotion without any preconceived plan of evoking emotion, and it might still be a bad poem.

It is now time to examine some of Collingwood's assumptions and conclusions. First, it is not at all clear that art necessarily "has something to do with emotion." One can think of many nonobjective paintings and pieces of music that are not expressive of emotion (or perhaps of anything else). If Collingwood were to try to answer this criticism by saying that such things are not works of art, he would be in the difficult position of maintaining that things ordinary usage calls works of art are not art. However, the answer that Collingwood would probably try to give the present criticism is that all expression involves emotion. This emerges when he gives an analysis of discourse, or speech.

> . . . it is a matter of fact that discourse in which a determined attempt is made to state truths retains an element of emotional expressiveness. No serious writer or speaker ever utters a thought unless he thinks it worth uttering.[48]

Presumably he thinks the same holds for painting, sculpting, and the like as well as for the literary arts. However, the concept of emotion is stretched so thin here that it becomes meaningless. When I say to my child, "Go brush your teeth," I always think it worth saying, but the remark is not always expressive of emotion. On some occasions, I am merely reminding him and no emotion is involved; on other occasions, when he offers resistance, emotion becomes involved and is usually expressed by the same remark uttered in a loud tone of voice. It simply is not true that every important remark expresses emotion, and Collingwood's attempt to ensure the presence of emotion only succeeds in emptying the concept of emotion of content. The point of this criticism is that the expression of emotion is not a *necessary* condition of art.

Another difficulty is that Collingwood's definition classifies as works of art an enormously large number of things that no one has the least inclination to think of as works of art. For example, "Go brush your teeth" said in a way that expresses emotion (exasperation) would be a work of art, presumably a poem, if the remark were not intended to evoke emotion. The theory is clearly much too broad. Collingwood's theory has the curious quality of being both too narrow and too broad. It claims that the plays of Shakespeare and many other works are entertainment and not works of art, and it rules out many other works as magic. Any theory that rules out the very paradigms of art is too narrow and hence defective.

One flaw in Collingwood's theory is that he mixes up two distinct senses of "work of art," both of which are sanctioned by ordinary usage—the classificatory and the evaluative senses. Earlier I illustrated the evaluative sense with the remark, "This painting is a work of art." Here the expression "work of art" is being used to say that the subject of the sentence is good or perhaps even magnificent. Unless the expression is being used evaluatively, it is redundant because the expression "This painting" establishes that the object referred to is a work of art in the classificatory sense. The classificatory sense is illustrated by a remark such as "This is a work of art," when the sentence is used to tell someone that a design is a work of art and not simply a product of nature, that a pile of metal is a work of art and not discarded junk, or that an object dug from the earth on an archaeological site is a work of art and not a stone. The evaluative sense is probably used much more frequently because there are not many occasions on which we need to use the classificatory sense in ordinary discourse. However, even if we do not frequently employ the classificatory sense in speech, it is embedded in our thought and plays an important role in the way we conceive the world around us. One way to show the existence and importance of the classificatory sense is to reflect on the fact that we frequently say that a work of art is bad; we could not do this if we were using only the evaluative sense. An adequate theory of art must distinguish these two senses of the term and give a coherent account of them. Such an account will be attempted in Chapter 8.

At the end of his book, Collingwood discusses what is apparently for him one of the paradigms of art, T. S. Eliot's "The Waste Land." With this poem in mind, he speaks of the role of the artist.

> His business as an artist is to speak out, to make a clean breast. But what he has to utter is not, as the individualist theory of art would have us think, his own secrets. As spokesmen of his community, the secrets he must utter are theirs.[49]

These final remarks reveal the motive behind his theory—to give an account of what might be best called "serious art." He calls it "art proper." If he had originally conceived of serious art, entertainment art, and magical art as three aspects of art, he would have been off to a better start. Even so, there would still be many difficulties in his theory. Collingwood is, however, making an important point about what art can do—it can reveal secrets and it can be expressive—but he is wrong in thinking that all art does this. He seizes on an important aspect of art but makes the mistake of thinking that that aspect is all there is to art. Instead of a theory of art, Collingwood has a theory of an aspect of art.

Each of the three philosophies of art discussed thus far has offered a definition of art, and in each case the definition has been specified in terms of characteristics that all works of art allegedly have in common: significant form, forms symbolic of human feeling, and the expression of emotion. The Wittgensteinian philosophy of art I will discuss in the next section challenges the traditional demand that works of art have something in common, an *essence*, which, if discovered, will serve as the defining characteristic of art.

Morris Weitz: Art as an Open Concept

The influence of Wittgenstein on the concept of aesthetic object has already been indicated, but his work on what has come to be known as the notion of *open concept* has had an even greater influence on the theory of art. An open concept is a concept for which there is no necessary condition in order for something to be an instance of that concept. Wittgenstein's frequently quoted example is that of *game*. He maintains that if we consider the whole range of games, say, from football to solitaire, we will not be able to discover any characteristic common to every game, and thus that there is no characteristic necessary for something to be a game. Wittgenstein's contention is that many, and perhaps even most, concepts are *open* and that philosophers have frequently been mistaken in trying to specify definitions for concepts in terms of necessary and sufficient conditions. It should be noted that Wittgenstein was not saying that there is anything wrong with open concepts, but simply that some concepts are open and that philosophers ought to take it into account in developing their theories.

In the early 1950s in a number of articles, philosophers began applying Wittgenstein's view of concepts to the philosophy of art. In the most well known and most reprinted of these articles, Morris Weitz argued that *art* is an open concept.[50] In stating his argument, Weitz distinguishes between the generic concept of art and the subconcepts of art. Weitz's argument consists of (1) an argument that purports to show that a subconcept of art, the novel, is an open concept and (2) the contention that all other subconcepts of art and the generic concept of art itself are open too. He says a consideration of such a question as "Is Dos Passos's *U.S.A.* a novel?" will show that the novel is an open concept. *U.S.A.* has certain features in common with other novels but has no regular time sequence and is interspersed with actual newspaper stories; of course, it is just these novelties that cause some people to question whether or not it is a novel. Weitz maintains that if we look at works that are unquestionably called "novels," we will find similar differences. He is suggesting that the class of novels is like the class of games, that is, the class of games as conceived by Wittgenstein. He then generalizes:

> What is true of the novel is, I think, true of every sub-concept of art: "tragedy," "comedy," "painting," "opera," etc., of "art" itself.[51]

According to Weitz, all the members of a subconcept of art—for example, tragedy—may not have a feature in common. Tragedy A and tragedy B may have features in common, tragedy B and tragedy C may also, and so on, but tragedy A and tragedy Z may not. Weitz's view is that tragedies have "family resemblances" among themselves but no common feature. It is, of course, possible on his view for all the members of a species of art to have a feature in common *at a given time*, but he contends that it is all but inevitable that some new work will be created that resembles many of the members of the subconcept but lacks the common feature. Weitz claims that when this kind of thing happens the new work is typically included within the subconcept despite its lack of the common feature and this shows that the subconcept is an open concept. He thinks the same holds for the generic concept of art. To show how far Weitz pushes his thesis, it may be noted that he maintains that "being an artifact" is not a necessary condition for the generic sense of "art." His reason is that we sometimes utter such statements as "This piece of driftwood is a lovely piece of sculpture." He reasons that if we are willing to classify a piece of driftwood as sculpture, that is, as a work of art, then artifactuality cannot be a necessary condition of art.

In addition to his thesis about the nature of the concepts of art, Weitz also maintains that, if we choose, we can close a concept by specifying a necessary condition or conditions and sticking to it or them. However, he warns that to do so "is ludicrous since it forecloses on the very conditions of creativity in the arts."[52]

For a long time Weitz's view seemed incontrovertible. Its relation to Wittgenstein lent it great prestige, and while not everyone found the argument persuasive and some attacked it, the conclusion did seem right to a very large number of philosophers.

In what follows it is maintained that Weitz's argument that "art" cannot be defined is defective, although it is left open as to whether all or some of the subconcepts of art such as novel, tragedy, ceramics, sculpture, painting, etc., lack necessary conditions *for their application as subconcepts.* For example, there may not be any characteristics common to all tragedies that would distinguish them from comedies, satyr plays, happenings, and the like *within the domain of art*, but it may be that there are characteristics that works of art have that would distinguish them from nonart.

The first obstacle to defining art is Weitz's contention that artifactuality is not a necessary condition for art. Most people assume that there is a sharp distinction between works of art and natural objects, but Weitz has argued that the fact that we sometimes say of natural objects such as driftwood that they are works of art breaks down the distinction. According to Weitz, there are works of art that are not artifacts. However, Weitz's argument is inconclusive because he fails to take account of the two senses of "work of art"—the evaluative and classificatory. There is a certain irony here because Weitz makes this distinction in his article, but he does not see that it undercuts his own argument. The evaluative sense of "work of art" is used to praise an object—for example, "That driftwood is a work of art" or "That painting is a work of art." In these examples we are saying that the driftwood and the painting have qualities worthy of notice and praise. In neither case do we mean that the object referred to by the subject of the sentence is a work of art in the classificatory sense: we are speaking evaluatively about the driftwood and the painting. It would be silly to take "That painting is a work of art" as a classificatory statement; ordinarily to utter the expression "That painting" is to commit oneself to meaning that the referent of the expression is a work of art in the classificatory sense. (The classificatory sense is used simply to indicate that a thing belongs to a certain category of artifacts.) We rarely utter sentences in which we use the classificatory sense because it is such a basic notion. We are rarely in situations in which it is necessary to raise the question of whether or not an object is a work of art in the classificatory sense. We generally know immediately whether or not an object is a work of art. Generally, no one needs to say, by way of classification, "That is a work of art." However, developments in art such as junk sculpture and found art may occasionally force such remarks. For example, I was once in a room at the Museum of Modern Art in which a work of art consisting of 144 one-foot-square metal plates was spread out on the floor. A man walked through the room and right across the work of art, apparently without seeing it. I did not, but I could have said, "Do you know that you are walking across a work of art?" The point is that the classificatory sense of "work of art" is a basic concept that structures and guides our thinking about our world. The whole point can perhaps be made clear by considering what would happen if one tried to understand the sentence "That painting is a work of art" in the classificatory sense. As indicated above, the expression "That painting" already contains the information that the object referred to is a work of art in the classificatory sense. Consequently, if the expression "That painting" is replaced in the sentence with its approximate equivalent, "That work of art which was created by putting paint on a surface such as canvas," the resulting sentence would be "That work of art which was created by putting paint on a surface such as canvas is a work of art." Thus, if one tries to understand this sentence by taking the last occurrence of "work of art" in the classificatory sense, the whole sentence turns into a redundancy. However, one would scarcely utter "That painting is a work of art" meaning to utter a redundancy, that is, simply to say that a work of art in the classificatory sense is a work of art in the classificatory sense. It is clear that what would generally be meant by such a sentence about a painting is that a work of art in the classifactory sense is a work of art in the evaluative sense. A parallel analysis could be given for the sentence about the driftwood, except that if one tried to understand "That piece of driftwood is a work of art" by construing "work of art" in the classificatory sense, a contradiction would result rather than a redundancy. It is, however, easy to understand this sentence construing "work of art" in the evaluative sense.

Weitz's conclusion that *being an artifact* is not a necessary condition for being a work of art rests on a confusion. What his argument proves is that it is not necessary for an object to be an artifact in order to be called (quite correctly) a work of art, when this expression is understood in the evaluative sense. It is, by the way, not at all surprising that the members of the class of objects that we find worthy of notice and praise do not all have a characteristic in common. Such a class would naturally be large and varied. Once we grasp the significance of the *two* senses of "work of art and see that Weitz's argument is misleading, we are free to reflect clearly on our understanding of the classificatory sense. And surely when we do so reflect, we realize that *part* of what is meant when we think of or assert of something (not in praise) that it is a work of art is that it is an artifact.

There are several other difficulties with Weitz's analysis of the concept of art. Weitz's account gives the impression that an object's resembling a prior-established work of art is the only way that something can become a work of art. If, however, this were the only way in which something could become art, an infinite regress of works of art resembling prior-established works of art would be required. There could be no first work of art because every work of art would require a prior-established work to resemble, and, consequently, there could not be any works of art. Some other way of becoming art is required to block the regress, and it seems plausible to think that this would have to be something becoming art by being crafted in some way, that is, by an *artifact* being created. Thus, what may be called "artifactual" art is required to block the regress. Furthermore, artifactual art has a kind of priority in that Weitz's "family-resemblance" art require the prior existence of artifactual art.

There is a further difficulty with Weitz's account. When traditional philosophers of art have theorized about art, they have always been interested in a particular class of human artifacts, so that artifactuality is a "built-in" necessary condition for art—"built-in" by their particular interest. Their main concern has always been to see what other features, if any, the class of artifacts they are interested in have in common. The fact that the kind of family-resemblance class Weitz describes can be generated by resemblance to prior-established works of art provides no reason to divert philosophers of art from their traditional task of theorizing about a particular class of human artifacts.

Part II

Aesthetics in the Twentieth Century— 1960s to Present

Chapter 7

A Change of Directions and New Developments

In the early 1960s, several philosophers published articles that signaled a new direction impacting both of the central organizing strains in analytic aesthetics, namely, the theory of the proper experience of art and the theory of the nature of art. Three of these articles—one by Marshall Cohen and two by me[1]—focus on the experience of art and two—one by Arthur Danto and one by Maurice Mandelbaum[2]—focus on the theory of art. What these five articles have in common was an emphasis on the cultural context within which art is embedded. Virtually all pre-1960s theories—the theory of beauty, taste theories, aesthetic-attitude theories, and theories of art—ignore the cultural context of art. These earlier theories, with the exceptions of Plato's theory of beauty and theory of art, which make central the metaphysical conception of the Forms, are organized around what I will call "notions of individual psychology," that is, notions of what persons do or undergo as individuals. Such notions contrast with cultural notions of what persons do or undergo as members of cultural groups. Simple examples of notions of individual psychology are perception and emotion. Of course, perceiving and having an emotion can be tied up with cultural matters, but, as such, they are individual phenomena. Noncultural animals perceive and have emotions. Simple examples of cultural notions are playing in a basketball game or receiving a degree from a university. Such activities are not possible without complex, ongoing cultural organizations as a context within which the activities take place.

A New Direction for the Experience *of Art*

In Chapter 3, three versions of the aesthetic attitude were examined. In Chapter 4, I discussed Beardsley's metacriticism. The aesthetic-attitude theories attempt to give an account of the proper experience of art and of the features of art to which appreciation and criticism are to be directed. Each of the three attitude theories claimed to identify the foundation for the proper experience of art, which each describes in terms of a particular notion of individual psychology—psychical distance, disinterested attention, or aesthetic perception. Each of the aesthetic-attitude theories also claims that its notion of individual psychology isolates the features of works of art to which appreciation and criticism are to be directed. Earlier, I tried to show that the attitude theories' notions of individual psychology are nonexistent.

Beardsley's metacriticism also emphasizes notions of individual psychology in attempting to isolate the features of artworks to which appreciation and criticism are to be directed; he calls these features "aesthetic objects." In his analysis, Beardsley speaks of the criteria of perceptibility and of the consideration of the basic properties of perceptual fields. These criteria clearly are based on notions of individual psychology. Earlier, I argued that Beardsley's criteria, although they do not involve nonexistent mental phenomena, cannot do the job of isolating "aesthetic objects." I believe that Beardsley's individual psychology criteria need to be aided by the introduction of cultural notions.

Aesthetic-attitude theorists claimed that a particular psychological state controls the thought and behavior of the experiencers of art; jealous husbands can attend to *Othello* if psychically distanced, children are disturbed by Peter Pan's request for applause because it destroys their psychical distance, and gallant spectators, if they are psychically distanced, do not attack stage villains. If, however, there are no such psychological states, what does control thought and behavior in the face of artistic phenomena?

Samuel Johnson's eighteenth-century answer was "The truth is, that the spectators are always in their senses, and know, from the first act to the last, that the stage is only a stage, and that the players are only players." Johnson is alluding to the knowledge of the nature of theater activity that each member of an audience has. Consider the cases of the attacker-spectator and Peter Pan's appeal. There is a general *rule* or *convention*, a cultural phenomenon understood by all, that audience members do not interact with a play's action. A gallant spectator who attacked a stage villain would be someone who flouts this convention out of ignorance of theater art or because of insanity. Such a spectator would not be someone who had lost the aesthetic attitude, although he could be someone who had lost his or her mind. When Peter Pan appeals for applause, it signals that the usual convention is being set aside and that a different convention is being put in place. Children catch on right away that there has been a convention shift, even if some aestheticians do not. A convention is by definition something that can be done in more than one way, and different plays have different conventions governing spectator participation. Reflection will reveal that there are many conventions involved in the presentation of the arts to their publics. Although the jealous husband at *Othello* case does not involve being in or losing the aesthetic attitude any more than the other two cases do, it does not directly involve theater convention either; the husband is just someone whose thoughts of his wife may cause him not to pay attention to the play.

Aesthetic-attitude theorists claim that being in the aesthetic-attitude reveals which characteristics of art belong to the aesthetic object of works, that is, which characteristics are to be appreciated and criticized. Beardsley makes a similar claim for perceptibility and other criteria. Both claims fail. What does direct attention to aesthetic objects of works of art? It is the background knowledge of theater—its nature as a cultural phenomenon and its conventions—that isolates the aesthetic objects of plays. The situation is the same in the other arts; it is the background knowledge of painting, literature, and the like, not the functioning of mechanisms of individual psychology, that guides people to the characteristics of art that are to be appreciated and criticized.

A New Direction for the Theory *of Art*

Difficulties in the open-concept analysis of *art* went unnoticed for a considerable period, and the unchallenged influence of this view paralyzed most philosophers of art. Attempts to theorize about the essential nature of art virtually ceased during the 1950s and the early 1960s. In the mid-1960s, however, two philosophers, Arthur Danto and Maurice Mandelbaum, independently and in different ways, opposed the prevailing Wittgensteinian view.

In 1965, Mandelbaum directly challenged Wittgenstein's argument about games and Weitz's argument about art and then suggested an inventive approach to philosophizing about art. He first argued that games have in common a certain kind of purpose: "the potentiality of . . . [an] absorbing non-practical interest to either participants or spectators."[3] Wittgenstein failed to notice this feature, Mandelbaum claims, because he was apparently concerned only with *exhibited*, easily-noticed characteristics such as whether a ball was used in the game or whether the game could be won and lost. Mandelbaum did not attempt to define art or its subconcepts, but he did make the acute suggestion that art may be definable in terms of some *nonexhibited* and less obvious characteristics, definable perhaps in terms of some relational features that relate an artwork to "some actual or possible audience."[4] Artifactuality, for example, is a relational, nonexhibited property, and perhaps this is also true of the other property or properties that distinguish art from nonart and which are involved in the definition of art.

In 1964, Danto published the first of a series of three articles.[5] In 1981, the material from these articles was incorporated into a book, *The Transfiguration of the Commonplace.*[6] In all these publications, Danto simply ignored the Wittgensteinian approach and began to theorize about art. Also, in all his works, Danto uses an important argument that he invented—the visually-indistinguishable-pairs argument. He envisions a pair of objects in which the two objects are visually indistinguishable but one object is a work of art and the other is not. One of his examples of such a pair is the case of Rembrandt's *Polish Rider* and a hypothetical canvas that has accidently been covered with paint in such a way that it looks exactly like the Rembrandt painting. Danto cites actual cases: Warhol's *Brillo Box* and a brillo box that looks exactly like it and Duchamp's *Fountain* and a urinal that looks exactly like it. In each case of pairs, the first object is a work of art, but the second object that look exactly like it is not. What, Danto asks, is responsible for the first object's being a work of art and not the second? It cannot be the artwork's appearance, because the two objects look exactly alike. Danto concludes that it must be some context that the first object is enmeshed in and that the second is not. (The visually-indistinguishable-pairs argument can be adapted to nonvisual art.)

In his 1964 article, *The Artworld*, Danto wrote, "To see something as art requires something the eye cannot descry—an atmosphere of artistic theory, a knowledge of the history of art: an artworld."[7] In this earliest article, Danto claimed that what makes the first object of an indistinguishable pair a work of art is that it is embedded in a context of artistic theory. (This context, he thought, is what makes any artwork an artwork.) It was never very clear what Danto meant by "artistic theory," but it was the indistinguishable-pairs argument that was important—because it showed that some kind of nonexhibited network of relations in which an object is enmeshed is what makes it a work of art.

Danto was apparently dissatisfied with his earliest account of the art-making context, because in his later articles and in his book he claimed that the art-making context is one that enables an object (1) to be about something and (2) to be subject to interpretation. Thus, in his later work, Danto replaces the earlier *art-specific*, art-making context that involves art theories with an art-making context (aboutness/interpretation) that is *linguistic-like* in nature.

Even if Danto's later claim about the linguistic-like, art-making context were true, he would not have a complete theory of art, that is, one that picks out all artworks and only artworks. Statue laws, scientific theories, directions for assembling machinery, and many other nonartworks are about something and subject to interpretation, so his claim captures nonartworks. In addition, there are many counterexamples to Danto's theory understood in this way; for example, although many artworks are about something, nonobjective paintings and instrumental music are not about anything.

At some points, Danto seems to have another account of the art-making context in mind, claiming that it is one that enables an object (1) to be the *sort* of thing that can be about something and (2) to be the *sort* of thing that is subject to interpretation. If the context is understood in this second way, then something could be art because it is the *sort* of thing that can be about something and subject to interpretation without being about anything and without being interpretable. Nonobjective paintings and instrumental music are not counterexamples to this claim, because they are paintings and musical pieces, and paintings and musical pieces are the *sort* of things that can be about something and subject to interpretation. If this second account is Danto's view, then his claim is that the class of artworks is a class of objects some of whose members are about something and subject to interpretation and some of whose members are not about something and not subject to interpretation. Understood in this way, the theory begins to sound vacuous. Danto's considered view, however, seems to be that artworks are about something and subject to interpretation.

Whatever Danto intends to say, his talk of aboutness and interpretation has interesting implications. Aboutness points in the direction of an *artist* as the intender of being about something, and interpretation points in the direction of a *public* as interpreter. Thus, his view(s) suggests that the role of artist and the role of public are part of the art-making context, although he does not specifically say this.

Chapter 8

The Institutional Theory of Art

Guided by the ideas in Mandelbaum's article and Danto's earliest article, beginning in 1969 with "Defining Art"[1] and culminating in 1974 with *Art and the Aesthetic*,[2] I worked out the earlier of two versions of the institutional theory of art. In response to a variety of criticisms of the earlier version, I presented a greatly revised, and I think improved, version of the institutional theory in my 1984 book, *The Art Circle*.[3] I will give accounts of both versions.

Traditional theories of art place works of art within simple and narrowly-focused networks of relations. The imitation theory, for example, suspends the work of art in a three-place network between artist and subject matter, and the expression theory places the work of art in a two-place network of artist and work. Both versions of the institutional theory attempt to place the work of art within a multi-placed network of greater complexity than anything envisaged by the various traditional theories. The networks or contexts of the traditional theories are too "thin" to be sufficient. Both versions of the institutional theory attempt to provide a context that is "thick" enough to do the job. The network of relations or context within which a theory places works of art I will call "the framework" of that theory.

All the traditional theories assume that works of art are artifacts, although they differ about the nature of the artifacts. There is, then, a sense in which the institutional approach is a return to the traditional way of theorizing about art, for in both of its versions I maintain that works of art are artifacts. By "artifact" I mean the ordinary dictionary definition: "an object made by man, especially with a view to subsequent use." Furthermore, although many are, an artifact need not be a physical object: for example, a poem is not a physical object, but it is, nevertheless, an artifact. Still further, things such as performances, for example, improvised dances, are also "made by man" and are, therefore, artifacts.

On the surface anyway, there is no mystery about the making of the great bulk of artifactual art; they are crafted in various traditional ways—painted, sculpted, and the like. There is, however, a puzzle about the artifactuality of some relatively recent works of art: Duchamp's readymades, found art, and the like. Some deny that such things are art because, they claim, they are not artifacts made by artists. It can, I think, be shown that they are the artifacts of artists. The two versions diverge over how artifactuality is achieved in the cases of Duchamp's readymades and their like.

The Earlier Version

The earlier version of the institutional theory of art can be summed up in the following definition from my 1974 book, *Art and the Aesthetic.*

> A work of art in the classificatory sense is (1) an artifact (2) a set of the aspects of which has had conferred upon it the status of candidate for appreciation by some person or persons acting on behalf of a certain social institution (the artworld).[4]

The notion of conferring status is the central notion in this earlier version. The most obvious and clear-cut examples of the conferring of status are certain actions of the state in which legal status is involved. A king's conferring of knighthood or a judge pronouncing a couple husband and wife are examples in which a person acting on behalf of an institution (the state) confers *legal* status. The conferring of a Ph.D. degree on someone by a university or the election of someone as president of the Rotary are examples in which a person or persons confer nonlegal status. What the earlier institutional definition of "work of art" suggests is that just as two persons can acquire the status of being married within a legal system and as a person can acquire the nonlegal status of being president of the Rotary, an artifact can acquire the status of candidate for appreciation within the cultural system called "the artworld."

How, according to the earlier version, is the status of candidate for appreciation conferred? An artifact's hanging in an art museum as part of a show or a performance at a theater are sure signs that the status has been conferred. These two examples seem to suggest that a number of people are required for the actual conferring of the status in question. A number of people are required to make up the cultural institution of the artworld, but only one person is required to act on behalf of or as an agent of the artworld and to confer the status of candidate for appreciation. The status in question is typically acquired by *a single person's treating an artifact as a candidate for appreciation.* Of course nothing prevents a group of persons conferring the status, that is, acting as an artist, but it is usually conferred by a single person, the artist who creates the artifact. In fact, many works of art are never seen by anyone but the persons who create them, but they are still works of art.

It may be felt that the notion of conferring status within the artworld, as conceived in the earlier version, is excessively vague. Certainly this notion is not as clear-cut as the conferring of status within the legal system, where procedures and lines of authority are explicitly defined and incorporated into law. The counterparts in the artworld to specified procedures and lines of authority are nowhere codified, and the artworld carries on its business at the level of customary practice. Still there is a practice and this defines a cultural institution. Such an institution need not have a formally established constitution, officers, and bylaws in order to exist and have the capacity to confer status. Some institutions are formal and some are informal.

Consider now the notion of appreciation. In the earlier version, the definition of "work of art" speaks of conferring the status of *candidate* for appreciation. Nothing is said about actual appreciation, and this allows for the possibility of works of art that are not appreciated. It is important not to build into the definition of the *classificatory* sense of "work of art" value properties such as actual appreciation; to do so would make it impossible to speak of unappreciated works of art and difficult to speak of bad works of art, and this is clearly undesirable. Any theory of art must preserve certain central features of the way in which we talk about art, and we do find it necessary sometimes to speak of unappreciated art and bad art. It should also be noted that not every aspect of a work of art is included in the candidacy for appreciation. For example, the color of the back of a painting is not ordinarily an object of appreciation. The reader will recognize that the question of which aspects of a work of art are to be included within the candidacy for appreciation has already been dealt with in Part I.

The earlier version of the institutional theory does not involve a special kind of *aesthetic* appreciation. In Part I it was argued that there is no special kind of aesthetic perception and there is no reason to think there is a special kind of aesthetic appreciation. All that is meant by "appreciation" in the earlier definition is something like "in experiencing the qualities of a thing one finds them worthy or valuable."

Both versions of the institutional theory of art have quite consciously been worked out with the practices of the artworld in mind—especially developments of the last hundred years or so, such as dadaism, pop art, found art, and happenings. The institutional theory and these developments raise a number of questions, and a few of these will be dealt with here.

First, if Duchamp can convert a urinal, a snowshovel, and a hatrack into works of art, can't natural objects such as driftwood also become works of art? Such natural objects can become works of art if any one of a number of things is done to them. One thing that would do the trick would be to pick a natural object up, take it home, and hang it on the wall. Another would be to pick it up and enter it in an exhibition. It was being assumed earlier that Weitz's sentence about the driftwood referred to a piece of driftwood in its ordinary situation on a beach and untouched by human hand. Please keep in mind that for something to be a work of art in the classificatory sense does not mean that it has any actual value. Natural objects which become works of art in the way being discussed are, according to the earlier version, artifactualized without the use of tools—the artifactuality is conferred on the object rather than worked on it. Of course, even if this is true, in the cases of the great majority of artworks, artifactuality is achieved by being crafted in some way. Thus, according to the earlier version, artifactuality can be achieved in two quite different ways: by being worked and being conferred. In the cases of things like Duchamp's readymades such as *Fountain*, a plumbing artifact has artistic artifactuality conferred on it and is a double artifact.

Note that according to the earlier version, two quite different kind of things can supposedly be conferred: artifactuality and candidacy for appreciation.

Second, a question that frequently arises in connection with discussions of the concept of art and which seems especially relevant in the context of institutional theory is, "How are we to conceive of paintings done by individuals such as Betsy the chimpanzee from the Baltimore Zoo?" Calling Betsy's products "paintings" here is not meant to prejudge that they are works of art; it is just that some word is needed to refer to them. The question of whether or not Betsy's paintings are art depends on what is done with them. For example, The Field Museum of Natural History in Chicago once exhibited some chimpanzee and gorilla paintings. In the case of these paintings we must say that they are not works of art. However, if they had been exhibited a few miles away at the Chicago Art Institute they *could* have been works of art—the paintings *could* have been art if someone at the Art Institute had, so to speak, gone out on a limb. It all depends on the institutional setting—the one setting is congenial for the creation of art and the other is not. (In speaking of institutional setting, I am not referring to the Art Institute as such but to an institutional practice.) According to the earlier version, what would make Betsy's paintings works of art would be some agent's conferring artifactuality and the status of candidacy for appreciation on them on behalf of the artworld. Despite the fact that Betsy did the painting, the resulting works of art would not be Betsy's but the work of the person who does the conferring. Betsy cannot do the conferring because she cannot see herself as an agent of the artworld—she is unable to participate (fully) in our culture.

Weitz charged that the defining of art or its subconcepts forecloses creativity. Some of the traditional definitions of art may have and some of the traditional definitions of its subconcepts probably did foreclose creativity, but neither version of the institutional account of art would. The requirement of artifactuality can scarcely prevent creativity, since artifactuality is a necessary condition of creativity.

How could there be an instance of creativity without an artifact of some kind being produced? The other requirement of the earlier version involving the conferring of the status of candidate for appreciation could not inhibit creativity; in fact, it encourages it. Since it is possible for almost anything whatever to be used to make art, the definition imposes no restraints on creativity. Weitz is probably right that the definition of some of the subconcepts of art have foreclosed creativity, but this danger is now a thing of the past. With the well-established disregard for established genres and the clamor for novelty in art, this obstacle to creativity probably no longer exists. Today, if a new and unusual work is created and it is fairly similar to some members of an established type, then it will usually be accommodated within that type, or if the new work is very unlike any existing works, then a new subconcept will probably be created. Artists today are not easily intimidated, and they regard art genres as loose guidelines rather than rigid specifications.

The earlier version of the institutional theory of art may sound like saying, "A work of art is an object of which someone has said, 'I christen this object a work of art.'" And it is rather like that; although this does not mean that becoming art, as conceived by the earlier version, is a simple matter. Just as christening a child has as its background the history and structure of the church, becoming art has as its background the Byzantine complexity of the artworld. Some people may find it strange that in the nonart cases discussed it appears that there are ways in which the conferring can go wrong, while there does not appear to be a way in which the conferring involved in producing art can be invalid. For example, an indictment might have been improperly drawn up, and the person charged would not actually be indicted. But nothing parallel seems possible in the case of art. This fact reflects the differences between the artworld and legal institutions. The legal system deals with matters of grave personal consequences and its procedures must reflect this; the artworld deals with important matters also, but they are of a different sort entirely. The artworld does not require rigid procedures; it admits and even encourages frivolity and caprice without losing its serious purpose. However, if it is not possible to make a mistake in the conferring involved in producing art, it is possible to make a mistake by conferring candidacy for appreciation. In conferring such status on an object, one assumes a certain kind of responsibility for the object in its new status; presenting a candidate for appreciation always faces the possibility that no one will appreciate it and that the person who did the conferring will thereby lose face. One *can* make a work of art out of a sow's ear, but that does not necessarily make it a silk purse.

The Later Version

The earlier version of the institutional theory is, I believe, defective in several respects, but the institutional approach is, I think, still viable. In the earlier version, I claimed, I now think mistakenly, that artifactuality is conferred on things such as

Duchamp's *Fountain* and found art. I now believe that artifactuality is not the sort of thing that can be conferred.

Typically an artifact is produced by altering some preexisting material: by joining two pieces of material, by cutting some material, by sharpening some material, and so on. This is usually done so that the altered material can be used to do something. When materials are so altered, one has clear cases that neatly fit the dictionary definition of "artifact"—"An object made by man, especially with a view to subsequent use." Other cases are less clear-cut. Suppose one picks up a piece of driftwood and without altering it in any way digs a hole or brandishes it at a threatening dog. The unaltered driftwood has been *made* into a digging tool or a weapon by the use to which it is put. These two cases do not conform to the nonnecessary clause of the definition "especially with a view to subsequent use" because they are pressed into service on the spot. There does seem to be a sense in which something is made in these cases. What, however, has been made if the driftwood is unaltered? In the clear cases in which material is altered, a complex object is produced: the original material is for present purposes a simple object and its being altered produces the complex object—altered material. In the two less clear-cut cases, complex objects have also been made—the wood used as a digging tool and the wood used as a weapon. In neither of the two less clear-cut cases is the driftwood alone the artifact; the artifact in both cases is the driftwood manipulated and used in a certain way. The two cases in question are exactly like the sort of thing that anthropologists have in mind when they speak of unaltered stones found in conjunction with human or human-like fossils as artifacts. The anthropologists conclude that the stones were used in some way because of, say, certain marks of the stones that they take to be traces left on the stones by that use. The anthropologists have in mind the same notion of a complex object made by the use of a simple (i.e., unaltered) object.

A piece of driftwood may be used in a similar way within the context of the artworld, that is, picked up and displayed in the way that a painting or a sculpture is displayed. Such a piece of driftwood would be being used as an artistic medium and thereby would become part of the more complex object—the-driftwood-used-as-an-artistic-medium. This complex object would be an artifact of an artworld system. Duchamp's *Fountain* can be understood along the same lines. The urinal (the simple object) is being used as an artistic medium to make *Fountain* (the complex object), which is an artifact within the artworld—Duchamp's artifact. The driftwood would be being used and the urinal was used as an artistic medium in the way that pigments, marble, and the like are used to make more conventional works of art. The driftwood used as a weapon and the urinal used as an artistic medium are artifacts of the most minimal sort. Duchamp did not confer artifactuality; he made a minimal artifact.

A second difficulty with the earlier account was pointed out by Monroe Beardsley. He observed that in the discussion surrounding the definition in the earlier version of the theory, I characterized the artworld as an "established practice," an informal kind of activity. He then goes one to point out that the quoted definition makes use of such phrases as "conferred status" and "acting on behalf of." Such phrases typically have application within formal institutions such as states, corporations, universities, and the like. Beardsley correctly notes that it is a mistake to use the language of formal institutions to try to describe an informal institution as I conceive the artworld to be. Beardsley queries, "does it make sense to speak of acting on behalf of a practice? Status-awarding authority can center in [a formal institution], but practices, as such, seem to lack the requisite source of authority."[5]

Accepting Beardsley's criticism, I have abandoned as too formal the notions of *status conferral* and *acting on behalf of* as well as those aspects of the earlier version that connect up with these notions. Being a work of art is a status all right, that is, it is the occupying of a position within the human activity of the artworld. Being a work of art does not, however, involve a status that is conferred but is rather a status that is achieved as the result of creating an artifact within or against the background of the artworld.

The later version claims (as does the earlier version) that works of art are art as the result of the position or place they occupy within an established practice, namely, the artworld. There are two crucial questions about the claim: is the claim true and if the claim is true, how is the artworld to be described?

This is a claim about the existence of a human institution, and the test of its truth is the same as for any other claim about human organization—the test of observation. "Seeing" the artworld and the works of art embedded in its structures, however, is not as easy as "seeing" some of the other human institutions we are more accustomed to thinking about.

Danto's visually-indistinguishable-objects argument shows that works of art exist within a context or framework, but it does not reveal the nature of the elements making up the framework. Moreover, many different frameworks are possible. Each of the traditional theories of art, for example, implies its own particular framework. For one example, Susanne Langer's view that "Art is the creation of forms symbolic of human feeling" implies a framework of artist (one who creates) and a specific kind of subject matter (human feeling). Langer's theory and the other traditional theories, however, fall easy prey to counterexamples, and, consequently, none of the frameworks they imply can be the right one. The reason that the traditional theories are easy prey for counterexamples is that the frameworks implied by the theories are too narrowly focused on the artist and the more obvious characteristics works of art may have rather than on *all* the framework elements that surround works of art. The result is that it is all too easy to find works of art that lack the properties seized on by a particular traditional theory as universal and defining.

The frameworks of the traditional theories do lead in the right direction in one respect. Each of the traditional theories conceives of the making of art as a human practice, as an established way of behaving. Consequently, the framework of each of these theories is conceived of as a cultural phenomenon that persists through time and is repeatable. The persistence of a framework as a cultural practice is enough, I think, to make the traditional theories themselves quasi-institutional. In every one of the traditional theories, however, there is only one established role envisioned and that is the role of the artist or the maker of artifacts. And, in every case, the artist is seen as the creator of an artifact with a property such as being representative, being symbolic, or being an expression. For the traditional theories the artist role is envisaged as simply that of producing representations, producing symbolic forms, producing expressions, or some such thing. This narrow conception of the artist role is responsible for the ease with which counterexamples can be produced. Since the traditional theories are inadequate, there must be more to the artist role than the producing of any, or even all, of these kinds of things that the traditional theories envisage. What an artist understands and does when he or she creates a work of art far exceeds the simple understanding and doing entailed by the traditional theories.

Whenever an artist creates art, it is always created for a *public*. Consequently, the framework must include a role for a *public* to whom art is presented. Of course, for a variety of reasons many works of art are never in fact presented to any public. Some works just never reach their publics although their makers intended for them to do so. Some works are withheld from their publics by their creators because they judge them to be in some way inferior and unworthy of presentation. The fact that artists withhold some of their works because they judge them unworthy of presentation shows that the works are things of a *kind* to be presented, otherwise, it would be pointless to judge them unworthy of presentation. Thus, even art not intended for public presentation presupposes a public, for not only is it possible to present it to a public (as sometimes happens), it is a thing of a type that has as a goal presentation to a public. The notion of a public hovers always in the background, even when a given artist refuses to present his or her work. In those cases in which works of art are withheld from a public, there is what might be called a "double intention"—there is an intention to create a thing of a kind that is presented, but there is also an intention not to actually present it.

What is an artworld public? It is not just a collection of people. The members of an artworld public know how to fulfill a role that requires knowledge and understanding similar in many respects to that required of an artist. There are as many different publics as there are different arts, and the knowledge required for one public is different from that required by another public. An example of one bit of knowledge required of the public of stage plays is the understanding of what it is for someone to act a part. Any given member of a public would have a great many such bits of information.

The artist and public roles are the minimum framework for the creation of art, and the two roles in relation may be called "the presentation group." The role of artist has two central aspects: first, a general aspect characteristic of all artists, namely, the awareness that what is created for presentation is art, and, second, the ability to use one or more of a wide variety of art techniques that enable one to create art of a particular kind. Likewise, the role of a public has two central aspects: first, a general aspect characteristic of all publics, namely, the awareness that what is presented to it is art and, second, the abilities and sensitivities which enable one to perceive and understand the particular kind of art with which one is presented.

In almost every actual society that has an institution of art-making, in addition to the roles of artist and public, there will be a number of supplementary artworld roles such as those of critic, art teacher, director, curator, conductor, and many more. The presentation group, that is, the roles of artist and public in relation, however, constitutes the essential framework for art-making.

Among the more frequent criticisms of the earlier version was that it failed to show that art-making is institutional because it failed to show that art-making is rule-governed. The underlying assumption of the criticism is that it is rule-governedness that distinguishes institutional practices such as, say, promising from noninstitutional ones such as, say, dog-walking. And it is true that the earlier version did not bring out the rule-governedness of art-making and this requires correcting. There are rules implicit in the theory developed in the earlier book, but unfortunately I failed to make them explicit. There is no point in discussing the rules governing art-making implicit in the earlier theory, but those of the present revised theory can be stated. Earlier I argued that actifactuality is a necessary condition for being a work of art. This claim of necessity implies one rule of art-making: if one wishes to make a work of art, one must do so by creating an artifact. I also claimed that being a thing of a kind that is presented to an artworld public is a necessary condition for being a work of art. This claim of necessity implies another rule of art-making: if one wishes to create a work of art, one must do so by creating a thing of a kind which is presented to an artworld public. These two rules are jointly sufficient for making works of art.

The question naturally arises as to why the framework described as the institutional one is the correct essential framework rather than some other framework. The frameworks of the traditional theories are clearly inadequate, but their inadequacy does not prove the correctness of the framework of the present version of the institutional theory. Proving that a theory is true is notoriously difficult, although proving that a theory is false is sometimes easy to do. It can be said of the present version of the institutional theory that it is a conception of a framework in which works of art are clearly embedded and that no other plausible framework is in the offing. For lack of a more conclusive argument that the institutional theory's framework is the right one, I will have to rely on the description of it I have given to function as an argument as to its rightness. If the description is correct, or approximately so, then it should evoke a "that's right" experience in the listener.

In the earlier version, I talked a great deal about conventions and how they are involved in the institution of art. I tried to distinguish between what I called "the primary convention" and other "secondary conventions" that are involved in the creation and presentation of art. One example of the so-called secondary conventions discussed there is the Western theatrical convention of concealing stagehands behind the scenery. This Western convention was there contrasted with that of classical Chinese theater in which the stagehand (called the property man) appears on stage during the action of the play and rearranges props and scenery. These two different theatrical solutions for the same task, namely, the employment of stagehands, brings out an essential feature of conventions. Any conventional way of doing something could have been done in a different way.

The failure to realize that things of the kind just discussed are conventions can result in confused theory. For example, it is another convention of Western theater that spectators do not participate in the action of a play. Certain aesthetic-attitude theorists failed to realize that this particular convention is a convention and concluded that the nonparticipation of spectators is a rule derived from aesthetic consciousness and that the rule must not be violated. Such theorists are horrified by Peter Pan's request for the members of the audience to applaud to save Tinkerbell's life. The request, however, merely amounts to the introduction of a new convention that small children, but not some aestheticians, catch on to right away.

There are innumerable conventions involved in the creation and presentation of art, but there is not, as I claimed in the earlier version, a *primary* convention to which all the other conventions are secondary. In effect, in the earlier version, I claimed that not only are there many conventions involved in the creation and presentation of art, but that at bottom the whole activity is completely conventional. But theater, painting, sculpting, and the like, are not ways of doing something that could be done in another way, and, therefore, they are not conventional. If, however, there is no *primary* convention, there is a primary *something* within which the innumerable conventions that there are have a place. What is primary is the understanding shared by all involved that they are engaged in an established activity or practice within which there is a variety of roles: artist roles, public roles, critic roles, director roles, curator roles, and so on. Our artworld consists of the totality of such roles with the roles of artist and public at its core. Described in a somewhat more structured way, the artworld consists of a set of individual artworld systems, each of which contains its own specific artist and public roles plus other roles. For example, painting is one artworld system, theater is another, and so on.

The institution of art, then, involves rules of very different kinds. There are conventional rules that derive from the various conventions employed in presenting and creating art. These rules are subject to change. There are more basic rules that govern the engaging in an activity, and these rules are not conventional. The artifact rule—if one wishes to make a work of art, one must do so by creating an artifact—is not a conventional rule, it states a condition for engaging in a certain kind of practice.

As I remarked earlier, the artifact rule and the other nonconventional rule are sufficient for the creating of art. And, as each rule is necessary, they can be used to formulate a definition of "work of art."

> A work of art is an artifact of a kind created to be presented to an art-world public.

This definition explicitly contains the terms "artworld" and "public" and it also involves the notions of *artist* and *artworld system*. I now define these four as follows:

> An artist is a person who participates with understanding in the making of a work of art.

> A public is a set of persons the members of which are prepared in some degree to understand an object which is presented to them.

> The artworld is the totality of all artworld systems.

> An artworld system is a framework for the presentation of a work of art by an artist to an artworld public.[6]

These five definitions provide the leanest possible description of the institution of art and thus the leanest possible account of the institutional theory of art.

To forestall an objection to the definition of "work of art," let me acknowledge that there are artifacts that are created for presentation to the artworld publics that are not works of art: for example, playbills. Such things are, however, parasitic on or secondary to works of art. Works of art are artifacts of a primary kind in this domain, and playbills and the like that are dependent on works of art are artifacts of a secondary kind within this domain. The word "artifact" in the definition should be understood to be referring to artifacts of the primary kind.

The definition of "work of art" given in the earlier version was, as I acknowledged, circular, although not viciously so. The definition of "work of art" just given is also circular, although again not viciously so. In fact, the definitions of the five central terms constitute a logically circular set of terms.

There is an ideal of noncircular definition that assumes that the meaning of terms used in a definition ought not to lead back to the term originally defined, but rather ought to be or lead to terms that are more basic. The ideal of noncircular definition also assumes that we ought to be able to arrive at terms that are primitive in the sense that they can be known in some nondefinitional way, say, by direct sensory experience or rational intuition. There may be some sets of definitions that satisfy this ideal, but the definitions of the five central terms of the institutional theory do not. Does this mean that the institutional theory involves a vicious circularity? The circularity of the definitions shows the interdependency of the central notions. These central notions are *inflected*, that is, they bend in on, presuppose, and support one another. What the definitions reveal is that art-making involves an intricate, co-relative structure that cannot be described in the straightforward, linear way envisaged by the ideal of noncircular definition. The inflected nature of art is reflected in the way that we learn about art. This learning is sometimes approached through being taught how to be an artist—learning how to draw pictures that can be displayed, for example. This learning is sometimes approached through being taught how to be a member of an artworld public—learning how to look at pictures that are presented as the intentional products of artists. Both approaches teach us about artists, works, and publics all at the same time, for these notions are not independent of one another. I suspect that many areas within the cultural domain also have the same kind of inflected nature that the institution of art has—for example, the area involving the notions of *law, legislature, executive,* and *judiciary.*

The ideal of noncircular definition holds also that sets of circular definitions cannot be informative. This may be true of some sets of definitions, but it is not, I think, true of the definitions of the institutional theory. For these definitions just mirror the mutually dependent items that constitute the art enterprise, and, thereby, informs us of its inflected nature.

In recent years Jerrold Levinson,[7] Noel Carroll,[8] Stephen Davies,[9] and others have published theories of art or drawn theoretical conclusions about art that relate in one way or another to the institutional theory of art.

Part III

Four Problems in Aesthetics

The core notions of beauty, art, and the aesthetic have been the focus of the previous chapters. These ideas organize and define the field of aesthetics. However, the philosophical problems generated by our thinking and talking bout art are many and varied. This part will be devoted to discussing some noncore problems of aesthetics. Some of them are closely related to the core questions and some are not; the relation of others to the core is unclear and awaits clarification. The terms "core" and "noncore" should not be taken as indicating the importance or urgency of the problems so designated. The attempt to discover a core for what is by common agreement an untidy discipline. The core provides a framework for orientation that gives us a sense of where we are as we work on the problems of aesthetics.

From the large number of noncore questions, I have selected four. These are (1) intentionalist criticism, (2) symbolism in art, (3) metaphor, and (4) expression. With the exception of metaphor, which involves only the literary arts, these questions cut across all of the arts. Each of the four has long been regarded by philosophers and critics as a most important question. Why they have been so regarded will, I think, emerge in the following discussions.

Chapter 9

Intentionalist Criticism

An artist always has an intention when creating a work of art, even when the work is a case of "accidental art." A painter intends to produce a certain kind of effect—luminosity, perhaps—or to represent a landscape. A composer intends to create a musical score that when performed will result in music that is majestic, gay, solemn, or has some other musical qualities. A poet intends a line or a whole poem to express a certain meaning. In accidental art, an accidental result is intentional if the artist intentionally leaves the result unrevised.

Many critics explicitly claim or assume that the artist's intention plays an important role in criticism. Intentionalist critics are not in universal agreement about the significance of the intention of the artist. Some think that an artist's intention is important *both* for understanding works of art and for evaluating works, while others deny the significance of the intention for evaluation. I will attempt to show that intentionalist criticism is fundamentally misguided.

Consider some generalized examples of intentionalist criticism.[1] According to an intentionalist critic, a painting must be taken as representing, say, a king because the painter intended it to represent a king. Suppose that the painting in question is an abstract one and it is difficult to make out what is represented in it. An intentionalist would try to determine what a painting represents by appealing to painter's intention. Or suppose it is a question of the meaning of a difficult line in a poem—difficult because it is obscure or ambiguous. The intentionalist claims that an artist's intention *determines* the meaning of a poetic line and thereby eliminates any ambiguity or obscurity. A somewhat more complicated but logically similar situation obtains with those arts in which performance is involved. An intentionalist will claim that a *correct* performance of a play is one that accords with the explicit stage directions of the playwright or, if stage directions are lacking, according to the intention of the playwright discoverable in some other way. Similarly, a musical score ought to be performed as the composer intended.

The attempt to use the intention of the artist as a criterion of *evaluation* is different from the question of how the artist's intention relates to understanding or correct performance. The intentionalist evaluational claim is that a work of art is good if its creator has succeeded in achieving what he intended to realize or bad to the extent that he fails to realize his intention. The evaluative use of the artist's intention faces a number of difficulties, but there are two difficulties that transparently undermine it. The first difficulty is a practical one, namely that it frequently is not possible to discover what an artist's intention was, so one cannot know if the intention has been realized or not. Shakespeare is a good example here; nothing is known of what his intentions were. Of course, the intentionalist need not say that the artist's intention is the *only* criterion for evaluation, even though he or she clearly wants to maintain that it is a prime one. The second difficulty is more theoretical in nature. An artist might have very modest intentions and as a result always realize her intentions: does that mean her work is always good? An artist might have extremely ambitious intentions and as a result never realize his or her intentions: does that mean his or her work is always bad? This second consideration shows that success in realizing intentions is not a useful criterion for the evaluation of works of art. As Beardsley has noted, an artist's success in realizing his intentions is at best a criterion of how good the artist is in doing what he or she wants to do.[2]

The question of the relation of the artist's intention to an understanding of the *meaning* of a work of art or some part of it cannot be dealt with so easily. "Meaning" is being used here to include such things as the meaning of a poetic line and representation in the graphic arts. The artist's intention and poetic meaning will be discussed in considerable detail. Then, an attempt will be made to show that the conclusion of this discussion can be construed generally for the various arts. An attempt will also be made to show how the generalized conclusion applies to the question of correct performance.

Perhaps the simplest way to indicate that a poet's intention is independent of the meaning of his or her poetic lines is to consider "computer poems." To produce such "poems," a computer must be programmed with a vocabulary, punctuation marks, spaces to separate words, and so on, which the computer randomly combines in a large variety of ways. Most of the combinations produced will be nonsense, but sooner or later the computer will type out,

The cat is on the mat.

The cat is very fat.

The meaning of this uninteresting poem would appear to be evident to anyone who understands English. However, no intention was involved in the production of the poem, because a computer does not have intentions. Of course, intentions are involved in the programming of the computer—a particular vocabulary is put into it and so on—but the computer puts the words together in a random manner, and no programmer's intention can be responsible for the word sequences produced. Given vocabulary enough and time, a computer would type out every poem ever written without intending anything.

The fact that we can construe a meaning for "computer poems" at least suggests that meaning and intention are independent. However, an intentionalist critic may not be impressed with computer poems and claim that it is impossible for an unintended string of words to have meaning. To avoid this objection, I will consider only intended strings of words that I will call utterances. Also, I will discuss the question quite generally, not restricting matters to literature. I will argue that if it were true that intention is required to determine meaning, then communication would be impossible. Since we do communicate, intentionalism must be false.

I will use the following example to illustrate communication. Antoine and Brennan are in a restaurant having soup when Antoine sees an insect land in Brennan's soup. Wishing to warn Brennan, Antoine says, "There is a fly in your soup." According to the intentionalist, intention determines meaning, so, on this view, Brennan can understand Antoine's utterance only if he knows what Antoine's intention is. How can Brennan come to know Antoine's intention? It might be suggested that we find out what a speaker's intention is by understanding his utterance and inferring his intention. The intentionalist cannot accept this common-sense solution because it requires understanding an utterance independently of intention. One prominent intentionalist faced with this problem claims that we *guess* what other people's intentions are when we hear their utterances and thus understand their utterances.[3] But if we guess independently of understanding others' utterances, we are guessing blindly. Of course, we sometimes infer what people's intentions are on the basis of their nonlinguistic actions, as, for example, one might infer what someone's intention is when the person is seen removing money from someone else's wallet. Unfortunately, for the intentionalist, the overwhelming majority of cases of utterances are not like this example. Inferring intentions behind utterances independently of utterances is not generally possible. On the intentionalist account, hearers do not have a general, effective way of discovering speakers' intentions, and, consequently, could not understand the bulk of the utterances they hear.

Suppose Antoine is an intentionalist and tries to help Brennan by making a declaration of his intention, saying, "I *intended* to say that there is an insect in your soup." Antoine's declaration of his intention will not help because, according to the intentionalist account, for Brennan to understand Antoine's declaration about his intention, Brennan would have to know Antoine's intention in uttering his declaration "I *intended* to say that there is an insect in your soup," and Brennan has no access to what would be a second intention on Antoine's part. Antoine could keep on declaring his intentions forever, but on the intentionalist view Brennan would never be able to understand him because a further intention would always be required. The declaration of intention as a way of fostering understanding would, on the intentionalist view, generate an infinite regress of intentions, which means that Brennan would never be able to understand what Antoine said.

Intentionalism stands refuted as a theory of how utterances are understood by hearers because on this view hearers have no effective way of knowing speakers' intentions. If intentionalism is refuted as a theory of how utterances are understood, it seems unlikely that it is a correct account of how utterances have meaning. Intentionalism might work as an account of how language could function for God-like creatures who can directly intuit the intentions of others. But of course such creatures would not need language of the kind used by human beings.

If intentionalism is false, how do we understand utterances? Consider ambiguous sentences as a test case. A sentence is ambiguous when it can be construed to have two or more meanings. An example of ambiguous sentences is, "I like my secretary better than my wife." This may be understood to mean either "I like my secretary better than my wife likes my secretary" or "I like my secretary better than I like my wife."

Although ambiguous word sequences are sometimes uttered, sentences are not typically ambiguous; if they were typically ambiguous, communication would be impossible. Sometimes the nonlinguistic conditions in which a sentence is uttered make the sentence unambiguous, as when someone says "I saw her duck" in the presence of a group that contains a young lady who has just ducked her head and no member of the family Anatidae is or has been present. Sometimes the other sentences that occur in the same discourse are sufficient to make a given sentence unambiguous, as when "I saw her duck" is immediately followed by "and its feathers were black and white." And sometimes nonlinguistic conditions and linguistic environment work together to make a sentence unambiguous. Of course, it sometimes happens that either or both of these is insufficient, and the sentence remains ambiguous. So a given sentence may or may not be ambiguous depending on the situation in which it occurs. We know how to guard against uttering ambiguous word sequences: we make sure that certain nonlinguistic conditions obtain, or we provide other sentences.

Lacking the appropriate conditions, a sentence on a certain occasion may be ambiguous, but that's just the way things turn out sometimes, even when one tries hard. Suppose I suddenly realize that what I said to you yesterday was ambiguous. I phone you and straighten things out. Still, what I said yesterday, taken by itself, remains ambiguous; what is no longer ambiguous after the phone conversation is what I *meant* (or intended to say) yesterday. With yesterday's conversation plus today's phone conversation, I have now succeeded in saying what I meant to say. When the sentences uttered yesterday and the sentences uttered today are taken as constituting a single disclosure, they mean what I meant all along.

I cannot make "I saw her duck" mean that I saw a duck that was a bird *simply* by uttering "I saw her duck" or by uttering "I saw her duck" and *intending* the bird interpretation. An act of intending will get me nowhere. What I have to do is utter "I saw her duck" and then do something else—point my finger, utter other sentences, or the like—or see that certain conditions obtain. Given (1) a discourse, (2) the nonlinguistic conditions under which the discourse was uttered, and (3) a specified language community, a sentence in the discourse will have a specific meaning or remain ambiguous.

The account of language and meaning given thus far has been developed in terms of "ordinary" situations, but when one turns to literature, the situation is different in certain important respects. First, there is a dramatic speaker in the case of literature, so that the typical literary situation is more complicated than the ordinary situation. In an ordinary situation there are simply a speaker and his or her utterances, but in a literary situation there are the author, the dramatic speaker (or speakers), and the utterances of the dramatic speaker. It is important not to confuse the author *of* a work with a dramatic speaker *in* the work. Shakespeare is the author of the play *Hamlet*, but the character Hamlet is one of the dramatic speakers in the play. In a novel the dramatic speaker is the person who tells the story, for example, Ishmael in *Moby Dick*. Of course, in many novels the dramatic speaker is not named and does not refer to himself. Second, literature is different with regard to the second of the three general conditions mentioned earlier for determining the ambiguity or nonambiguity of sentences. The first and third conditions seem to hold for both ordinary and literary situations.

1. *The discourse condition.* In happy cases, we have the complete discourse—a complete conversation, a complete treatise on astronomy, a complete poem, a complete novel. These cases are happy because when we have a complete text, we have all there is to have for determining whether or not a sentence is ambiguous, so far as this condition is concerned. In unhappy cases, we either know the discourse is incomplete or cannot tell whether or not it is complete. These cases are unhappy because, although we can determine whether a given sentence is ambiguous or not relative to the possibly incomplete discourse, we know that our determination of ambiguity might change if we had the complete discourse.

3. *The-knowledge-of-a-language condition.* In happy cases, we know the language of some language community—twentieth-century American English, some regional variation of twentieth-century American English, sixteenth-century Elizabethan English, some regional variation of sixteenth-century Elizabethan English, and so on—in terms of which we can understand a discourse and determine whether or not a given sentence is ambiguous. In unhappy cases, we lack to some degree or other knowledge of the language in terms of which we are to understand a discourse.

It must be made clear what is involved in the knowledge-of-a-language condition and what is and is not involved in the inquiry necessary to find out what a word, phrase, or sentence means in a discourse in a certain language. In order to understand a given sentence in a discourse written in sixteenth-century English, I may have to do research into the meaning of a certain word. But in finding out what that word means in sixteenth-century English, I am not inquiring into what the sixteenth-century author of the discourse in question meant by the word. (I am ignoring the differences between the meanings of words and the meanings of sentences here.) The distinction between what a speaker meant by her utterance and what her utterance means is crucial here. It is conceivable that the discovery through, say, some historical record of what an author meant by a word would serve as a clue to what the word means in the language of the author's day. But the distinction I am insisting on still remains: what a particular author meant by a word or an utterance on a particular occasion of its use does not give that word or utterance its meaning in a language. To think otherwise is to get things backwards. The meaning of a word or an utterance in a language comes first, and a particular speaker can then use that meaning on a particular occasion to mean something. The order spoken of here is logical order, not a temporal order.[4]

We now come to the second general condition—a condition in which ordinary and literary situations differ: the nonlinguistic conditions under which the discourse is uttered. In ordinary situations, these conditions would be such things as pointing one's finger, the fact that the hearer can see who the speaker is, the fact that a member of the family Anatidae is present, and so on. But in literary situations with poems and novels, the question of nonlinguistic conditions does not arise. A dramatic speaker in a novel or poem cannot point a finger at a member of the family Anatidae or at a woman present, because although such dramatic speakers can *refer to* things outside the world of the literary work, they cannot *point* to such things. A hearer (a reader) cannot see who the speaker is because dramatic speakers in a novel or poem cannot be seen. A reader can be *told* what such a dramatic speaker looks like even though a dramatic speaker can never be seen, but this is a linguistic matter and not a question of nonlinguistic conditions. The point is that sentences in a literary situation—that is, in poems, novels, and the like—do not typically have nonlinguistic contexts. Consider the contrasting ways in which the same sentence might function in an ordinary situation and a literary one. In an ordinary situation, the utterance of the sentence "Twas on yonder hill that the battle was fought" is not ambiguous with regard to the referent of "hill" if only one hill is visible. However, it is ambiguous if two hills are visible and nothing is done to indicate which hill is being referred to. But if "Twas on yonder hill that the battle was fought" occurs in a literary work, there cannot be any ambiguity of reference that involves a nonlinguistic context of the utterance. Of course, there may be an ambiguity of reference *within* the story of the work as, for example, when a second character says, "Which of those two hills?" Although there is a reference context established by the utterances that make up a literary work, this kind of context does not exist independently of the discourse and is very different from the context of ordinary situations.

My point is that the nature of literary works is such that they do not typically have nonlinguistic contexts as ordinary discourse does. (Some ordinary situations wholly or partially lack nonlinguistic contexts—e.g., phone conversations.) There is nothing necessary about this; it is merely a fact of our *practice*, or way, of literary life. It could have been that all our literary works were such that in order for all the sentences in them to be unambiguous they would have had to be performed in specific geographical locations or replicas of such locations or in geographical locations or their replicas that possessed certain kinds of features. Of course, some of our literary works do require such settings—namely, plays and movies—and a full discussion of literature would require a detailed treatment of such works. But I am concerned with literary works such as poems and novels that are typically experienced (read) without any nonlinguistic context. Our practice is that these literary works ordinarily do not have nonlinguistic contexts. Consequently, an author of a poem or novel ordinarily must fail or succeed in having dramatic speakers mean what he or she intends them to mean without depending on the presence of a nonlinguistic context. One possible kind of exception to this might be the case of a novel set in a specific, well-known geographical location. In this case, the knowledge of the geographical terrain may be thought of as a condition that the dramatic speaker has made sure obtains and which may serve to make some sentence in the discourse unambiguous.

The main point here is that meaning is a *public* matter, not a matter of what an author or, more generally, a speaker intended in the privacy of his or her mind. So if an author tells us what his poem means but it is not possible to discover that meaning in the poem independently of the author's statement, then it cannot be claimed that the poem means what its author claims it means. The fact that the author had certain intentions in mind when writing out the words of the poem does not guarantee that those intentions are embodied in those words. Authors and ordinary speakers alike sometimes fail to say what they mean to say, and although an appeal to intentions can help clear up what was meant by the original words, such an appeal cannot change the meaning (or meaninglessness) of the original words. To forestall one possible misunderstanding, it should be made clear that an author may act as a critic to explicate, interpret, and even evaluate his own work, and he may be a good or bad critic. The anti-intentionalist denies that an author has a privileged position as a critic because of the author's intimate knowledge of his or her own intention (critics can only work with the public meaning they find in the literary work).

Representation in the visual arts is similar to meaning in literature insofar as the artist's intention is concerned. An artist's intending that his design represent an apple or a woman or Churchill does not accomplish anything. It is the properties of the design itself that determine what it represents. True, an artist or anyone else acting as a critic might call our attention to certain properties of the design that we have not noticed and enable us to see that the design represents (or perhaps suggests) a certain object or person. But this simply means we had failed to take account of what was publicly there to see and in no way need involve the intentions of the artist.

The interpretation of symbols in painting and literature is also a public matter. Symbols such as halos have a conventional, public meaning similar to the way in which words have public meaning. It is true that symbols are sometimes created or established by a work of art, but this is done in a public way by having the symbol play a certain role in the painting or literary work. The meaning of a symbol is not established by the artist's intention.

The question of correct performance and the artist's intention is different from the above because more than understanding is involved. In addition, two distinct problems are involved in performance: (1) in a playscript or musical score, there is always some leeway, for the artist never specifies exactly how each element is to be performed; and (2) in a given performance, actual stage or score directions may be ignored, or certain elements (a passage, a scene, an act) may be omitted. The advice of the intentionalist critic to follow the intention of the artist is vacuous in the first case, because if there is leeway for the performer, *there is leeway*.

However, the second case is different. If something is omitted, then the intention of the artist is knowingly flouted by the performer (director, composer, arranger, i.e., whoever has the responsibility for the performance). In this case, the intentionalist critic feels that violence has been done to the work of art. It is true that the identity of the work has been disturbed and perhaps even radically changed. But what of it? If a critic is concerned with the description, interpretation, or evaluation of the performance of a work, what difference does it make that the performance the critic experiences and talks about is derived by altering an existing work? The critic can still explain and evaluate the performance he or she has experienced. The critic might say, among other things, that the performance would have been better if something were added at a certain point, and he might or might not be specific about what was missing. If the missing element in a performed work well known to the critic corresponds to some element omitted by a performer, director, and so on, then the critic might be very specific and correctly say that the omitted element was just what the performed work needed. On the other hand, in a given case the critic might correctly say that the performed work was better without the element in question.

The point is that the critic must talk about and evaluate the performed work. The critic may also speculate about why a performed work is good or bad. In some cases, he or she can correctly say that if the artist's intention had not been flouted, the performed work would be better. But the badness of the performed work would not be due to flouting the artist's intention; it would be due to the *specific change* the director or conductor made. When one undertakes to alter the identity of art, one incurs the dangers inherent in creative work—namely, the danger of creating an inferior thing. However, there is also the possibility of creating something positively good, and this makes the chance worth taking.

From the point of view of the criticism of performed works of art, it is what meets the eye and the ear that is described and judged. It is the uncut *Hamlet*, a cut version, a version in modern dress, and so on, that is described and judged, not

Shakespeare's intentions. Criticism is concerned with helping us understand art and distinguish good art from bad, and the intentions of artists do not have a privileged role to play in the carrying out of either task.

Chapter 10

Symbolism in Art

Symbols are associated in the minds of some with the occult and magic. The connection is not a necessary one, and there is nothing magical about the way symbols function in art. There is nothing mysterious about the symbolic process, although in given cases the process may be very complicated. There is also nothing inherently valuable about symbolism in art—symbolism is a means of conveying meaning and it can be done well or clumsily. Symbolism can be tastefully and economically employed, but it can be overdone and heavy-handed. Symbolism can enhance a work of art, or it can be a burden.[1]

The symbols we deal with most frequently are words. The account given of symbols here is, however, not concerned with words but with symbols in art. I am concerned here with symbols as they occur in paintings, poems, plays, and so on. Literary works are built up out of symbols (words), but I am interested in the symbols that result from the description that words provide. In a painting, something, e.g., a lamb, is depicted, and the depicted thing in turn may function as a symbol of something, e.g., of Christ. Similarly, in a literary work something is described, and it is the described thing that may function as a symbol. Words and symbols in art have in common the symbolic function of bearing meaning, and the account of symbolism given here will exhibit this common feature. An account of the symbolic functioning of words, however, would be more complicated than an account of symbolism in art and will not be undertaken here.

Before attempting to formulate a definition of symbolism in art, it will be helpful to give several examples of such symbolism and describe how they work. Gören Hermerén, drawing on Panofsky, cites the following case of symbolism.[2] In a Jan van Eyck painting, a throne is depicted; on its armrest there is a brass figure of a pelican. The pelican is a traditional Christian symbol for Christ. This is an interesting case because the pelican seems like such an unlikely candidate for this particular symbolism. The basis for the symbolism is the belief stated in a bestiary of the twelfth century that the pelican is a devoted parent. According to the bestiary, the young strike their parents with their wings and the parents strike back and kill them. After three days, however, the mother pelican pierces her breast, pouring out her blood over the dead bodies of her young, and this brings them back to life. The attribution to the pelican of the power to revive life serves as the basis for the representation of a pelican to symbolize Christ, to whom similar powers are attributed.

For a present-day example of symbolism, consider Hemingway's short story, "A Clean, Well-Lighted Place." In the opening sentence of the story, an old man is described as "an old man who sat in the shadow the leaves of the tree made against the electric light." A dozen or so lines later it is said of him, "the old man sat in the shadow of the leaves of tree that moved slightly in the wind." A few lines later he is described simply as "the old man sitting in the shadow." The thrice-repeated image of sitting in the shadow is clearly a symbol of approaching death and nothingness.

Isabel Hungerland cites an example of symbolism from the movie *Lost Horizon*.[3] As the High Lama of Shangri-La dies, the camera focuses on a lighted candle that is extinguished by the wind. We know the High Lama has died when the candle goes out because the extinguished candle symbolizes his death.

In the Grünewald Isenheim altarpiece, "The Crucifixion," a lamb stands at the foot of the cross. The lamb carries a small cross on its shoulder held with its right front leg. The lamb with cross is clearly a symbol, presumably for the sacrifice of Christ, which is also the main subject of the painting. The cross itself is a symbol for Christianity, the flag is a symbol of a nation, and the eagle on a U.S. quarter is a symbol of certain characteristics attributed to the nation, such as strength and nobility.

If these are taken as genuine cases of symbolism, then certain features can be noted about symbolism. (1) A symbol does not, as some assume, have to be concrete, that is, nonabstract. Words are not concrete. No doubt most symbols in art are concrete, but in formulating a definition of "symbol" only characteristics uniformly true of symbols can be used. (2) The things that symbols symbolize are quite varied—for example, a person (Christ), an event and a state (death and nothingness), an event (the High Lama's death), an action (Christ's sacrifice), institutions (Christianity and a nation), and qualities (strength and nobility). There seems to be no reason to try to limit the types of things that can be symbolized. (3) In the case of visual art a symbol does not depict what it symbolizes, and in the case of literary art a symbol does not describe what it symbolizes. Symbols convey meaning in a more indirect way than depiction and description, but they build on and enhance depiction and description. (4) A symbol "stands for" in some establishable way that which it symbolizes. A symbol serves to transfer someone's thought to something other than itself, and the transfer is not a random association. The transfer depends on certain features of the symbol that give it a place in a certain meaning system. (5) None of the symbols cited is a natural sign, such as clouds signifying rain or smoke signifying fire. Natural signs depend on causal relations between sign and thing signified. Natural signs are usually distinguished from symbols, presumably because a symbol achieves the status of being a symbol as the result of some person's action, whereas a natural sign signifies quite independently of anyone's action. In the case of a natural sign, one merely notes causal regularities. However, there is a certain vagueness here and one must be cautious.

Perhaps a definition may now be attempted, but, as Hungerland notes, the variety of ways that the word "symbol" has been used is so large that probably no definition could cover them all.[4] What has to be done is to focus on a set of examples that one hopes is representative of the bulk of the uses of "symbol" and whose members one hopes are sufficiently similar to provide a basis for a definition.

> Something is a symbol if and only if for some person or group of persons that thing stands in some establishable way for some other thing and that thing (which is the symbol) does not depict or describe the other thing (that which is symbolized) and the relationship between the thing which signifies and the thing signified is not simply that of a natural sign.

The most important question raised by this definition is that of the *establishment* of the standing-for relation. Perhaps the best way to explain this is to begin by talking about firmly established symbols such as the cross. The cross has for hundreds of years had a central place in Christian ceremonies because of the manner of the martyrdom of Jesus. Such symbols as the cross are a kind of capital for artists to draw on. The artist can count on all the members of his audience knowing what the cross signifies if he uses it in his work. Such symbols are very much like common words that all members of the community know the meaning of. However, all this talk about the cross or other firmly established symbols does not show how symbols are established, but only that they are established symbols. How, for example, was the cross established as a symbol? One can only speculate about the details of its establishment. At some time, some early Christians must have drawn or fashioned a cross in the presence of other Christians who knew the story of Jesus' martyrdom in order to enhance a ceremony or perhaps establish his identity as a member of the sect or for some other purpose. In any event, because of the use of a cross in one of the basic events of Christian history, the depicted or fashioned cross became established as a symbol of Christianity. Thus, some early Christian by action established the *convention* that the cross is a symbol, and the convention was accepted and used by members of the Christian community. In time the symbolic significance of the cross became known to non-Christians as well.

Conventions may be established in both formal and informal ways. Flags as symbols of nations are probably most often established in a formal way. No doubt, at some early moment in the history of the United States, some member of Congress proposed that a flag with thirteen stars and thirteen stripes, and so on, be adopted as the flag of the United States, and the proposal was accepted by a majority vote of Congress. However, the establishment of most symbols is informal and consists in some person using something in such a way as to show that it is being used to signify a certain thing.

Artists can employ already established symbols in their work, but just as they create stories, paintings, and plays, artists also create symbols. Artists employ a variety of devices to help establish something as a symbol and no doubt there are some devices as yet not invented, but the following examples will serve to illustrate the ways in which devices are used to help establish new symbols. One way is to depict a very unusual or impossible event in a painting that otherwise depicts an ordinary or historical event. In the Grünewald painting "The Crucifixion," the lamb carrying a little cross on its shoulder supported by holding its leg around the bottom of the cross is a case in point. Even if the lamb were not already an established symbol, this depiction in the context of this painting would clearly serve to establish it as a symbol. In some cases when descriptions of unusual or impossible events are given in literary works, they function as symbols.

Another device is to give a depiction or a description a prominent place in the work. The lamb in the Grünewald painting is an example of this device also; it is located in the center foreground of the painting at the foot of the cross. In the Hemingway story, the old man is described as sitting in the shadow in the very first sentence. The end of a work is another prominent place; other prominent places would be relative to the plot or other formal characteristics. Additional devices are repetition and juxtaposition. The description of the old man sitting in the shadow is given three times at the opening of the Hemingway story, and in the story darkness is frequently juxtaposed with light, which here signifies life and youth. Juxtaposition, whether repeated or not, may serve to establish a symbolic relation. The lamb in the Grünewald painting is shown right next to the crucified Christ, whom it symbolizes.

Such devices alone, however, cannot establish something as a symbol: a thing must have or be believed to have certain appropriate characteristics in order to function as a symbol of a given other thing. Appropriately presented in a work of art, it is relatively easy to make a lamb a symbol of Christ and his sacrifice, for it is believed that lambs have such prominent characteristics as meekness, which is also attributed to Christ, and it is a well-known historical fact that lambs were a traditional sacrificial animal for the Jews. In the case of the old man sitting in the shadow, the easy association of darkness with death and the relation of the phrase to "the valley of the shadow of death" in the Twenty-third Psalm provide a sufficient basis for the described situation to function as a symbol. The basis of a pelican symbolizing Christ is the power attributed to it to revive life. The fact that no one now believes the pelican has this power does not prevent it from functioning as a symbol of Christ. It is not likely, however, that a present-day artist would use a pelican as such a symbol, although he or she might use a lamb.

In general, it takes both formal devices and a thing with appropriate characteristics to establish that thing or make it function as a symbol. Not every depicted lamb is a symbol of Christ or anything else. A lamb in a painting of Little Bo Peep probably would not symbolize anything. Symbols are context dependent. The way the elements of a work of art work together to enable one element to function as a symbol is well illustrated by the example of the candle and the High Lama. A candle burning and then going out is similar in certain respects to a person being alive and then dying, but these similarities by themselves cannot establish a symbolic relation. The extinguished candle is also similar to a tire that goes flat, but in this instance it is not a symbol of a tire going flat. The extinguished candle is exactly similar to another extinguished candle, but one is not a symbol of the other. Similarity is not enough; it is the treatment in the context of the work that picks out the relevant similarities and establishes the symbolic relation. In the movie there is first a shot of the High Lama, who is obviously at the point of death. The camera then cuts to a shot of a candle flickering before an open window. The wind coming through the window blows the candle out. The extinguishing of the candle symbolizes the death of the High Lama because the immediate temporal juxtaposition of the two shots provides the linkage between them and brings out the relevant similarities that establish the symbolic relation. Given another context, the extinguishing of a candle might symbolize a tire going flat.

An artist may try to establish something as a symbol and fail, because he does not put the elements of his work together properly or does not provide certain crucial elements. If the film editor of *Lost Horizon* had mistakenly placed the candle shot far removed from the death scene, then it would not have functioned as a symbol of the High Lama's death, although it would still have the aura of being a symbol. It is also possible and probably frequently occurs that artists place things in their works that have the aura of being symbols but in fact do not succeed in being symbols. Masses of such "symbols" in a work of art would lend to it the appearance of significance. Perhaps some of the strange things in surrealist art are this kind of "symbol." Beardsley says that Kafka's "In the Penal Colony" has the "air of being deeply and richly symbolic without symbolizing anything in particular, or at least anything that you can formulate in other words."[5]

But what is the point of symbols in art? What function do they serve? Most fundamentally, symbols in art convey meaning or information. The image of sitting in the shadow conveys the meaning "is near death." The depicted lamb with cross on its shoulder conveys the meaning "the crucified Christ." The extinguished candle conveys the information "the High Lama is dead." In some cases the meaning conveyed might be grammatically best formulated as a statement (the candle), in other cases as an adjectival phrase (the lamb with cross), in still other cases as a predicate (the shadow), and in still other cases in other ways. The point is that in one form or other meaning is conveyed.

The information conveyed may be additional information or it may be redundant. In the case of the extinguished candle, additional information is conveyed—when the candle goes out we know for the first time that the High Lama is dead. The lamb with the cross bears redundant meaning, for the central focus of the painting is the depiction of the crucified Christ. One would probably want to say that the meaning conveyed by the image of sitting in shadow is also redundant because the old man's situation is made abundantly clear by the straightforward nonsymbolic aspects of the story. It is probably the case that the large majority of symbols are redundant and most symbols could be dispensed with without any loss of meaning. One could, for example, simply show the High Lama dying or say the old man feels the nearness of death.

But this technical kind of redundancy is not a defect in art, or even in ordinary speech. The redundancy of ordinary speech ensures that what we say is understood. The redundant meaning of symbols in art adds a thickness and richness of texture to a work of art. Symbols can at once add to the complexity and maintain or increase the unity of a work of art. Consider the Grünewald painting without the lamb with cross. Then add the lamb to the painting. With the lamb the painting is more complex than without the lamb because it has more elements. The lamb maintains or perhaps increases the unity of the painting because the symbolic meaning of the lamb fits in with the other elements and the main theme of the painting. Of course, not every symbol will enhance a work of art: a given symbol might tend to make a given work incoherent, and too many symbols, even if coherent, may spoil a work.

Symbols typically serve to emphasize and reinforce the main theme or themes of a work. In some cases, symbols properly used give a work a brooding intensity similar to that given by repeated chant. The kind of effect supplied by symbols could not have been achieved by simple repetition in the basic mode of expression (depiction or description). Such repetition would be boring or even silly: imagine replacing the lamb with cross at the foot of the cross with a small depiction of the crucifixion. Also in some instances, the symbol further serves to emphasize certain specific features of what is symbolized—in the instance of the lamb with the cross, the meekness of Jesus and the sacrificial nature of the event. Symbols work in subtle and complicated ways.

The impact of symbols is not simply the result of the fact that they convey meaning in a manner different from depiction or description; the economy with which they function is important too. A symbol may not, like the proverbial picture, be worth a thousand words, but it may be worth many words or much depiction. A symbol packs a great deal of information into a small compass. And an established symbol serves to sum up a lot of significant history and experience—it is a repository of meaning.

There is at least one sort of thing for which the word "symbol" is used that might be expressed better in a different way. For example, it is sometimes said that Willie Loman in *Death of a Salesman* is a symbol of a certain kind of man or a certain kind of life. To say that Willie Loman is a symbol means that the character and his actions *stand for* a certain kind of man or life and *transfer* our thought to that kind of man or life. Putting the matter in these terms, however, fails to do justice to the experience of this play. Willie Loman does not stand for a certain kind of man or life; he is a fictional *example* of that kind of man or life. Willie Loman is an illustration or exemplification rather than a symbol. An example is more powerful and direct and less subtle than a symbol. Both exemplification and symbolization serve to call our attention to certain kinds of things and each has its place in art. However, there is not, I think, any good reason for calling exemplification a kind of symbolization.

Chapter 11

Metaphor

Metaphor has probably attracted more critical attention than any other figure of speech. This attention is partly a function of the great frequency with which metaphors occur in poetry. If poetic language is to be understood, an account of metaphor must be given. Metaphors also occur in prose, and not just in "literary" prose. Metaphors are used by everyone—sportswriters, scientists, philosophers, business people. And they are as much a feature of speech as of written language. Metaphor is a pervasive and powerful aspect of language. It is, therefore, highly desirable to have an account of how metaphors function, or to have what is sometimes called a "theory of metaphor."[1]

The word "metaphor" is sometimes used in a very broad sense, but here it refers to certain kinds of sentences and phrases within sentences. The following is a list of sample metaphors:

1. The chairman ploughed through the discussion.
2. A smokescreen of witnesses.
3. Light is but the shadow of God.[2]
4. The smoke is briars.[3]

Note that certain words in these phrases and sentences—"ploughed" and "smokescreen," for example—stand out as metaphorical and contrast with the other words in the expressions.

In order to understand metaphor, it will be helpful first to discuss another figure of speech—simile. Discussion of this figure will provide a background and an opportunity to develop some terminology with which to analyze metaphor. A simile, according to the traditional account, means literally what it says and explicitly compares one thing with another. For example, "The boy runs like a deer" is a simile that asserts of a certain boy that certain features of his running resembles the running of a deer. Of course, not every feature of a deer's running is being predicated of the boy's running—for example, running on four legs. This example is an *open* simile in that the hearer must figure out from the context—the other words in the sentence and the other sentences in the discourse of which the sentence is a part—which features of a deer's running are being attributed to the boy. A *closed* simile specifies the respect or respects in which the two things compared are alike. The open-simile example can be closed by adding a few words—"The boy runs like a deer with respect to grace" or, more idiomatically, "The boy runs as gracefully as a deer."

Similes are, then, literal. What is meant by "literal"? A word is used literally when it is used in one of its dictionary senses. The literal meaning of a sentence is the meaning it has as a function of the literal meanings of the words in it. A basic question about metaphor can now be asked: is metaphor a species of literal language like simile?

The oldest and most widely held view, one that can be traced back to Aristotle, is that a metaphor is a disguised simile that makes an implied comparison. Several other theories of metaphor have been advanced, but they lack the plausibility and influence of the disguised-simile theory and will not be discussed here.[4] According to the disguised-simile view, a metaphor has meaning in a literal, although somewhat roundabout, way. Max Black calls this theory "the comparison view"[5] and Beardsley designates it "the object-comparison view."[6] The reason for using the word "object" is to bring out that the theory maintains that a metaphorical word literally refers to an object or process that is then compared by the hearer to the object or process referred to by the nonmetaphorical words. Consider the detailed account that the object-comparison view would give of the metaphor embedded in the sentence "the defense attorney presented a smokescreen of witnesses." A hearer would understand the word "witnesses" to refer to certain witnesses (objects) and the word "smokescreen" to refer to a smokescreen. The hearer would then compare the two referents and work out what is being said by means of a comparison. The object-comparison theory claims that the way metaphorical words mean depends on both of two aspects of words. First, words have *senses*, or meanings that are specified in terms of other words. The sense of a word is given in a dictionary. Second, some words and expressions *refer* or purport to refer to objects or processes. A sense of the word "cat" is "a carnivorous mammal (Felis catus) . . . etc." The referent of "cat" in "The cat is on the mat" is a nonlinguistic object, namely, a particular cat.

The problem with the object-comparison view is that although, for example, the referent of "witnesses" is clear enough—it is the group of witnesses presented by the defense attorney—the referent of the metaphorical word "smokescreen" is a mystery. Which smokescreen is being referred to so that a comparison can be made? Clearly no particular smokescreen is being referred to as is the case in the sentence "Remember the smokescreen that was laid down before we went into Omaha Beach." In this sentence "the smokescreen . . ." functions as a referring expression and purports to refer to a particular smokescreen (object). The word "smokescreen" in the metaphorical expression does not refer; it functions like, say, "large number" in "a large number of witnesses," namely, to modify the word "witnesses." In short, the complete function of "smokescreen" *in the metaphorical expression* is carried out simply in terms of the sense of "smokescreen" without referring. In the literal sentence "John is a student," the proper name "John" refers to some particular person (object), but "a student" does not refer to anything; it simply applies a sense of the word to the subject of the sentence. Of course, in some sentences "a student" may have a referring function—for example, in "A student left a package." When a word is used in a sentence or a phrase, its sense is always used, but a word does not refer unless it is used to do so. In "Monkeys are mammals," the word "monkeys" refers to the *class* of monkeys, and something is said about each member of the class referred to. In "Jocko and George are monkeys," the sense of "monkeys" is used, but "monkeys" does not refer to anything. "Jocko" and "George" refer to two individuals, who incidentally happen to be monkeys. In the metaphorical sentence (about a human being), "John is a sheep," the metaphorical expression "a sheep" functions just as "a student" does in the first literal sentence and as "monkeys" does in "Jocko and George are monkeys." That is, "a sheep" applies a sense (metaphorical in this case) to a subject of a sentence and has no referring function.

The main point of these remarks is that even in those cases in which it might be thought that the object-comparison account might work best—namely, cases in which the metaphorical expression is a noun or a noun phrase—it does not work. Even in these cases, the metaphorical word does not refer and hence does not designate a referent to which something can be compared. In a sentence such as "My uncle is like your uncle" both "My uncle" and "your uncle" refer and designate two objects that can be compared, and we may say that the sentence is a comparison. It should be clear by now that metaphors are not comparisons. Beardsley presents an argument against the object-comparison view that fits in nicely with the above. He considers a line from T. S. Eliot's poem "East Coker":

> frigid purgatorial fires
> of which the flame is roses, and the smoke is briars.[7]

In the metaphor "the smoke is briars" the object-comparison view would be that "briars" refers to briars and that we get the meaning of the metaphor by comparing the smoke and its properties with briars and their properties in order to understand what is being said about the smoke. However, an important part of the meaning of "briars" in this case comes from the way the crown of thorns figures in the Bible story of the crucifixion. It is impossible to work out the meaning derived from the Biblical association by reflecting on briars and their properties—their scratchiness, and so on. The word "briars" has acquired a nonliteral meaning as a result of an historical event, and such meaning can be exploited by the poet. This meaning is not idiosyncratic or private to the poet; it derives from a well-known event and is public. Mythological stories are as good as historical events for providing the foundation for this kind of meaning. Note that this argument shifts the emphasis away from objects and their properties to words and their meanings.

The object-comparison theory is not only mistaken about reference, it is more complicated than it needs to be. In the comparison view, a metaphor operates in two stages: in the first stage the metaphorical word, say, "smokescreen" *by virtue of its meaning* refers to an object; in the second stage the object referred to is compared to some other object. In the view advanced by Beardsley, which he calls "the verbal-opposition theory," it is maintained that metaphorical words function completely at the level of the applying meaning without referring to an object.

According to the verbal-opposition view,[8] words have their primary, or dictionary, meanings, and when these senses are used, literal expressions result. In addition to these primary meanings, words have other meanings. Some of these secondary meanings are the result of what Max Black calls "systems of associated commonplaces."[9] Some of the associated commonplaces are associations such as briars with Jesus' crown of thorns, and some involve characteristics commonly (truly or falsely) attributed to some thing. For example, it is commonly believed that wolverines are fierce. Such meanings are common capital from which we can construct metaphors. Other secondary senses are generated by the metaphors and the contexts in which they occur. For example, the metaphorical meaning of "smokescreen" in "a smokescreen of witnesses" is generated by an abstraction of the dictionary meaning of "smokescreen" from "a curtain of heavy smoke, often produced by chemicals, used as a concealing screen, as for naval vessels" to something less specific like "a device for concealing something." In addition to abstraction, there are many ways in which secondary meanings are generated, but the significant point is that (some) words have or can come to have meanings other than their dictionary meanings.

How are secondary senses activated to mean what they mean in a particular metaphor? Beardsley speaks of a logical opposition between the literal words and the metaphorical word that rules out a literal interpretation of the meaning of the metaphorical word and shows that the word must be understood in a nonliteral way. I am not sure if logical *opposition* is the best way to put it, but he is probably on the right track. In any case, what goes on in understanding a word metaphorically is basically the same as what goes on in understanding a word literally. A given word may, for example, have three distinct literal meanings, with each sense being numbered in the dictionary. However, when this word is used literally in a sentence, it is not numbered to indicate which of the literal senses it means. We have to figure out which literal sense fits the sentence and its context. If this cannot be done, the sentence is ambiguous or obscure. The same kind of sorting process is involved when a word is used metaphorically in an expression: each one of the literal meanings is in one way or another ruled out, and in the search for the meaning that fits we must go on to the "list" of nonliteral senses that the word may already have. If the nonliteral "list" fails us, we go on to try to find what new meaning is created by the metaphor and its context. Of course, I do not mean to suggest that we go through the process in such a mechanical way; I am just specifying the elements that are involved in the process.

Let me examine the kind of process that we go through in understanding the metaphorical sentence "The chairman ploughed through the discussion." A metaphorical sentence typically contains substantive words (nouns, verbs, adjectives) that are literal and substantive words that are metaphorical, as does this example. However, which words are metaphorical and which literal cannot be known *until the whole sentence is understood*. Assume that we read through a sentence one word at a time, absorbing the information in each word as we come to it. I realize that we normally absorb larger chunks at a time than this, but we do go through a written sentence from left to right absorbing the information contained in chunks of some size or other. As we go through a sentence, at various points certain options are opened up to us and other options are closed off, although what appeared to be closed options at an earlier point may be opened up by information that comes further along in the sentence. When we come to "The" in our sample sentence, several options are opened. For example, it and the words immediately following it may constitute a definite description such as "the man on the corner" or an expression referring to a class of individuals such as "the whale (is a mammal)." The occurrence of "The" closes off or makes improbable certain options. When we come to "chairman," the two options mentioned still remain. "The chairman" may be a definite description (or part of one) that refers to a person who presides at a meeting or who holds a certain kind of administrative job, or it may refer to the class of chairmen as in the sentence "The chairman is the main administrative officer in an academic department." When we come to "ploughed," it seems most probable that "The chairman" is a definite description, but the second possibility is not entirely ruled out. "Ploughed" is the metaphorical word in the sentence. However, we are not yet in a position to say that it is. There is nothing about being a chairman that rules out ploughing a furrow in the earth or ploughing through the sea (say, with the chairman being pulled through the water by a rope) or any other of the literal meanings of "ploughed." The word "through" seems to rule out ploughing a field for cultivation, for we would say "ploughed the field" for that, but ploughing through water, a watermain, an oil pipeline, an electrical cable, and so on, remain as possibilities. When we come to "the" and "discussion" everything (or almost everything) falls into place, and we understand the sentence, see that it a metaphorical sentence, and realize that "ploughed" is a metaphorical word in this context.

None of the literal senses of "to plough," with one possible exception, fits in such a way as to make the sentence make sense as a literal sentence. The one dictionary sense that is not ruled out by the other words in the sentence is "to proceed laboriously." To take care of this possibility, assume a context for the sentence that rules out this literal sense and requires that the sentence be understood metaphorically to indicate that the chairman dealt ruthlessly and the like with the matters considered in the discussion he chaired.

How do we know to read "ploughed" metaphorically and not some other word or words? There is no general answer to this question. One just has to see what options for understanding are available, given the words in a particular sentence. And of course it is not simply the words in the sentence in question that may be important. The context of the sentence—the spoken or written sentences connected with the sentence in question, the tone of voice or gesture with which the sentence is uttered if it is a spoken sentence, and so on—is frequently crucial. Earlier I gave "John is a sheep" as an example of a metaphor, but there are contexts in which it would be a literal sentence. For example, if someone said, "I have three pet animals: a pig named Jack, a cat named Tom, and one named John who is covered with wool. John is a sheep." In this context it is clear that a literal sense of "sheep" applies.

Sentences such as "John is a sheep" and "Richard is a lion," which are often cited as examples of metaphors, are not really metaphors at all—they are at best "dead metaphors." For example, one of the senses of "lion" given in the dictionary is "a person felt to resemble a lion especially in courage, ferocity, dignity." "Sheep," "bear," "cat," and the like have similar senses specified in the dictionary. Thus, to say of some human being that he is a lion is to assert literally that the person is courageous, ferocious, or dignified. (Given the presence of the locution "felt to resemble" in some of these senses, one might be tempted to say that some dead metaphors are similes. But perhaps a better way to conceive of them is to say that dictionaries have been influenced by the object-comparison theory of metaphor in stating some of the senses that produce dead metaphors.) Presumably at some time in the past, "lion" did not have this sense as a literal meaning, and at that time "Richard is a lion" could have been a metaphor. A problem arises about dating the time at which a particular sense became literal. Dictionaries, which I used initially in specifying when a sense is literal or not, are of fairly recent origin, and "lion," "sheep," and so on, must have been used in the way they are currently used for centuries. So although we cannot date the death of "Richard is a lion" as a metaphor, it must have been a very long time ago. Metaphors are born, age in direct proportion to their popularity, and finally reach the dictionary —the graveyard of forgotten metaphors. There is a conceptual problem here too, because the distinction between literal and nonliteral senses of words ultimately depends on actual usage, which is only reflected by dictionaries and reflected always with a time lag. Still, the use of dictionaries is the only practical way for determining the literal senses of words.

I have just said that "Richard is a lion" is a dead metaphor, and as a sentence that asserts that the person named by "Richard" is courageous, and so on, it *is* a dead metaphor. It is, however, always possible to revive the sentence as a metaphor, although it will not be an assertion about courage. For example, given a certain context, "Richard is a lion" might be used to say that someone named Richard has a large amount of flowing, tawny-colored hair. The raising of dead metaphors points up the importance of context in understanding the meaning of sentences—metaphorical or literal.

At the beginning of this chapter a traditional account of simile was given. This account maintains that words are used literally in similes. The question was then posed, "Are metaphors literal like similes?" It is now clear that metaphors are nonliteral; that is, metaphorical sentences and phrases depend on the nonliteral functioning of some words or words in them. Metaphor differs from simile, at least as simile is usually understood.

Reflection on the theory of metaphor advanced here suggests to me that perhaps the traditional view of simile as a comparison is wrong too. Perhaps "like a deer" in "The boy runs like a deer" and "like a red, red rose ..." in "O my Luve's like a red, red rose." do not refer and hence do not designate an object for comparison. However, this question will not be pursued here, and readers will have to follow it up on their own.

Chapter 12

Expression

It was argued in Chapter 5 that the nineteenth-century theories of art as the expression of emotion are inadequate, and in Chapter 6 an examination of Collingwood's version of the emotional-expression theory yielded the same result. It seems reasonable to suppose that any theory claiming a *necessary* connection between art and the expression of emotion will fail. There have been other kinds of expression theories—art as the expression of wishes, as the expression of unconscious desires, and so on—but these theories have not been nearly as popular as the emotion version. These other theories fail for reasons similar to those cited in regard to the emotion version.

However, even if art cannot be defined in terms of the expression of emotion, it is certainly true that in some sense art frequently expresses emotion. It is an important problem in aesthetics to work out in what sense or senses emotion is expressed by art. Consider first two examples of the account usually given of the expression of emotion in ordinary situations outside of art. A person's beaming face expresses joy. In this situation it is typically assumed that two basic elements are involved: (1) the face with a particular expression on it and (2) the emotion the person is feeling. A person's bitter remark expresses her anger (or some other emotion depending on the context). Again it is typically assumed that two basic elements are involved: (1) the bitter remark and (2) the emotion the person is feeling. In each of these examples there is something public—the face and the remark—and something private, or not observed by spectators or auditors—the felt emotion. It is quite natural to take this picture of ordinary situations as the model for explaining what it means to say that art expresses emotion. When this is done, one is led to look in the artistic situation for something public that is the vehicle of expression and for something private that is expressed by this vehicle. It should be noted that the nonart cases cited are cases in which there are actual emotions felt and a person behaves in such a way as to express his or her emotion. It is quite possible for someone to behave in an expressive way without any felt emotion, as in acting.

There are three basic items in the artistic situation: (1) the artist, (2) the art the artist creates, and (3) the audience that experiences the work. Works of art are, of course, public, and it is natural to assume therefore that they are public vehicles for expression. The artist and audience offer private locations for felt emotions that may stand in relation to works of art. Thus, given the typical assumptions about expressing, two possibilities are immediately suggested: (1) art expresses the emotion of the artist, and (2) art expresses (evokes) emotion in the audience.[1] If a case cannot be made for one of these two theses, the notion that a privately felt emotion is involved when art expresses emotion will have to be given up. In order to avoid certain complications introduced by arts in which representation typically occurs (to be discussed later), these two possible theses will be discussed as they apply to music. I will develop my argument by talking about the expression of sadness or joy, assuming them to be typical emotions.

First, consider the possibility that when we say that a particular musical passage expresses joy or sadness, we mean that the music expresses the joy or the sadness of its creator. Call this possibility the "artist thesis." It might at first appear that the kinds of argument used against intentionalist criticism could also be brought to bear against the artist thesis—namely, that to refer to the artist's emotion is to talk about something that is distinct from the work of art. Such an argument would be relevant from the point of view of the philosophy of criticism, which is concerned with aesthetic objects. However, the question must be treated in the wider context of the philosophy of art, and, from this point of view, it might conceivably be true that art that expresses joy or sadness does in fact express the joy or sadness of its creator. There are, nevertheless, good reasons to think that the artist thesis is false. In arguing against the artist thesis, it should be admitted at the outset that a given piece of sad music might have been composed during a time when its composer was sad and that the composer's sadness was in part responsible for the sadness in the music. In such a case, it would be reasonable to say that the music served to express the sadness of the composer. However, the artist thesis demands a great deal more. It demands that all music expressing sadness be written by a composer in a sad frame of mind, all music expressing joy be written by a composer when he or she is happy, and so on.

The first difficulty the artist thesis meets is a practical one, namely, the impossible task of empirically confirming that all music expressive of sadness has been or will be written by composers when they are sad. There are little or no data available about the state of mind of composers at the time they compose. So we certainly cannot *know* that the artist thesis is true. The second difficulty the artist thesis must meet is that there is no compelling reason to think that sad music must be written by a person feeling sad. Given a musical passage that all agree expresses sadness, there is no reason to think a person had to be sad in order to write down that particular sequence of notes. It is very easy to imagine a composer in a happy frame of mind being given the commission to write a piece of music that expresses sadness for some sad occasion. Such a composer, if he or she is competent, ought to be able to do the job required. It must certainly be the case that the artist thesis is false. Thus, although on an occasion when we know that a composer feeling sad composed a sad piece of music we could use the locution "the music expresses sadness" to convey the information that the music expressed the composer's emotion, this cannot be what we generally mean when we say that a particular musical passage expresses sadness.

Consider now what may be called "the audience thesis," namely, the possibility that when we say that a musical passage expresses sadness, we mean that the music evokes the emotion of sadness in the members of the audience that hear the music. The audience thesis would have to meet some rather complicated and sophisticated objections concerning the problem of how a specific emotion such as sadness may be aroused by something as unspecific as music. Some simpler arguments, however, show that this thesis is false. Music that expresses sadness may evoke sadness in a hearer, and this seems to occur with some frequency. However, music expressive of sadness certainly does not *always* evoke sadness; for example, a person might listen to a piece of music that expresses sadness, agree that it expresses sadness, and simply be too happy at the moment to feel sad. This particular argument becomes clearer when music expressive of gaiety is considered: a person in a sad frame of mind can seldom have gay feelings evoked by music that expresses gaiety. In fact, such music may make a sad person even sadder. Even if one were to specify that the relevant emotions are evoked by the music in a person in a normal frame of mind (assuming that normal could be adequately characterized in this context), it does not seem plausible that such a person would always be made sad or happy or whatever. Thus, we might on a given occasion use the locution "the music expresses sadness" to convey the information that a piece of music evokes sadness in a certain individual. However, this is not what we generally mean when we say that a particular musical passage expresses sadness.

If the artist and audience theses are false, there is no private location for felt emotions in connection with music expressing emotion. Consequently, the explanation of how music can express emotion must be given in terms of public phenomena, and the explanation must not contain reference to any felt emotion, that is, to any particular actual emotion. The sadness expressed by music does not have the "depth" that the sadness expressed by a sad face has when the sad face is genuine and there is a sad feeling "behind" it. This lack of depth means that the sadness of music does not stand in relation to any particular instance of sad feeling. It is perhaps also worth noting that whereas one can be deceived by a "put-on" sad face into thinking that there are sad feelings behind it, one cannot be deceived in the same way by sad music, for there is nothing behind the music that necessarily stands in relation to its sadness.

If sad music does not necessarily stand in relation to some particular instance of sad feelings, then it is unnecessary and misleading to use the verb "expresses" when we want to say what we generally mean when we use the locution "the music expresses sadness." It is misleading because "express" is a relation verb, and its use in this case strongly suggests that there is a relation between the music and some other particular thing. Consequently, the word "express" should be avoided in favor of locutions such as "the music is sad" or "the music has a sad quality." This way of speaking makes it clear that a quality of the music itself is being referred to. Even this kind of usage is not without a minor inconvenience: it might mislead someone who does not realize that the statement is metaphorical into thinking that it is being asserted that some music is literally sad. But what we are doing when we say that the music is sad is to call attention to a certain quality of the music by way of a metaphorical attribution. As we saw in the last chapter, there is nothing wrong with metaphor; in fact, it is a very useful and powerful aspect of language. Frequently when we say music is sad, gay, and so on, we are referring to qualities of music for which we have no literal words.

The avoidance of "express" in favor of "is" or "has" also has the advantage of bringing about a certain theoretical simplicity. Words such as "majestic," "delicate," "vigorous," and "sprightly"—words that do not refer to emotional states or emotions—are used to describe music by means of "is" or "has." We say that music is majestic or vigorous or sprightly or the like. Emotion words like "sad" or "gay" and nonemotion words like "delicate" or "sprightly" may now be handled in the same way. As long as "express" is used in connection with emotion words, the impression is given that emotion words function differently from nonemotion words. It turns out, however, that emotion words and nonemotion words (of the general type mentioned) are both instances of metaphorical description when applied to qualities of music.

Having reached the conclusion that descriptions of qualities of music are cases of metaphorical attribution, this conclusion should be reviewed in the light of some of the results of the preceding chapter on metaphor. From the point of view of usage, it may well be the case that a number of the kind of words discussed in this section have developed literal senses that apply to music. "Sad" and "gay," for example, have been applied with such great frequency to music that we no longer have the feeling of metaphor when they are so used. We may not find these literal senses listed in dictionaries yet—there is always a certain time lag. Although it is a difficult matter to decide, "sad" and "gay" seem to apply as literally to music as "allegro," "has a fast tempo," and so on. Whether the words under discussion all apply to music metaphorically or whether some apply literally and some metaphorically is not really the most important point. The main conclusion of this argument is that these words describe characteristics of music rather than characteristics of the composer or audience.

The qualities of music referred to by such terms as "sad" probably cannot be characterized in a general way. That is, it may very well be the case, for example, that all pieces of sad music do not have a common feature. Probably most sad music is rather slow-paced, but there might be sad music that is not. And, of course, not all slow music is sad—a certain slow-paced piece might be majestic or stately or even be without any definite character. Still, with certain pieces of music, "sad" will be the best term available for referring to a particular quality of the music; "majestic" will be the best term available for other pieces; and so on.

Music is not the only art with qualities that can be usefully referred to by such terms as "sad" and "gay." For example, people frequently speak of nonrepresentational paintings as sad, gay, lively, delicate, and the like. And, of course, areas in a representational painting may be similarly described; for example, someone might aptly speak of the color of a represented piece of clothing as being painted with a delicate shade of blue or with a gay combination of red and yellow. Similar cases can be found in the other arts.

The problem treated in this chapter has been discussed entirely in terms of non-representational aspects of the arts: musical passages, nonrepresentational paintings, and colors in representational painting. Of course, color in a painting may be representational, but the kind of descriptions under discussion do not relate to the representational function of color, only to its various qualities. The reason for restricting the discussion to nonrepresentational aspects is that representation raises complications: is a sad face in a painting sad in the same way that sad music is sad? A depicted face *expresses* sadness in the same way that a real face *expresses* sadness, whereas music is best described as *being* sad. The sad face in a painting is depicted as standing in relation to the sad feelings of the depicted person, whereas sad music does not necessarily stand in relation to any particular sad feelings.

Part IV

The Evaluation of Art

Chapter 13

Twentieth-Century Theories of Evaluation

When critics evaluate a work of art, they do not simply say that it is good or bad; they generally give reasons to back up their evaluation. Sometimes the reasons offered seem to support the evaluational judgment and sometimes they seem to fail to do so. The important point at this juncture is that it appears that *evaluational judgments* can be supported by *reasons* and that reasons are important for art criticism. Some philosophers take evaluative conclusion and reasons to be connected by general *principles* such that the evaluative conclusions are deduced as conclusions from general principles and reason statements. Evaluative conclusions, critical reasons, and critical principles will be focal notions in my accounts of the various theories of art evaluation I will discuss. Some of these theories claim that principles and reasons are irrelevant to evaluational conclusions, but some do not.

Traditionally, the *defining* of basic evaluational terms has been the central focus of evaluational theories. For the most part, the word "good" will be used throughout this discussion of evaluation as the value term for which the philosophers under consideration will give an account. The value vocabulary of critics is much richer and contains a host of terms such as "magnificent," "exquisite," "beautiful," and the like. For the sake of brevity, I will ignore this usage.

Because of the limitations of space, I can discuss only the most important evaluational theories—important either because the theory has been widely held, because it has been philosophically prominent, or because it seems particularly promising.

I will discuss eight theories that divide into two phases. The first phase consists of five theories that are traditional in the sense that they focus on the notion of defining basic terms for the evaluation of art, although some deny that such terms can be defined. The second phase consists of three theories in which the defining of basic terms for the evaluation of art is deemed unnecessary. The view that I will call (1) *personal subjectivism* proposes to define basic evaluational notions in terms of psychological states of a person (subject); this theory claims that there are no critical principles and that reason-giving is essentially a pointless activity. The view I call (2) *intuitionism* claims that basic evaluational terms are indefinable and refer to nonempirical properties; the theory claims that principles and reasons are unnecessary or not called for. The view I term (3) *emotivism* claims that evaluational terms are not definable, do not refer to anything, and merely express emotions; this theory maintains that there are no critical principles and that evaluations cannot be logically supported, although "reasons" that persuade can be given. The view I label (4) *relativism* claims that evaluational terms function in complex ways; the theory claims that there are principles relating reasons to evaluation conclusions, but that ultimately the principles of criticism are chosen rather than justified. The view I call (5) *critical singularism* holds that although the giving of reasons has a function in criticism, evaluational terms do not really evaluate. According to this view, there are no critical principles and so there is no problem of justifying principles. (6) *Monroe Beardsley's instrumentalist theory* of art evaluation is not organized around the question of the definition of evaluational terms as the above theories are; this constitutes a sharp break with traditional theorizing and the beginning of a new phase in theorizing about the evaluation of art. Beardsley's theory attempts to show how works of art are to be evaluated in terms of their capacity to produce valuable consequences. This theory attempts to provide an justification for reasons and evaluative principles within an instrumentalist framework. (7) *Nelson Goodman's instrumentalist theory* also claims that works of art are to be evaluated in terms of their capacity to produce valuable experience, but Goodman conceives of that valuable experience very differently from the way in which Beardsley does. Finally, I will present (8) my own instrumentalist views of critical principles, reasons, and evaluative conclusions.

Personal Subjectivism

Subjectivist theories attempts to *define* the basic term "good" for the evaluation of art. What distinguishes subjectivist theories from other theories that try to define this expression is that they attempt to define "good" in terms of the attitude of subjects or persons. There are as many different possible versions of the subjectivist theory as there are ways of classifying people. For example, the following would be a nonpersonal subjectivist definition: "good" means "is liked by all human beings." Such expressions as "is liked by upper-class people," "is liked by the proletariat," "is liked by my family," and so on, would also yield nonpersonal subjectivist definitions if anyone wished to use them to try to define the basic value term. However, because all versions of subjectivist theory face the same basic difficulties, I will discuss only one.

It seems reasonable to discuss the most widely held subjectivist theory, namely, personal subjectivism, which asserts that "good" means "is liked by me." The word "me" in the definition refers, of course, to whichever speaker utters a sentence that contains the term "good" or a synonym for it. According to this theory, "good" contains an implicit reference to any person who uses the expression. This view has been held by some philosophers[1] and held or assumed in a less conscious and explicit way by many people. Henceforth, I will use the term "subjectivism" to refer to the personal "liked by me" variety of subjectivism.

There are a number of reasons why this definition seems plausible. First, there is a close and important relation between the goodness of a work of art and liking it. Of course, the fact that there is a close relation between the two notions does not mean that they have the same meaning. For example, it might just be that it is desirable that whatever is judged good be liked. Second, what has been called "the whirligig of taste"—the fact that what is thought good in art from age to age may change, the fact that what is thought good in art by a person has frequently varied during the person's lifetime, and so on—gives comfort to subjectivism. If subjectivism were true, then one would expect that what is held to be good would vary widely, since it is admitted by all that likings are subject to wide variation. Nevertheless, it is clear that such variation of taste does not *prove* subjectivism true. A number of things might account for the variation—immaturity, being uninformed, and so on, in the cases of the changes both in a particular individual and in many individuals of a certain period.

From a logical point of view, subjectivism has an interesting consequence: it makes critical disputes impossible. Suppose two critics, Jones and Smith, are disputing about a painting. Jones claims the painting is good and Smith claims it is not. The dispute has the appearance of being about the painting, but if subjectivism were true, they would be not talking in a straightforward way about the painting and there is no dispute. If "good" means "is liked by me," then when Jones says the painting is good he is saying, "I (Jones) like the painting," and when Smith says the painting is not good, he is saying, "I (Smith) do not like the painting." The statements "Jones likes the painting" and "Smith does not like the painting" can both be true at the same time without any conflict. The two statements are not about the same thing. (Some forms of subjectivism do not have this consequence. If "good" means "is liked by the majority of the human race," then if Jones and Smith disagree, they are at least talking about the same things and in principle the dispute could be settled by a large-scale inquiry into the likes of human beings.)

The considerations that make subjectivism plausible are clearly not conclusive reasons for thinking it true; and if it were true, critical disputes would have a different logical structure than seems to be presupposed by the activity and remarks of critics—disputing critics seem to think that they are arguing about the same thing and not simply asserting their own likings. There are several arguments showing that subjectivism is probably false.

The first argument is really an expansion of the above remark about the logical structure of critical disputes. Critics almost always give reasons to support their evaluation, and we often find such reasons helpful in understanding the evaluations and in deciding whether we think the evaluations justified or not. In the first place, it does not make much sense to say that evaluations are justified or unjustified, if "good" is identical in meaning with "liking." Ordinarily we do not justify our likings—they just are. If asked to justify why I like ice cream, I might say, "Because it is sweet." But this is just a way of saying I *like* sweet things or of being more specific about what it is *about* ice cream I like. If asked to justify why I like a painting, I might point out various aspects that I like. But all this seems very different from the justification of evaluations. Still, the subjectivist will no doubt find these remarks beside the point. He or she will say that these remarks only make sense because it is assumed that subjectivism is false and that begs the whole question.

A second argument against subjectivism derives from the fact that we sometimes admit that we like something we judge not to be good. Furthermore, we sometimes judge something good but do not like it. Neither of these two would be possible if subjectivism were true. For example, if subjectivism were true and we liked something, it would be impossible not to judge it good, and similar considerations apply to the second case. It must be noted parenthetically that this argument does not necessarily apply to nonpersonal versions of subjectivism, in which "good" is not defined in terms of a particular person's likes. The subjectivist might still reply that we only *think* that we are making the kinds of judgments cited and that we are confused about our language.

The third argument against subjectivism is G. E. Moore's open-question argument—discussed in Chapter 6— which is supposed to prove that *no* definition of "good" can be given.[2] Formulated against subjectivism, the argument runs as follows. If "good" means "is liked by me," then an evaluation of a work of art such as "This painting is good" is equivalent in meaning to the statement "This painting is liked by me." The open-question argument maintains that when one is faced with statements such as "This painting is liked by me," one can *always* sensibly ask, "Yes, I understand that you like the painting, but is it a good painting?" If subjectivism were true, such a question would be silly, for it would reduce to "Yes, I understand that you like the painting, but do you like the painting?" Since the question is not silly, subjectivism must be false. However, the subjectivist might point out, as some philosophers have done against Moore, that the general applicability of the open-question argument presupposes the truth of Moore's own view that "good" cannot be defined and names a simple unanalyzable, non-natural property. The subjectivist can maintain that (1) it is true that the application of the open-question argument shows that many definitions of "good" are incorrect, but (2) it only shows that all definitions are wrong if Moore's theory is true and that has not been proven, and that (3) subjectivism is in fact true.

However, the open-question argument does suggest a conclusive line of argument against subjectivism. This argument depends on our careful reflection on how we use language, specifically evaluational language and language used to describe our psychological states. Even though we may not be able to give a complete analysis of what "good" means or how we use the term, it is clear that it is not identical in meaning with "is liked by me" or for that matter with any phrase of the "is liked by . . ." type. Saying something is good and saying something is liked play two very different roles in our linguistic activities. Briefly, to say that something is good is to say that it has satisfied certain standards; to say that something is liked is to make a statement about a psychological fact. We use statements about goodness to do one kind of job and statements about likes to do quite a different one.

As a last resort, the subjectivist might say that this theory is not about the way that we actually use language now but that he or she is attempting to *reform* language in order to give us a better way to talk. The subjectivist might claim that his reform would give us a simple and straightforward way of verifying our evaluations—I can verify if something is good by discovering if I like it. Such attempts at reform are misguided, however, for the main purpose of a theory of evaluation is to throw light on and explain the practice of critical reasoning and evaluation that is part of our ordinary linguistic behavior. It is true that a great deal of nonsense is spoken about art and the evaluation of art, but surely the whole practice of evaluating art and the basic terms of the practice are not in need of radical reform. The subjectivist's "reform" reduces the whole business of the evaluation of art to the liking of art, which virtually eliminates the need of giving reasons for evaluations. The reform simply dismisses rather than explains what needs to be explained.

Intuitionism

What I am calling intuitionism has its origins in Plato's theory of beauty, and is similar in important ways to G. E. Moore's theory of evaluation.[3] And some such theory as intuitionism is presupposed by critics and ordinary persons who think that properly made critical evaluations are true and make no reference to the psychological states of subjects or other ordinary empirical properties. However, I am not claiming that intuitionism is Plato's or Moore's theory; it is simply a generalized statement of the type of theory of which Plato's and Moore's theories are instances.

Intuitionism maintains that in addition to their natural or empirical properties such as being of a certain color, size, and shape, or consisting of certain tones, sounds, and so on, works of art and natural objects may also possess a nonnatural or nonempirical value property, variously referred to by such terms as "beauty," "aesthetic value," and "aesthetic goodness." (This discussion will be concerned only with *beauty*.) According to intuitionism, the nonempirical property of beauty is unanalyzable and therefore indefinable. That is, the word "beauty" denotes a logically primitive entity that cannot be analyzed into parts in the way that, say, "man" supposedly can be analyzed into *rational* and *animal*. The meaning of beauty cannot be conveyed to someone by a definition or a verbal description, and the meaning of the word "beauty" can be learned only by experiencing beauty. In this respect, the term "beauty" is supposed to be like an empirical color term such as "red," whose meaning, it is generally maintained, can only be learned by experiencing the empirical property of redness. Empirical properties and the nonempirical property of beauty are apprehended by different modes of knowing: empirical properties are perceived and known by the ordinary modes of sense perception—sight, hearing, touch, and the like—while nonempirical properties are apprehended by an entirely different way of knowing called "intuition." Intuition, of course, depends on the ordinary modes of knowing in the sense that the ordinary modes must provide the mind with information about the empirical properties of an object before the mind can intuit whether or not the object also possesses the nonempirical property of beauty and to what degree. But whereas ordinary perception is sensuous, intuition is not. It is this contention of intuitionism that the object of intuition is not an empirical property or set of empirical properties that makes intuitionism (ethical or aesthetic) so controversial and endlessly debated. The lack of an empirical check on the correctness or incorrectness of particular alleged intuitions is the root of the controversy.

The most attractive feature of intuitionism is that the theory promises an objective way of evaluating works of art. There is much unresolved disagreement over what works are aesthetically good or beautiful, and intuitionism promises that such disputes are in theory resolvable. According to it, beauty is a property of an object and is *there* to be experienced by anyone who has the capacity to apprehend it. Beauty is as objective a property of a thing as is its color or size, although it is not known in the same way that color and size are known. If intuitionism were true, in a dispute about whether or not an object is beautiful, one of the disputants must be right and one wrong because an object either has the property of beauty or it does not. A person who is wrong in such a dispute according to the theory is blind to beauty (although perhaps not in all cases), that is, the individual lacks the intuitive power to apprehend beauty in the case in question. It would of course be possible, given the theory, that a person can correctly claim that an object possesses beauty and yet lack the capacity to know that it does—a person might correctly guess that it possesses beauty or claim that it does on the authority of someone who has the relevant capacity.

To flesh out intuitionism more completely, it can be noted that a person might have the capacity to intuit beauty in certain kinds of art, say, paintings and not have the capacity in the case of other kinds of art, say, music. The capacity might be even more limited in a given person; for example, someone might be able to intuit the beauty in representational paintings but not in nonobjective paintings. This point makes clear that the capacity to intuit beauty claimed by intuitionism is not a simple easily obtained ability. Some people might not possess it at all and some might possess the capacity to intuit beauty but not develop the abilities to discriminate acutely in connection with empirical properties and their relations. In order to intuit beauty in paintings, one must learn to discriminate between subtle colors, learn to be aware of composition, and so on. Similar considerations hold for the other arts. In short, to bring out the ability to intuit beauty, one must first develop many other abilities.

Another characteristic of intuitionism is that it supposes that beauty is intuited on a case-by-case basis and that no general conclusions follow from the cases of beauty experienced. For example, all the paintings that possess the nonempirical property of beauty need not have any empirical property in common. And if, in fact, it turned out that all existing beautiful paintings do have one or a set of empirical properties in common, all the beautiful paintings that subsequently may come into existence might very well not have that property or set of properties. According to intuitionism, the capacity to intuit beauty is always necessary in order to know that a given work of art or natural object possesses beauty. There are no empirical indices that people who lack the capacity can use to identify objects that possess beauty. The intuiting of beauty is analogous to the perceiving of a particular color, say, red. There is no *perceptual* property other than redness that all red things have in common, so there is no perceptual index that a color-blind person who cannot distinguish red can use to infer that something is red or not. If it were the case that all red things were square and all square things were red, then the color-blind person would be able to infer which things are red and which are not because even though he could not discriminate red, he could discriminate squareness.

With one, perhaps trivial, exception, reason-giving is not possible if intuitionism were true. Given this theory, the proposition that would have to be supported by reasons would be of the general type "X is beautiful." However, according to the theory, there is nothing that is correlated with beauty, so there is nothing other than beauty that can serve as a reason for thinking a thing beautiful. The only "reason" for thinking a thing beautiful is knowing that it possesses beauty by way of intuition. The trivial exception alluded to is the case in which it is known that X is beautiful and Y is exactly similar to X in all its properties and in all the relations among its properties. In this case, it could be said that the fact that Y is exactly similar to X and X is beautiful is a reason for thinking that Y possesses beauty.

As noted earlier, the most attractive feature of intuitionism is that it promises an objective way of settling disputes in aesthetic matters. However, the assurance of objectivity is purchased at a very high price. The basis of the objectivity is the alleged nonempirical, indefinable property of beauty, which, since it is nonempirical, must be known by a special mode of knowing—intuition. First, the knowledge and appreciation of beauty is available only to those who have the capacity to intuit it. This objection, however, is not a criticism of the truth of the theory but only states an inconvenient aspect of it. Second, many people are suspicious of intuition as a mode of knowledge: it seems so tailor-made to solve a given problem in aesthetics. Intuition is supposed to be a mode of knowledge that has but one object—beauty. Admittedly, there is a parallel moral theory that maintains that intuition has moral goodness as its object, but, even so, the number of types of objects of intuition is embarrassingly small when compared with the great multitude of objects of ordinary empirical knowledge. It is easy to see how intuition could be abused and used as a refuge for knowledge claims that cannot really be substantiated, and this makes people suspicious. Nevertheless, it is not possible to prove that intuitionism is false. The intuitionist can always argue that anyone who disputes his or her claim simply lacks the capacity to intuit beauty (or to intuit moral goodness if the intuitionist is defending moral intuitionism). By the very nature of the claim, the intuitionist puts this theory outside the range of refutation; still, this fact does not prove the theory true, nor does it inspire confidence in it.

Emotivism

The emotive theory is an account of evaluation that arose within logical positivism, a philosophical movement that had great influence in the period from about 1930 to 1950. Logical positivism claims that all knowledge is either empirical, as are the truths of science, or tautological, as are the truths of pure mathematics. Logical positivism flatly rejects the claim of intuitionism that there are nonempirical, nontautological truths that state moral and aesthetic evaluations and are known to be true by means of intuition. The logical positivist considers intuition a philosophical device invented to give moral and aesthetic evaluations the appearance of being truths.

A. J. Ayer, a British philosopher, formulated a well-known statement of emotivism in 1936, and the account given here is based on his views.[4] Ayer rejects Moore's and all other versions of intuitionism as unempirical, but he adopts Moore's open-question argument against all attempts to define the basic evaluation terms. Ayer formulates his version of the open-question argument against both subjectivism and hedonism, which he apparently takes to be typical of theories attempting to define "good" or some other moral word in terms of empirical notions. Having shown, he thinks, that subjectivism and hedonism are incorrect, he assumes that the same argument can be used successfully against any attempt to define "good."

Let us consider his argument against hedonism. The hedonistic view he attacks claims that good can be defined in terms of pleasure, that is, that the word "good" is identical in meaning with the word "pleasure" or with some variant of it such as "pleasant." Thus, "X is good" has the same meaning as "X is pleasant," according to this theory. The great advantage of hedonism is that, if it is correct, moral and aesthetic evaluations then are really empirical propositions about pleasure and can be verified or falsified. The theory of evaluation would turn out to be a part of empirical psychology. Unfortunately for hedonism, Ayer claims, it is not self-contradictory to say, claim, or hold that there are some pleasant things that are not good, that is, to hold that some pleasant things are bad. If hedonism were true, that is, if "good" and "pleasant" were identical in meaning, then it would be self-contradictory to say that some pleasures are not good. That is, if hedonism were true, then we would be able to substitute "good" for "pleasure" in the sentence "Some pleasures are not good" and the self-contradictory sentence "Some goods are not good" would result. However, since "Some pleasures are not good" is not self-contradictory, hedonism must be false. Ayer uses exactly the same argument against subjectivism.

What criterion is Ayer using in saying that "Some pleasures are not good" is not self-contradictory? If someone said, "Some bachelors are married," we would say that the sentence is self-contradictory because of the way in which we use or understand the word "bachelor." In other words, part of the meaning of "bachelor," as we use the term, is unmarriedness. In short, the inconsistency of a given sentence in a given language is shown by appealing to the meanings of the terms in that language. What Ayer is maintaining, then, is that the subjectivist and hedonist definitions do not comprehend the diversity of ways in which we use such terms as "good" in English or any other natural language. His method is to find a sentence that seems perfectly sensible to ordinary users of English and show that the sentence would be inconsistent given a certain definition. Ayer's most general claim is that he can produce a counterinstance sentence for any proposed definition of basic value terms. This claim is justified only if it can somehow be "seen" that the uses of "good" and other such terms in English are so diverse that no definition could encompass them.

Ayer asserts that of course we could construct a language in which the hedonist definition is adequate or a language in which the subjectivist definition is adequate, but neither of these languages would be English and English is the language in which we make our moral and aesthetic evaluations. Insofar as ethics and aesthetics are concerned at least, Ayer is an "ordinary language" philosopher. That is, he maintains that ordinary language usage is the criterion for the correctness or incorrectness of definitions.

If "good" or any other basic value term does not refer to a primitive, unanalyzable property known by intuition or cannot be defined in terms that refer to empirical properties, then how does "good" function? It would seem that all the ways have been ruled out in which "good" could function in a sentence by *referring* to something by virtue of which the sentence would be true or false. Ayer's conclusion is that evaluative sentences are not capable of being either true or false and that evaluative terms simply serve to express the feelings—pro or con—of the persons who use them. According to Ayer, when a person says of a painting she is looking at, "This painting is beautiful," the person is not asserting or saying something about the painting, she is simply expressing her pro feelings about the painting. Uttering the sentence in question amounts to saying, "This painting—hurrah!" The sentence "This is a bad painting" amounts to saying, "This painting—bah!" Ayer's theory is sometimes referred to as the Bah-Hurrah Theory.

There is some danger of confusing Ayer's view with the version of subjectivism that tries to define "good" in terms of "is liked by me." However, according to this version of subjectivism, "X is good" means "X is liked by me," and that is either true or false; according to subjectivism, evaluative terms refer and evaluative sentences assert something about the world that is either true or false. According to emotivism, however, evaluative terms are simply expressive, and evaluative sentences do *not* assert anything. However, there is a respect in which emotivism is similar to the "liked by me" version of subjectivism. If two persons disagree, one saying, "This painting is beautiful" and the other claiming, "This painting is not beautiful," the disagreement is only apparent and not real. The first person is expressing his pro attitude toward the painting and the second is expressing her con attitude toward the painting, but neither is really *asserting* anything. Since nothing is being asserted by either person, there is no disagreement. The impossibility of disagreement over evaluations contrasts with the disagreements we can have over facts. For example, if two people disagree about, say, the color of an object, each is making an assertion or a claim about a feature of the empirical world. And, of course, it is possible in principle to settle a dispute over facts. However, according to emotivism, a disagreement over values cannot be settled by discovering some proposition to be true.

Nevertheless, disagreement over values can be resolved in the sense that, as the result of a debate, a closer look at the painting, a threat, flattery, or whatever, one of the parties may experience a change in attitude. Also, according to Ayer, attitudes may be influenced directly by the uttering of evaluational sentences. When Jones says, "This painting is beautiful," he not only expresses his feelings toward the painting, but he may excite pro feelings in others. It is possible, then, that the mere uttering of an evaluational sentence may bring about sameness of attitude or feeling.

To give a *reason* in criticism is to cite some feature of a work of art in support of an evaluational statement about the work, that is, a reason is a statement that is evidence that the evaluation is true. Since emotivism claims that evaluations are not capable of being either true or false, there is no straightforward way of giving reasons if emotivism is true. If a critic says that a play is bad because it is tedious, she is not, according to emotivism, giving a reason for the truth of "The play is bad," although knowledge of the tediousness of the play may make someone adopt a con attitude toward it. However, if critics cannot, according to emotivism, give reasons for evaluation, they can give what might be called "persuaders." An important consequence of this feature of emotivism is that whereas those philosophers who support reason-giving distinguish between good and bad reasons, there is no way to distinguish between good and bad persuaders. Anything that a critic might say or do—cite a feature of a work of art, make a threat of bodily harm, kick someone—might result in someone having a change of attitude. If, however, there is no distinction between good and bad persuaders from the point of view of being evidence for the truth of evaluative conclusions and anything may function as a persuader, then evaluative criticism is clearly not a rational activity. Of course, one persuader may be more effective than another, but this sense of betterness and worseness does not have anything to do with the truth of evaluations in the emotive view.

An important criticism of Ayer's version of emotivism is that its analysis of evaluation is too simple. A number of later emotivists attempted to remedy this defect by arguing that evaluations have a descriptive aspect and perhaps an imperative aspect as well. The best known of these emotivist analyses is C. L. Stevenson's *Ethics and Language*.[5] Some of the central features of emotivism will reappear in relativism, the next evaluational theory I will discuss.

Relativism

The view that I am calling "relativism" is an adaptation of some of the basic features of the moral philosophy of R. M. Hare[6] to the problem of evaluation in criticism. Relativism is similar to the view of Bernard Heyl.[7] The logical foundation of relativism lies in the type of analysis that Hare gives of good. This analysis purports to be a description of our use of the term "good" in both moral and nonmoral contexts: Hare claims that "good" functions in the same way regardless of context. If Hare is right, there would seem to be no reason why an account of "good work of art" cannot be formulated.

Hare, like Ayer, uses a version of Moore's open-question argument to show that no descriptive term or terms such as "pleasant," "I approve," or the like has the *same meaning* as "good." Consequently, no set of statements consisting only of descriptions of something can *entail* that something is good. But whereas Ayer makes no serious attempt to discover how evaluative language actually works and quickly concludes that "good" does not have any cognitive meaning and is merely expressive of feelings, Hare examines evaluative language carefully and at great length and concludes that the meaning of "good" is its *commending* function. He claims (1) that what is common to all normal uses of "good" in any context is that a commendation is being made and (2) that there is nothing else common to such uses. Hare's claim is clearly about how we use evaluative words; like Ayer, he is an ordinary-language philosopher on this point. Hare distinguishes between *the meaning* of "good," which is not context-dependent, and *the criteria* of "good," which are context-dependent. Although we always commend when we use "good," the criteria we use when applying "good" vary from context to context. In both cases, when we say "That is a good watch" and "That is a good radio," we are commending, but we use one set of criteria for watches and another set for radios. The characteristics that make a radio good are different from those that make a watch good.

The evaluation of watches and radios is relatively easy and straightforward because there is widespread agreement about the criteria of goodness for watches and radios. The same cannot be said about art criticism, so it is a good idea to illustrate the theory first with easy examples. Consider what is involved in correctly saying, "This is a good watch." First, one is commending a particular watch. Second, one is affirming that a particular watch satisfies all (or some sufficient set) of the criteria of good watches. If the evaluation is challenged, the person who made the evaluation is committed to giving justifying *reasons*, that is, to *showing* that the watch satisfies the criteria for goodness in watches. As reasons, it might be pointed out that the watch keeps accurate time, is small in size, and so on. It is important to note that in asserting that something is a good watch, one is *committing* oneself to a certain criterion or certain criteria and thereby to a principle that embodies the criterion or criteria. Thus, if one judges a particular watch *A* to be good, then one is committed to saying of any watch exactly like *A* that it is good also. Of course, exact likeness is not required in the case of watches (and in the great majority of other things) because certain features, for example, shape in most instances, are irrelevant to goodness in watches. Hare claims that evaluation is a *deductive* procedure involving general principles. This feature may be illustrated as follows:

1. All watches that have properties *A*, *B*, and *C* are good.
2. This watch has properties *A*, *B*, and *C*.
3. Therefore, this watch is good.

(In this illustration, the first premise is a principle.) The contention that evaluation is a deductive procedure from general principles is really identical with the contention that saying *X* is good commits the sayer to a general principle of goodness for things of type *X*. The first way of formulating the contention starts "at the top" with given or established principles from which the particular evaluation is deduced. The second way of formulating the contention starts "at the bottom" with the particular evaluation that one wishes to make; the making of the particular evaluation *generates* the general principle for all relevantly similar cases. We start at the top when evaluating such things as watches and radios for which there are established principles of goodness that every evaluator accepts. We start at the bottom when we wish or find it necessary to evaluate something for which there are no established principles or the person making the evaluation rejects the established principles. The fact, if it is a fact, that starting at the bottom generates and commits one to general principles that cover all relevantly similar cases shows that evaluative language cannot be used lightly.

The function of principles, whether moral, critical, or otherwise, is to furnish a rational framework for evaluation. Because of their generality, principles provide a stability that might not be achievable if one proceeded from case to case without trying to relate the cases in any way. Also, principles can be taught in the sense that one person can state a principle for another and the hearer can understand it. There is, of course, no guarantee that hearers will accept as a principle what they hear and understand. Principles provide a procedure for helping to ensure consistency; that is, insofar as a critic uses principles, he or she will treat similar cases similarly. To say of two exactly similar cases that one is good and the other bad would be a case of inconsistency. It is worth noting that individuals may not be able to formulate explicitly the principles that they hold and use. The test of whether or not a person uses principles in evaluating is whether or not the person evaluates cases similarly that are similar in the relevant respects. A person's evaluations may satisfy this test without his realizing that they do; one does not have to understand about principles in an abstract way in order to have and employ principles. In fact, a person may learn to use a principle in a given context by observing someone else's particular evaluations without either of them being able to formulate the principle that has been passed on.

According to relativism, the principles of criticism cannot themselves be justified—they are themselves the ultimate grounds of aesthetic justification. What, then, can be said of the principles of criticism that people hold and use? Relativism's answer is that principles come to be held as the result of the *decision* of the holder. The decision may be a conscious one or it may be a result of "picking it up" from one's cultural environment. Hare calls both of these ways of coming to hold a principle "decisions" because both are cases of accepting a principle without deducing it from already held premises or without inducing it as probable from premises. Principles are neither true nor false; they simply embody decisions to commend certain types of things.

Hare says that criteria (and hence principles) are necessarily involved with goodness. He also argues that the meaning of "good" is its use to commend. According to Hare, commending is an action done by an individual on his own initiative and from his own principles, and one can decide to commend or not to commend. Criteria and principles go together to produce generality, commending and decision go together to relate the generality to an individual person. The decision aspect provides a means for change in or of principles. One changes a principle by deciding (consciously or not) to commend in a different way from the way one has in the past, that is, by predicating "good" on the basis of different criteria.

It would also be consistent with relativism if everyone were to agree on the same set of critical principles. What makes a view relativistic is that its principles are not themselves justified but are decided for.

If the relativists are correct about the logical status of critical principles, are there any considerations that might be kept in mind when deciding on principles and might tend to result in general agreement on principles? Perhaps the best that can be said in this regard is that critics should be widely acquainted with the arts to which they apply their critical principles. However, if the past is any guide, there seems to be scant hope that even well-informed critics will agree completely. Still, there is nothing that rules out the possibility of widespread or even complete agreement. I suspect, however, that many relativists see the possibility of complete agreement as a stagnant situation in which both art and criticism would have lost their vitality.

Critical Singularism

Some philosophers have argued that principles play no role in the criticism of art.[8] These philosophers agree that critics do give reasons and that to do so is a proper function of criticism, but they maintain that a reason does not involve a principle. They contrast reason-giving in criticism with reason-giving in morality and in the evaluation of such things as watches and radios. To give a reason to justify an act as morally right or a watch as good involves a principle, but works of art, they contend, are very different from moral actions and watches. In fact, they claim the difference is so great that works of art cannot be evaluated at all. Critical singularism is an evaluational theory in that it is an account of how evaluational language functions when applied to art, but it maintains that such language when applied to art serves no evaluational purpose. When a critic says of a work of art that it is good and gives a reason for saying so, the reason does not serve to justify calling the work "good." According to the critical singularist, the reason functions to call some quality of the work of art to the attention of the person who reads or hears the critic's remark. Once attention has been called to a quality of a work, the reader or hearer can appreciate that quality, if he or she can discriminate it. Evaluative terms simply play a role in a process whose sole function is to call attention to the various qualities of works of art.

Critical singularists seem to rely on two arguments in rejecting the relevance of principles in art criticism. The first argument is that works of art are unique and that, consequently, it is impossible to say that one work is better than another—each work of art is in a class by itself, and it is senseless to try to compare one work with another. The first problem with this argument is to find out what is intended. Every object or event is unique in the sense that it is just the thing it is, but this cannot be what the critical singularists have in mind because they wish to say that works of art are unique in a way that other things are not. Perhaps they wish to maintain that every work of art is different in some respect from every other work of art; in this sense, works of art would contrast with mass-produced watches, each of which is exactly like the others. Even so, works of art clearly have similarities and fall into classes—for example, the class of paintings, the class of statues, and so on—and into subclasses of the broader classes—for example, the subclass of representational painting, the subclass of comedies, and so on. Many works of art are highly individual, but they are not unique in the sense maintained by the critical singularists.

The second argument of the critical singularist is that a quality cited as a merit (a reason) in one work of art may not be a merit or may even be a defect in another work of art and that, consequently, there cannot be a general principle involving such a quality applicable to all works of art. As we will shortly see, Beardsley has an effective argument against the critical singularist's contention that principles are not possible because a reason cited as a merit in one work of art may not be a merit or even a defect in another work.

Chapter 14

Monroe Beardsley's Instrumentalism

As noted earlier, Beardsley's theory for the evaluation of art is not organized around the question of how "good" is to be defined for aesthetic or artistic contexts. In fact, he does not even try to define such terms. The first concern of Beardsley's theory is to show how critical reasoning works, that is, how—by employing the notion of instrumental value—critical evaluations of works of art can be logically derived from critical principles and reason statements. Beardsley's theory of evaluation consists of two related parts: an account of critical reasoning about the arts which he calls "the general criterion theory" and an account of the nature of artistic value that can be called "the instrumentalist theory of artistic value." His instrumental theory of artistic value forms the foundation of the general criterion theory.[1]

I will first consider Beardsley's account of critical reasoning. The central feature of his theory is the contention that critical reasoning about the arts presupposes general principles on which evaluational conclusions about particular works of art *deductively* depend.[2]

The necessity of general principles has been vigorously debated. Critical singularists have correctly pointed out that certain features are merits in one work of art, but are not in other works of art (sometimes they are even defects). Consequently, they have argued that there are no general principles involving *such features*. Their argument is that if feature X is sometimes a merit and sometimes not, then a general principle "*X* is always a merit" cannot be true. (Critical singularists have also drawn the stronger conclusion that there are no general principles at all.)

Beardsley's answer to this argument is that there does not have to be a general principle for *every* feature that can be correctly cited as a merit. First, it is frequently misleading to speak of single features in isolation from other features. Feature *A* may be a merit in a work of art when the work also possesses features *B* and *C*. However, feature *A* may not be a merit when the work lacks *B* and *C* and possesses features *M* and *N*. Features frequently work together in clusters, and some combinations of features will work together while others will not. Thus, in understanding why a single feature helps make a work of art good, one must frequently see how that feature combines with others. In Beardsley's view, there does not have to be a general principle for every feature that can be correctly cited as a merit. When features work together to make works good, they are secondary to more basic good-making features. The more basic good-making features are the *primary* features that generate general principles. Beardsley writes, "For example, suppose the touch of humor (the gravedigger's gags [in *Hamlet*], the drunken porter at the gate [in *Macbeth*]) is a merit in one context because it heightens the dramatic tension, but a defect in another context, where it lets the tension down."[3] Clearly a touch of humor is not a *general* merit, but notice that in the cases cited it is a merit because it increases dramatic tension, and in the supposed case in which it lets down dramatic tension it is a defect. Perhaps dramatic tension is always a merit, at least in dramas. Dramatic tension is an instance of *intensity*, which, Beardsley claims, is a primary criteria. He also claims that there are two, and only two, other primary criteria—*unity* and *complexity*. He argues, but he does not pretend to have shown conclusively, that any reason that can correctly be cited as a general or primary merit can be subsumed under either unity, intensity, or complexity. Thus, according to Beardsley, only the presence of unity *or* intensity *or* complexity *always* makes for value in a work of art. Consequently, Beardsley explicitly claims that there are three, and only three, critical principles, each with one of the primary merits as its subject. They are

"Unity in a work is always good in some degree."

"Intensity in a work is always good in some degree."

"Complexity in a work is always good in some degree."

It is important to note at this point that Beardsley explicitly asserts that any moral or cognitive aspect that a work of art may have is irrelevant to its evaluation as art. He claims that only the aesthetic properties of unity, intensity, and complexity contribute to the value of art as art. In Beardsley's view, in order for an aspect of art to be relevant to artistic value, it must have the capacity to contribute to the production of aesthetic experience. The three aesthetic aspects of art function to produce aesthetic experience (and in so doing make no reference to the world outside aesthetic experience). On the other hand, according to Beardsley, moral and cognitive aspects of art do not contribute to producing aesthetic experience (and because they refer to the world outside the aesthetic experience may even interfere with the production of aesthetic experience). The details of why Beardsley thinks that there are only three primary merits and why moral and cognitive aspects of art cannot be merits will become clear when his conception of aesthetic experience is explained later.

The following simplified dialogue will serve as an example of the structure of critical reasoning. It is simplified because only one primary feature is involved. A complete case would involve a detailed discussion of each of the primary features and would be much richer in details cited and described.

CRITIC: Cezanne's "The Sainte Victoire, Seen from the Quarry Called Bibemus" is a good painting.

QUESTIONER: Why?

CRITIC: Because its colors are harmonious and its spatial design of planes and volumes is tightly organized.[4]

QUESTIONER: True, but why does that make the painting good?

CRITIC: Because each of these two is an instance of unity and unity in a work of art is always a good thing.

The critic's remarks can be reorganized to show the deductive nature of this reasoning.

1. Unity in a work is always good in some degree.   Principle

2. This painting's colors are harmonious   By observation
    and its spatial design of planes and
    volumes is tightly organized.

3. This painting is unified.   From 2 or by observation

4. This painting is good in some degree.   From 1 and 3

It is clear that the deductive reformulation of the critic's remarks does not say as much as the original remarks. Originally it was concluded that the painting is good but in the reformulation it is concluded only that the painting is good in some degree, which is a much *weaker* conclusion. The original remarks as stated, however, are not deductively valid. The mere presence of some unity does not ensure the *strong* conclusion that the work that possesses it is good, but only the *weak* conclusion that the work is good in some degree.

Similar simplified deductive reconstructions of the reasoning of critics can be made with regard to matters other than unity. Beardsley mentions the use of humor in *Macbeth* (the drunken porter at the gate) to increase dramatic tension (intensity). A reconstruction of critical reasoning involving this point might go as follows:

1. Intensity in a work is always good   Principle
   in some degree.

2. There is a touch of humor in *Macbeth*   By observation
   which, together with the other elements
   in the play, makes *Macbeth* intense.

3. *Macbeth* is intense.   From 2

4. *Macbeth* is good in some degree.   From 1 and 3

The conclusion of this argument is also a *weak* one. The reader can see how a reconstruction for complexity would go and also see that a conclusion derived from the complexity principle would be a weak one.

Beardsley concludes that there are three general principles and that deductive conclusions can be drawn from them. These principles—either individually or all three together—do not suffice to deduce the *strong* conclusion that a work of art is *good*. As long as the evaluative predicate in the principles is the weak, unspecific predicate "is good in some degree," it is not possible using the principles to deduce a conclusion that has the strong, specific predicate "is good." The evaluational predicate in the conclusion of a valid deductive argument cannot be stronger that the evaluative predicate or predicates that appear in the premises.

After it has been shown how Beardsley's theory of critical reasoning connects with his instrumentalist theory of artistic value, it will be shown how his overall theory provides for the formulation of deductive arguments in which a strong conclusion that a work of art is *good* can be drawn.

I will now give an account of Beardsley's instrumentalist theory of artistic value, which is supposed to provide the foundation for the general criterion theory. Following an old and widely held tradition, Beardsley maintains that a specific kind of experience—aesthetic experience—can be isolated and described. For Beardsley, the value that aesthetic experience possesses is the source of artistic value; works of art are (instrumentally) valuable because they can produce aesthetic experience that is valuable. Aesthetic experience is typically caused by aesthetic objects such as plays, paintings, poems, and the like, but may sometimes be caused by football games, sunsets, and other nonartworks. I am concerned only with aesthetic objects that are works of art.[5]

Aesthetic experience has a subjective pole—the person or subject who has the experience—and an objective pole—the object (a work of art) that the experience is an experience of. Beardsley analyzes the *subjective* features of aesthetic experience in terms of five categories. The first characteristic is of the person undergoing the experience: such a person has his or her *attention firmly fixed* on an object that controls the experience. This concentration contrasts with, say, the loose play of ideas in daydreaming. Second, the experience itself is marked by some *intensity* in which energies are focused on a rather narrow field of concern. This intensity may not be a full-blown emotion of the ordinary sort, but if the intensity does involve an emotion, it will be tied to some element of the aesthetic object. The concentrated intensity of the experience tends to shut out alien elements such as coughs in the theater, scratch noises on a record, thoughts of unpaid bills, and the like. Third, the aesthetic experience is *coherent*, or hangs together, to a relatively high degree. "One thing leads to another; continuity of development, without gaps or dead spaces, a sense of overall providential pattern of guidance, an orderly accumulation of energy toward a climax, are present to an unusual degree."[6] Fourth, the experience is *complete*. "The impulses and expectations aroused by elements within the experience are felt to be counterbalanced or resolved by other elements within the experience, so that some degree of equilibrium or finality is achieved and enjoyed. The experience detaches itself, and even insulates itself, from the intrusion of alien elements."[7] Coherence and completeness can be subsumed under *unity*. Aesthetic experience is quite unified; by contrast, ordinary experience is diffuse. The fifth and last of the characteristics of aesthetic experience is *complexity*. "The range or diversity of distinct elements that ... [the experience] ... brings together into its unity, and under its dominant quality"[8] is the measure of its complexity. The elements referred to here are the various affective and cognitive elements of the experience. These elements are subjective in that they are elements of experience that depend on the subject (a person) of the experience.

According to Beardsley, the subjective characteristics of aesthetic experience itself turn out to be three in number: unity, intensity, and complexity. The subjective unity, intensity, and complexity of the *experience itself* are caused by objective characteristics of the perceived work of art. Beardsley claims that the perceived characteristics of art that cause aesthetic experience will themselves all be instances of perceived unity, intensity, and complexity. Thus, the perceived objective unity, intensity, and complexity of artworks (aesthetic objects) cause a further kind of subjective unity,[9] intensity, and complexity of experience. For example, if I look at a painting and notice its unity (experience its unity), this in Beardsley's view can cause me to have unity of experience. In using the expression "unity of experience," I am trying to indicate that the caused unity is distinct from the unity perceived in the painting. The perceived intensity and complexity of an aesthetic object are also supposed to be able to cause intensity and complexity of experience. Beardsley's theory gives the following picture of aesthetic experience. Someone perceives an aesthetic object. The perceived characteristics of the aesthetic object will cause the perceiver to have an experience that includes the perceived (objective) characteristics of the object plus feelings, expectations, and other subjective features caused by the object. The perceived objective unity of a work of art will cause a subjective unity of the experience. The subjective unity of the experience may consist of, say, an expectation and its fulfillment or a set of similar (unified) feelings. Aesthetic objects have their various degrees of unity, intensity, and complexity that can be seen, heard, or understood (in, e.g., literary works), and aesthetic experience itself has its additional subjective unity, intensity, and complexity which is caused by the perceived unity, intensity, and complexity.

Objective unity, intensity, and complexity and subjective unity, intensity, and complexity can be thought of as the basic properties of aesthetic experience as conceived of by Beardsley. In Beardsley's view, there are also secondary properties of aesthetic experience that derive from some of the basic properties. He notes that the intensity of the experience tends to shut out elements alien to the experience. He also claims that the coherence and completeness of the experience cause it to insulate and detach itself from elements alien to the experience. Beardsley then claims that because of these phenomena aesthetic experience is a detached experience. In concluding this, Beardsley is agreeing with Schopenhauer and the aesthetic-attitude theorists, but he disagrees with them about the source of the detachedness. They claimed that some feature of the mind—aesthetic consciousness, disinterested perception, or the like—causes aesthetic experience to be detached. Beardsley claims the detachedness of the experience derives from the nature of some of the basic properties of the content of aesthetic experience.

The alleged detached nature of aesthetic experience causes Beardsley to claim that moral and cognitive aspects of art are irrelevant to the evaluation of art. On his view, the detachedness of the experience nullifies the moral and cognitive aspects of art that refer to the world outside aesthetic experience so that they fail to function in the aesthetic experience of art. Speaking metaphorically, aesthetic experience has a sharp edge that severs the referential relation to the world beyond it.

Since each of the three objective elements and each of the three subjective elements of aesthetic experience can vary by degrees, on Beardsley's view, a given experience may be more unified, more intense, or more complex than another. Thus, two aesthetic experiences may be compared by the magnitudes of each of the six characteristics, but they may also be compared by the magnitudes of all six characteristics taken together. Of course, such magnitudes cannot be assigned exact mathematical measures, although in many cases it can be determined which of two experiences has the greater magnitude. According to Beardsley, what is important, however, is that it *can be determined* that a given experience has a greater or lesser magnitude, and this is what is significant for determining whether a certain aesthetic object is good or not.

At this point Beardsley draws two important conclusions. The first is the observation that aesthetic experience as he conceives of it is an instrumentally valuable thing because it has the capacity to produce something that is valuable. Let this observation be granted for the moment. In his view, aesthetic experience may not be the best thing (the highest value), but it is a valuable thing. The second conclusion is that an aesthetic experience of a fairly great magnitude is good. This second conclusion presupposes (1) that the magnitude of aesthetic experience can be estimated—for example, one aesthetic experience can be seen to be of low magnitude, another aesthetic experience can be seen to be of fairly great magnitude, and so on—and (2) that aesthetic experience of a fairly great magnitude is instrumentally good because it has the capacity to produce something that is good. Let this conclusion be granted for the moment. The stage is now set for Beardsley's definition of "good aesthetic object," that is, "good work of art," in terms of the notion of aesthetic experience. This definition will tie together his theory of critical reasoning (principles, reasons, and evaluational conclusions) and his theory of artistic value.

> "X is a good aesthetic object" means "X is capable of producing good aesthetic experiences (that is, aesthetic experiences of a fairly great magnitude)."[10]

Note that the definition is stated in terms of capacity, so that a good work of art need not always produce a good aesthetic experience. Such an experience can be produced only when the work is experienced by someone who is susceptible (not color-blind, not tone-deaf, properly trained, and so on). Note also that in defining "good aesthetic object," that is, "good work of art," Beardsley has not defined "good." "Good" appears on both sides of the definition. If Beardsley's theory is correct, he has succeeded in dealing with one of the most difficult questions that theories of artistic evaluation have faced in the past, namely, the problem of defining "good." Given his definition of "good work of art," Beardsley can now give an account of critical reasoning as a deductive procedure.

The defining part of the definition equates good aesthetic experiences with aesthetic experience of a fairly great magnitude which amounts to asserting the following general principle:

1. Aesthetic experiences of a fairly great magnitude are always good.

Beardsley's account makes use of the notion of the instrumentally good, an idea that everyone accepts. This notion can be stated in a general way as follows.

> If a thing is capable of producing something good, then that thing is instrumentally good.

This notion can be applied to works of art to generate the following premise:

2. If a work of art is capable of producing a good aesthetic experience, then the work of art is instrumentally good.

In a given case, someone might be able to see that a particular work of art can produce an aesthetic experience of a fairly great magnitude, so that the following premise would be generated.

3. This work of art can produce an aesthetic experience of fairly great magnitude.

With these three premises, the following argument can be constructed.

1. Aesthetic experiences of a fairly great magnitude are always good.

2. If a work of art is capable of producing a good aesthetic experience, then the work of art is instrumentally good.

3. This work of art can produce an aesthetic experience of fairly great magnitude.

From premises 1 and 3 it follows that

4. This work of art can produce a good aesthetic experience.

From premises 2 and 4 it follows that

5. This work of art is instrumentally good.

The conclusion of this argument is a strong one, that is, one that applies the strong predicate "is good." Conclusions such as this one contrast with the conclusions of earlier arguments that apply the weak predicate "has some good in it." Examples of other strong principles, given Beardsley's theory, are "Aesthetic experiences of less than fairly great magnitude are always not good" and "Aesthetic experiences of a fairly low magnitude are always bad."

Strong principles such a "Aesthetic experiences of a fairly great magnitude are always good" are derived by being inductive generalizations based on repeated observations that aesthetic experiences of fairly great magnitude are invariably good. Weak principles such as "A unified work always has some good in it" are derived from Beardsley's view that a unified work has the capacity to contribute to the production of a valuable experience, specifically, aesthetic experience.

In Beardsley's theory, strong principles serve to produce strong conclusions, which are typically the kind of evaluative conclusions that critics make. In his theory, weak principles have a kind of explanatory function; weak principles fit logically with reason statements to support weak conclusions and thereby to show that the characteristic of a work of art that a reason statement refers to contributes to the value of that work.

As noted, in Beardsley's view, works of art have instrumental value because they have the capacity to produce aesthetic experience, which in turn is valuable. What kind of value does aesthetic experience itself have? Beardsley's answer is that aesthetic experience's value is also instrumental; he claims that aesthetic experience has the capacity to produce general well-being. If this is the case, Beardsley will have avoided the possibility of *relativism* because it will just be a fact that aesthetic experience has the capacity to produce or not produce well-being. That is, the value of aesthetic experience will not depend on persons' liking or valuing it, and, hence, does not make aesthetic experience's value relative to persons' liking or valuing. Beardsley's view is that aesthetic experience is valuable because it can produce a certain kind of consequence, and this is not something that persons can differ over in the way that they can differ over liking (valuing) or not liking (valuing).

I turn now to a critical evaluation of Beardsley's theory, focusing on his claim that aesthetic experience, as he describes it, is the basis for art evaluation. It will be shown that nondetached experiences are proper experiences of art; this will undermine Beardsley's theory and thereby show that he has not proven that cognitive, moral, and referential aspects of art generally can be excluded from the evaluation of art. It will also be shown that referential aspects can be vitally important in proper experiences and, hence, in the evaluation of many works of art.

Consider the experience of reading *The Adventures of Huckleberry Finn*. Does this experience have the detached nature that Beardsley attributes to aesthetic experience? There are references in the novel to Illinois, Missouri, the Mississippi River, and the Ohio River. The novel has a clear moral point of view in its depiction of the institution of slavery in the United States. Of course, Beardsley would not deny that the references and the moral point of view are there, but his theory requires that they make no contribution to the experience on which the evaluation of the novel is based because it is claimed that the detachedness of that experience (aesthetic experience) nullifies references to the actual world.

If, however, we reflect on the experience of reading *The Adventures of Huckleberry Finn*, we will see that nothing about that experience nullifies the references. Moreover, the novel's references to historical places and practices in the United States play an important and necessary role in our experience of the work. In fact, the novel's references typically tend to heighten the reader's awareness of aspects of the actual world. One of the reasons that this novel is regarded as a *great* novel[11] and *better* than, for example, *The Adventures of Tom Sawyer* is because of its confrontation of the morality of slavery. There are many examples of works of art in which references play an important role in our experience of them.

Referential aspects of art play an important role in our experience of art in the way just described. Referential features are also sometimes responsible for the *aesthetic*, nonreferential properties that the artworks have. Consider the central event of *The Adventures of Huckleberry Finn*—Huck and Jim floating down the river. It is important that it is the real Mississippi River that is referred to—a river that flows between the slave state of Missouri and the free state of Illinois (subject, however, to the fugitive slave laws) and that flows on south into the heart of slave territory. The realities referred to underlie the mounting tension in the novel that results from the southerly drift of the raft and contributes to the *intensity* of the novel and the experience of it. Note that intensity is one of Beardsley's three primary aesthetic properties. There are many examples of works of art in which references support aesthetic qualities.

Examples of the kind just described show that Beardsley's account of the proper experience of art, namely, as detached experience, is wrong as a generalization. It was shown that the experience of works like *The Adventures of Huckleberry Finn* are not detached because their references are not nullified by the nature of the experience that is proper to them. And, it was also shown that the recognition of the references in artworks can be important for a proper experience of the works.

There are of course many instances of works of art that make no references—nonobjective paintings and many musical pieces, for example. Are the proper experiences of such nonreferring works instances of detached experience? Beardsley's paradigm case of detachedness of experience is the experience of an object with references in which the references have been nullified by the aesthetic experience of it. It has been shown that nullification does not occur in such cases. If detachness does not occur in the case of art that makes references, the question of detachness does not even arise for works that make no references. So, it appears that both the proper experiences of referential works and nonreferential works are not to be thought of as detached. Of course, both kinds of experience are usually sharply focused, but that is quite different from being detached.

Beardsley's instrumentalistic theory of artistic value is inadequate because its centerpiece—his account of the experience proper to works of art—fails. Since the instrumentalist theory of artistic value is supposed to support his general criterion theory of evaluative principles, Beardsley's account of critical principles is in jeopardy. His account of strong principles, which directly involves aesthetic experience, clearly will not do. Even weak principles, as Beardsley conceives of them, are tied closely to his conception of aesthetic experience. Thus, if the notion of general principles as relevant to art criticism is to survive, another way of supporting them must be discovered. If support cannot be found, then a view of principles something like the view discussed in the section entitled "Relativism" will obtain, namely, that principles are not rationally supported but simply decided for. I think that support for general principles can be found, but they will have to be formulated in a somewhat different way from the way in which Beardsley formulated them.

Chapter 15

Nelson Goodman's Instrumentalism

Nelson Goodman has sketched the broad outlines of an instrumentalist theory, which also proposes to evaluate art on the basis of its ability to produce aesthetic experience.[1] Goodman's conception of aesthetic experience is, however, very different from Beardsley's.

Beardsley claims that aesthetic experience is detached. He claims that works of art are properly experienced within a detached experience and that references art makes to things outside itself are nullified during that aesthetic experience. Since the references of art are nullified and cannot function in an aesthetic experience, works must be evaluated on the basis of their nonreferential aspects. Goodman, in contrast, maintains that works of art are symbols, that art is essentially cognitive and is to be experienced as standing in cognitive relation to things outside itself. For Goodman, art is to be evaluated on the basis of its cognitive efficacy, that is, on how well it signifies what it signifies.

Beardsley starts with an account of aesthetic experience as detached and uses it to generate an account of the evaluation of art. Goodman begins with a theory of art as symbol and uses it to generate an account of the evaluation of art.

The claims that make up Goodman's evaluational theory are as follows: (1) Every work of art is a symbol that symbolizes by means of either description, representation, expression, exemplification, or some combination of these four. (2) Symbols are for cognizing. (3) "The primary purpose [of art] is cognition in and for itself; . . . [art's] . . . practicality, pleasure, compulsion, and communicative utility all depend on this." (4) Art is to be evaluated by how well it serves its cognitive purpose.[2]

Goodman's evaluational scheme is not as complete as an instrumentalist theory as Beardsley's is. Beardsley claims art is instrumentally valuable because it can produce aesthetic experience that is instrumentally valuable because it can produce general well-being. Goodman claims art is instrumentally valuable because it can produce cognitive experience that is valuable, but he does not attempt to show why cognitive experience is valuable.

The incompleteness of Goodman's account makes it difficult to know how evaluational principles for his theory would be formulated. On a theory of the kind he seems to have in mind, I assume that it would generate principles if it were worked out in detail.

Goodman's evaluational theory contradicts Beardsley's theory at almost every point. For Goodman, the experience of art is cognitive and not insulated from the remainder of experience. A work of art refers unimpededly to things outside the immediate experience of the work, although this may be a somewhat misleading way of putting it since, for Goodman, the experience of art does not have an "edge" such that things can be inside or outside it.

Underlying his claim about cognitive efficacy is the claim that all art is referential: unless a work of art is referential, the question of cognitive efficacy cannot arise for it. Thus, if there are nonreferential artworks, they cannot be evaluated according to Goodman's scheme. Goodman must show that there are no nonreferential works of art. The most obvious candidates for nonreferential works of art are ones that come from the domains of nonobjective painting and instrumental music. It is crucial for Goodman to show that nonobjective paintings, which do not refer in any of the usual ways (representationally, for example), do in fact refer.

Goodman maintains that a characteristic, such as the dominant color of a nonobjective painting, is referential because it *exemplifies* itself. Beardsley maintains a work can have value by merely *possessing* a color that is, say, very intense, while Goodman maintains that, with respect to such a color, a work can have value only because the color it possesses refers by means of exemplification.

The issue, then, is whether the aesthetic value of works of art is always a function of the reference of their properties or whether in some cases their value may result from the simple possession of properties that do not refer.

Consider the following five objects: each is a flat rectangle two feet by four feet, each is a gorgeous shade of blue, and all are visually indistinguishable from the distances at which they are seen. Three of the objects are paintings side by side on a wall. The fourth, on the floor below the paintings is a bundle of rug sample bound together labelled "Rug Samples." The viewer sees only the topmost sample. The fifth object is a hole in the wall above the paintings through which the clear blue sky is seen.

The rug sample both possesses and exemplifies its blue color, that is, it both is a gorgeous blue and refers to, say, rug rolls of the same color. The well-established practice of choosing carpets based on such samples makes the reference possible. Everyone would agree that exemplification occurs here. That is, everyone agrees that a rug sample is a sample. The painting on the left is titled *The Blue Sky*. This painting is representational and, hence, on Goodman's view symbolizes, that is, refers.

The painting in the middle is titled *Cerulean Blue*. This painting would presumably not be representational, but it does exemplify a shade of blue. The title provides a context analogous to that provided by the practice that surrounds rug selection. Let it be granted to Goodman that reference occurs here too.

Move now to the hole in the wall. The two-by-four-foot rectangle of gorgeous blue is visually indistinguishable from the other four objects. However, this fifth object is neither a work of art nor a work of rug selection, it is just a section of sky. There can be no question that it merely possesses its color and does not exemplify its color and that it is gorgeous, that is, has aesthetic value. This is a clear case of the aesthetic experience of a bit of nature. Nothing needs to be granted Goodman in this case because no art is involved.

Move finally to the third painting, the one on the right. It is titled *#1*. According to Goodman, the blue of this painting exemplifies itself and it is in virtue of this symbolizing that it has whatever aesthetic value it has. It is not clear to me that Goodman presents any argument for the claim that properties such as the blueness in this nonobjective painting exemplify. What he does do is to talk first about such things as tailor's swatches, pointing out that they exemplify some of their properties (color, texture, pattern, etc.) but not other properties (shape, having pinked edges, etc.). He then moves on to nonobjective paintings, pointing out that some of their properties are aesthetically important (color, pattern, etc.) and that some of their properties are not aesthetically important (e.g., being owned by a certain person). He says that the aesthetically important properties of such paintings are shown forth, exhibited, and so forth. He then concludes that the important properties that are shown forth are exemplified and that the unimportant properties are not. Although this conclusion is consistent with what he has said, it does not follow from what he has said. What does follow is that there is something that distinguishes aesthetically important properties from aesthetically unimportant ones. More argument is required to show that that something is exemplification and that exemplification even occurs in such cases. Goodman needs to show that some kind of context (analogous to the practice surrounding rug samples) surrounds works of art and is specifically responsible for allowing exemplification. That this can be shown seems unlikely to me, especially in light of the fact that Goodman has made no move to do so.

Goodman's remarks give no more reason to say that the blue of *#1* exemplifies than to say that the blue seen through the hole in the wall exemplifies. So there is no reason to think that the aesthetic value #1 has derives from exemplification or any other kind of reference. If *#1* has aesthetic value, it may well be because of the property of blueness it possesses. So, if #1 has aesthetic value, Beardsley rather than Goodman seems to be right about why it has the value it has.

There is another argument that shows that Goodman's view cannot have the generality he claims for it. Suppose it is granted that *#1*, and every other nonobjective painting, exemplifies. Granted this claim, would Goodman's view that it is in virtue of exemplification that such paintings have whatever aesthetic value they have be acceptable? Suppose that *#1* is a gorgeous blue and exemplifies the gorgeous blue. Let it be granted for the moment that #1 has aesthetic value because it exemplifies the gorgeous blue. #1 must also have additional aesthetic value, because it is visually indistinguishable from the section of blue sky that has aesthetic value without exemplifying.

There is another difficulty with Goodman's claim about cognitive efficiency as the criterion of artistic merit. Assume again that *#1* has the value it has because its gorgeous blue exemplifies its color. Consider, however, a second nonobjective painting that like *#1,* is uniformly colored but is uniformly colored a dull, drab, muddy, brownish-grey. The second painting exemplifies its color just as well as the first painting, because a painting is supposed to exemplify its dominant color. There is, however, good reason to think that the first painting is superior. Thus, there has to be more to the evaluation of these two paintings than exemplification. Put another way, according to Goodman's theory, every nonobjective, uniformly colored painting will have exactly the same value if the value of such paintings derives solely from exemplification, but surely all such paintings do not have the same value.

What is it then that makes art valuable? Beardsley and Goodman agree on one thing, namely, that art is valuable insofar as it can produce valuable experiences. That is, they agree that artistic value is instrumental value. I believe that they are right about the instrumental nature of artistic goodness.

Given that artistic value is instrumental value, what conclusions can we draw about the evaluation of art on the basis of the analyses and criticisms of Beardsley's and Goodman's views that have been given so far?

First, Beardsley is right that some aspects of works of art are instrumentally valuable because they can produce valuable experiences without referring to anything outside the experience of the work of art. Examples of such aspects are the gorgeous blue of #1, the intense combinations of colors in many of Van Gogh's paintings, and the unity of form in a sonnet. Goodman is just wrong that an aspect of a work of art must refer in order to be valuable.

Goodman is right, however, that some aspects of works of art are instrumentally valuable because they can produce valuable experiences in which these aspects are experienced as standing in relation to things outside the immediate experience of the work. Examples of such aspects are the references in *The Adventures of Huckleberry Finn* to specific geographical locations and the depiction of the social and legal relations between slave and nonslave in the pre-Civil War United

States. Beardsley is just wrong that an aspect of a work of art cannot be valuable to the experience of that work in virtue of its reference.

Both Beardsley and Goodman suffer from the philosopher's passion for theoretical neatness and simplicity. Each wants a theoretical explanation for the value of art that involves only one kind of feature: possession in Beardsley's case and referentiality in Goodman's. Beardsley's inability to recognize the value of reference derives from the view of aesthetic experience as the only proper product for the instrumentality of art—a view he inherited. The traditional picture of the aesthetic experience of a work of art goes like this: the work and the person or subject who is experiencing it are surrounded by an impenetrable, psychological wall "secreted" by the subject that experientially nullifies all relations that the work has to things outside the experience. Aspects of works of art may, and frequently do, refer, but a "proper" subject of aesthetic experience cannot take account of such references.

The roots of Goodman's inability to recognize the value of possessed properties are not so clear. His view that works of art are symbols, that is, have reference, has something to do with it. There is, however, nothing about being a symbol that prevents aspects of a symbol from having value independently of its symbol function.

Chapter 16

Another Kind Of Instrumentalism

Beardsley and Goodman are right that the only reasonable basis for the evaluation of art is its capacity to produce valuable experiences. Why else would human beings have invented the institution of art if not to create objects (instruments) with the capacity to produce experiences that they regard as valuable. The central questions are "What is the nature of the valuable experiences or what are the natures of the valuable experiences if there is more than one kind of valuable experience?" and "What kind of value do the experiences have or what kinds of values do the experiences have if there is more than one kind of value?" For reasons already given, the valuable experience cannot be aesthetic experience as traditionally conceived, that is, as a detached experience. In addition, the experiences of artworks do not *all* have the high degree of similarity of structure that Beardsley envisaged. Since there is no specific kind of highly structured experience of art that is produced by *all* artworks, it cannot be concluded that any given work of art is instrumentally good as a whole because of its capacity to produce a particular kind of structured experience that is good as a whole. It seems more promising to focus on the valuable experiences of various valuable aspects of artworks such as unity, intensity, and other aesthetic qualities as well as nonaesthetic, referential aspects. In this conception, aspects of works of art are valuable because they have the capacity to produce valuable experiences of these aspects. It remains to be seen what kind of value the experiences themselves have. Proceeding in this way promises to provides a way for evaluating the various aspects or parts of artworks, but it also remains to be seen how evaluation of artworks as a whole is to be accomplished.

I will focus first on the experience of aesthetic qualities; later I address the experience of referential aspects of art. What *kind* of value do the experiences of aesthetic qualities of artworks have? Such experiences may sometimes has instrumental value, when, for example, an experience of an aesthetic properties produces or helps to produce, say, a feeling of well-being or some other kind of valuable consequence. Instrumental value, however, is not the kind of value an experience of an aesthetic quality typically has for us. Typically, when the experience of an aesthetic quality is valuable it is *intrinsically* valuable, that is, valued for its own sake independently of anything it might lead to. Moreover, on those occasions in which an experience of an aesthetic quality does have instrumental value, it does so because the intrinsic value of the experience is responsible for the instrumental value, that is, the intrinsic value is first produced and then it in turn produces the further benefit. So, the kind of value that experiences of aesthetic qualities have that is relevant for the evaluation of art is *intrinsic value*, that is, value that the experiences have for persons independently of any consequences of the experiences.

Proceeding in this way, a specific aesthetic quality of a work of art, say, unity, would have instrumental value as a result of its capacity when perceived to produce an intrinsically valued experience of unity. If this is the case, then the following weak principle is generated: "Unity in a work of art is always (instrumentally) good in some degree" (because perceived unity can produce an intrinsically valued experience of unity). Every aesthetic quality with the capacity to produce an intrinsically valued experience generates a weak principle of this kind. Negative aesthetic qualities such as garishness would have instrumental disvalue because of their capacity to produce intrinsically disvalued experiences, and they would generate negative principles such as "Garishness in a work is always (instrumentally) bad in some degree."

With the instrumentalism under discussion, weak principles are justified because the characteristics of artworks they refer to can produce intrinsically valued experiences. With this kind of instrumentalist theory, the threat of relativism arises at the level of valued experiences because it is possible that persons might differ over how they intrinsically value the experiences of specific aesthetic qualities. If the experience of a particular aesthetic property is intrinsically valued by one person and the experience of the same aesthetic property is intrinsically disvalued by another, then the two person's experiences would support different principles involving that aesthetic property and they would lack a basis for critical reasoning involving that property.

Although relativism with respect to some particular aesthetic property is always a possibility, virtually all aesthetic properties are valued in the same way by everyone. Everyone values experiences of unity, experiences of elegance, experiences of intensity, and so on. Thus, while it is theoretically possible for relativism with regard to aesthetic properties to arise, there is little real danger that it will. Of course, if relativism with regard to a specific aesthetic quality does arise between two persons, the possibility of their sharing a principle involving that quality and a basis for critical reasoning involving that quality evaporates.

A given aesthetic property might be out of place in a particular work of art—for example, elegance might not fit with the other characteristics of a work, a high degree of unity might destroy or interfere with another aesthetic property, and so on. Thus, while everyone values experiences of unity, elegance, and the like as such, it may not be possible in a given case to have both the experience of elegance and the experience of some other particular aesthetic property. Consequently, it is best to formulate critical principles in a qualified way. For example, the unity principle must be formulated in the following way:

> Unity in a work of art (in isolation from the other properties of the work) is always valuable.[1]

This principle is universally justified because everyone values the experience of unity as such. There will be as many aesthetic principles as there are aesthetic qualities that are universally valued or disvalued. For example, the following are aesthetic principles.

> Elegance in a work of art (in isolation from the other properties of the work) is always valuable.

> Garishness in a work of art (in isolation from the other properties of the work) is always disvaluable.

By the way, the fact that there is virtually universal agreement about aesthetic qualities does not imply virtually universal agreement about the overall evaluations of works of art insofar as aesthetic properties are concerned. Artworks typically involve a number of aesthetic properties, and even if everyone agrees about the value of each individual aesthetic property of an artwork, it is still possible to disagree over how aesthetic properties of a particular work go together. Judgments of the overall value of a works of art are much more complicated than judgments of individual aesthetic properties. Judgments of the overall value of works of art will be discussed later.

Consider now the value of cognitive properties that support aesthetic properties. The example of this discussed earlier is the case in which references to the Mississippi River and other geographical items are responsible for the aesthetic property of intensity in *The Adventures of Huckleberry Finn*. Such cognitive properties are instrumentally valuable because they produce aesthetic qualities that themselves are instrumentally valuable for producing the intrinsically valuable experiences of aesthetic properties. Such cognitive properties do not generate principles, but they support aesthetic properties that can generate principles.

Cognitive properties can be valuable in a more direct way. Those aspects of the world of a work of art that are true to actuality in some way or present a true proposition are valuable because we intrinsically value the experience of such aspects. It does not follow from this that fantasy and the like lack value. However, if a work attempts to be realistic and fails to be, then the aspects in question would be intrinsically disvalued. Such cognitive aspects generate the following principles.

> Truth to actuality is some respect in a work of art (in isolation from the other properties of the work) is always valuable.

> Presenting a true proposition by means of a work of art (in isolation from the other properties of the work) is always valuable.[2]

These principles are generated because we intrinsically value the experiences of truth to actuality and true propositions.

In his essay, "Of the Standard of Taste,"[3] the eighteenth-century philosopher David Hume discusses another way in which cognitive properties of art can have disvalue (and by implication a way in which cognitive properties can have value). Hume cites a French play in which religious bigotry is presented in an approving way. Hume reasons that since religious bigotry is a moral defect, the approving presentation of it in a work of art is also a moral defect, and if an aspect of a work of art is morally defective, it is a defect in the work of art, that is, is an artistic defect. Such cognitive properties generate the following principles.

> The approving representation in a work of art of anything valuable (morally or otherwise) (in isolation from the other properties of the work) is always valuable.

> The approving representation in a work of art of anything disvaluable (morally or otherwise) (in isolation from the other properties of the work) is always disvaluable.

These principles are generated because we value experiences of the representations of valuable things and disvalue experiences of the representations of disvaluable things. The value or disvalue that the representations have derives from the value or disvalue of the things depicted. What kind of value or disvalue the valuable and disvaluable things that are depicted by the representations have and how they come to have it are not the concern of the aesthetician.

Finally, concerning the evaluation of particular aspects of works of art, any argument constructed with the weak principles discussed will have a weak conclusion. The following is an example of such an argument.

Unity in a work of art (in isolation from the other properties of the work) is always valuable.

This work of art is unified.

Therefore, this work of art is valuable, that is, has some degree of good in it.

Such arguments can never produce a strong conclusion with a specific evaluation predicate such as "good," but they can serve to indicate the source of value in a particular work of art.

I move now from the topic of the evaluation of particular properties of works of art to comparing the overall value of one work of art to that of another.

Consider first how this can be done according to Beardsley's theory. In his view, the overall value of any work of art can be compared to the overall value of any other work because all works are to be evaluated according to their capacity to produce a particular kind of valuable experience, namely, aesthetic experience. On Beardsley's view, the magnitude of an aesthetic experience can be estimated; in turn, the magnitude of a work of art's capacity to produce aesthetic experience can be determined by the magnitude of the aesthetic experience it actually produces. Thus, for example, in his view, the value of a painting could be compared to the value of an opera; one would compare the differential capacities of the two works for producing aesthetic experience. Such a comparison can be illustrated in the following way. Assume a scale of 1 to 5 in which 5 stands for the greatest capacity that a work of art can have for producing an aesthetic experience. With such a scale, a comparison *matrix* can be constructed with a "*p*" marking the ranking the painting and an "*o*" marking the ranking of the opera.

$$5$$
$$4p$$
$$3o$$
$$2$$
$$1$$

The comparison matrix illustrates a case in which the painting is better than the opera. (Note that the numbers in the matrix are ranking numbers, not numbers that can be added, multiplied, or divided. Thus, a rank of 4 is a higher value than a rank of 2, but the 4 is not twice as valuable as the 2.)

Since Beardsley's view has been shown to be defective, if the overall values of works of art are to be compared, it will apparently have to be done on the basis of the values of the particular, multiple properties of works of art.[4] To simplify matters, I will consider only aesthetic properties. There are some *standard* aesthetic properties that all works have—for example, unity and complexity. All works can, therefore, be compared with regard to unity and complexity. Suppose that works *A* and *B* have only the valuable (aesthetic) properties of unity and complexity and that work A is more unified and more complex than B. In this case, it is possible to see that the overall value of *A* is greater than the overall value of *B*. Suppose, however, that works *X* and *Y* have only the aesthetic properties of unity and complexity and that work *X* is more unified than *Y* but that *Y* is more complex than *X*, then it is impossible to say which work has the greater overall value. So, even in the cases in which two works have the same two (or more) valuable properties and only those properties, it is sometimes possible but not generally possible to compare overall values. Of course, in the great bulk of cases, pairs of works do not share their valuable properties. Suppose work *M* is unified, complex, elegance, and somber and work *N* is unified, complex, comic, and fast-paced; it will not be possible to compare the overall values of these two works—it will be a apples-and-oranges situation. Thus, in the great majority of the cases, it will not be possible to compare the overall values of works of art.

In those cases in which comparisons of overall value can be made, such a comparison can be illustrated with the following comparison matrix for the case of works *A* and *B* discussed above. In this particular case, there were only two valuable properties—unity and complexity. Assume a scale of 1 to 3 in which 3 represents the greatest possible unity or complexity possible. Assume that work A has a unity ranking of 3 and a complexity ranking of 2 and that work B has a unity ranking of 2 and a complexity ranking of 2. The following comparison matrix can be constructed.

$$(U3,C3)$$
$$(U3,C2)—(U2,C3)$$
$$(U2,C2)$$
$$(U2,C1)—(U1,C2)$$
$$(U1,C1)$$

Work B falls exactly in the middle of the comparison matrix and work A falls in the line above it to the left, which illustrates that work *A* is better overall than *B*. (This matrix represents all possible works that have just the valuable properties of unity and complexity when a 1-to-3 scale is used. Thus, some positions in the matrix may not represent actual works of art but only possible ones.)

How are ranking scales and positions for matrices arrived at? Focus on three works of art: *A* is more unified than *B* and *B* is more unified than *C*. To rank these three works with regard to unity a scale of 1 to 3 is required. If a fourth work is examined and discovered to be equal in unity with one of the first three, then a scale of 1 to 3 will still suffice. If a fourth work is examined and discovered to have greater unity than any of the first three, then a scale of 1 to 4 will be required. The scale to be used for a given property will depend on the number of distinctions that can be discovered in works of art for that property.

I move on now to the topic of the specific evaluations of works of art. If all works of art do not produce a particular kind of valuable experience so that there are strong principles, that is, principles with strong predicates such as "good," how is it possible to arrive at specific evaluations of works of art such as "This work is good"? Again, first consider how this is done, according to Beardsley's theory. On this view, every work of art has the capacity to produce an aesthetic experience of some magnitude. For purposes of illustration, I will use a magnitude scale of 1 through 5, with 5 being the greatest possible capacity. Thus, every work will fall somewhere on the following scale.

5

4

3

2

1

The scale serves as an evaluational *matrix* for every work when a pair of asterisks is placed on each side of the value ranking a particular work has. According to Beardsley, a good work of art is one that can produce an aesthetic experience of fairly great magnitude, which, I judge, would be a work that would fall at about the 4 point on the scale. Thus, for Beardsley's theory, an evaluational matrix for a particular good work would look like this.

5

★4★

3

2

1

Of course, the evaluation matrix for Beardsley's theory, with its dependence on the capacity to produce aesthetic experience, cannot be used. Can there be evaluational matrices for works of art with multiple valuable properties that are valued independently of one another according to their capacities to produce valuable experiences?

I think the answer is "Yes." but the matrices will have to be much more limited that the matrix for Beardsley's theory. For Beardsley, there is a single matrix into which any work can be placed because of its capacity (shared by all works) to do a *single* thing. When, however, works of art are viewed as things with multiple valuable properties, the evaluational matrices will be more complicated. And when those properties are not shared by all works, there will have to be many, many matrices. For all practical purposes, each actual work of art will have to have its own evaluational matrix that will consist of all actual and possible works with which it shares valuable properties and with which it can be compared.

Let me illustrate how this would work for a work of art with three valuable properties *A*, *B*, and *C* each of which has a scale of 1 to 3. Assume the work has the following ranking values: *A*1, *B*2, and *C*3. To simplify, I will omit the letters and represent the assumed work as (1,2,3). I will identify the assumed work in the matrix by placing asterisks on each side of its representation. I will call the work whose matrix this is "the base work." The matrix goes as follows.

$$(3,3,3)$$
$$(3,2,3)—(2,3,3)$$
$$(2,2,3)—(1,3,3)$$
$$\star(1,2,3)\star$$
$$(1,2,2)—(1,1,3)$$
$$(1,2,1)—(1,1,2,)$$
$$(1,1,1)$$

First, the pairs of works in the matrix that are separated by a dash are not comparable to one another. Not every possible work with these three properties appears in the matrix because some, for example, (3,3,2), is not comparable to the base work. All the actual or possible works in the matrix are comparable to the base work. (Remember that the numbers in the matrices are ranking numbers.)

To say that a work of art is excellent would be to say that it falls at the top or very close to the top of its matrix. To say that a work of art is good would be to say that it falls near the top but not at the top and so on with all the other specific evaluations that we make of works of art. Such specific evaluations do not purport to say as much as specific evaluations in Beardsley's theory. His theory attempted to show how works could be judged good, excellent, and the like with regard to all works of art. The evaluational matrices I have worked out show only what can be judged good, excellent, and the like with regard to all the actual and possible works of art to which the work judged can be compared, that is, those that share the valuable properties of the work.

In talking about evaluational matrices, I have talked as if the valuable properties of works of art are completely independent and never interact, but they do sometimes interact. The question is how can a case in which interaction occurs be represented so that it can go into a evaluational matrix? To go into a matrix a work's valuable properties have to be represented in the form such as (*A*3,*B*2,*C*1), but if *A* and *B* interact positively it looks as if the representation would have to be (*A*3 interacts positively with *B*2,*C*1) and this representation will not go into a matrix. The problem can be resolved by representing the value that results from *A* and B interacting positively as AB and representing the valuable properties as (*A*3,*B*2,*A*B2,*C*1). This representation cannot go into a matrix with (*A*3,*B*2,*C*1) for obvious reasons, but that is no problem because any representation of a work's valuable properties generates its own evaluational matrix.

I do not claim that when critics reason and make specific evaluation judgments about works of art that they have actual evaluational matrices in mind. But critics do evaluate particular aspects of works and compare works with shared valuable properties and thus, I think, approximate in an informal way what would go on with formal matrices. My account is a tidier and idealized philosopher's version of what actually goes on in criticism.[5]

Concluding Remarks

In this chapter, I first discussed five views that I call "traditional" theories of evaluation: personal subjectivism, intuitionism, emotivism, relativism, and critical singularism. These theories are organized around the question of the definiton of basic evaluational terms in that each gives a positive or negative answer to the question of whether such terms can be defined.

However, I regard the instrumentalist approach to art evaluation as more promising than any of the traditional theories. Instrumentalist theories make no attempt to define basic evaluational terms and rely on the notion of instrumental goodness, a notion understood and accepted by everyone. I discussed three instrumentalist theories: Beardsley's, Goodman's, and my own view. What the three instrumentalist theories have in common is that they all claim that works of art are instrumentally valuable because of the valuable experiences they can produce. The three theories differ in their accounts of the nature of the valuable experiences. Beardsley claims the valuable experience is a detached aesthetic experience. Goodman claims the valuable experience is of a cognitive nature and is not detached. I claim that the valuable experience is not detached and is more complicated than Beardsley and Goodman conceive it to be. In the case of Beardsley and myself, we also differ over the kind of value the valuable experiences themselves have; Goodman is not explicit about the kind of value the experiences have.

I have also focused throughout Part IV on the question of whether principles and reasons play a role in the various theories. Beardsley's theory is particularly useful because it is so completely worked out that it illustrates all the elements of an instrumentalist, evaluational theory. The roles of principles and reasons is plainly illustrated in Beardsley's theory and thus provides a clear guide for thinking about this topic. In this final chapter, I attempt a kind of synthesis of Beardsley's and Goodman's theories that I supplement by introducing as necessary the notion of the intrinsic valuing of some experiences of art and the notion of weak principles as the only kind of evaluational principles possible. Because I claim that weak principles are the only ones available for the evaluation of art, I also introduce a new way for trying to account for how overall evaluations of artworks are arrived at.

Epilogue

In Parts I, II, and IV, I have tried to relate the odyssey of the central and organizing notions of aesthetics and the changes and displacements they have undergone from ancient Greek times to the present. In their Greek beginning, the central notions were the theory of beauty and the imitation theory of art. In this story, I have identified six instances of revolutionary change in which these two central notions have been transformed or at least radically altered. One such change occurred in the eighteenth century, two took place in the nineteenth century, and three have occurred in the twentieth century.

The theory of beauty began as an objective theory, that is, one in which beauty was held to exist independently of human subjects. This objective theory in one form or another was the dominant view for more than two thousand years. In the eighteenth century, theories of taste seized center stage. With the advent of these theories, taste, a characteristic of human subjects, displaced objective beauty as the theoretical central notion, and beauty became one of many notions such as sublimity, novelty, and the like that were subsumed under the subjective notion of taste. With this new focus on human faculties, aesthetics took a subjective turn. Theories of taste were, however, objective to an extent because each one specified some feature or features of the objective world that supposedly trigger the faculty of taste. Hutcheson, for example, specified uniformity in variety as the relevant feature of the world. Of course, although the older, objective theory of beauty was displaced from the center of theoretical attention, it has continued to exist as is evidenced by the discussion of intuitionism in Part IV.

The second revolution of my story took place in the nineteenth century. At this time, aesthetics took an even more subjective turn when the notion of taste was replaced by the notion of the aesthetic attitude. Aesthetic-attitude theories focus entirely on the human subject by making aesthetic consciousness, psychical distance, disinterested attention, or the like do all the theoretical work with no aspect of the objective world determining anything.

The third revolution of my story also took place in the nineteenth century. This was the expression theory's replacement of the imitation theory of art, which had remained supreme in its almost subliminal way for over two thousand years. Once the imitation theory had been challenged, the production of philosophies of art became a fairly active endeavor.

The fourth revolution of my story took place in the twentieth century. The theory of beauty was from the beginning a theory for the evaluation of art, and it set the question for all subsequent evaluational theories in its line of descent, namely, "Can beauty (or the basic evaluational term otherwise conceived) be defined?" This fourth revolution began in the late 1950s with Monroe Beardsley's rejection of the traditional request for a definition of a basic evaluational term in favor of an evaluational theory that placed instrumental value at the heart of the theory of art evaluation. It is, by the way, worth noting that eighteenth-century theories of taste in conceiving of certain features of the world as productive of pleasure to a degree anticipate Beardsley's instrumentalism.

The fifth and sixth revolutions are also twentieth-century affairs and are related in that both depend on the abandonment of concepts of individual psychology in favor of the use of cultural concepts. The fifth revolution occurred in the theory of the proper experience of art, which has its roots in the line of theories that runs from the theory of beauty to theories of taste to aesthetic-attitude theories. Theories of taste and aesthetic-attitude theories had been developed using concepts of individual psychology (aesthetic consciousness, psychical distance, and the like) and in the 1960s several philosophers challenged these theories and began trying to substitute theories that characterized the proper experience of art in terms of cultural conventions, rules, and roles.

The sixth revolution occurred in the philosophy of art. The expression theory and all the theories of art of the first half of the twentieth century were developed in terms of concepts of individual psychology, and in the 1960s several philosophers challenged the traditional theories and began developing accounts that characterize the nature of art in terms of cultural phenomena—art theories, institutions, and the like. All the three twentieth-century revolutions are ongoing affairs. No doubt there are revolutions yet to come.

Notes

Chapter 1

1. See I. A. Richards, *Practical Criticism* (New York: Harcourt Brace, 1929), *The Philosophy of Rhetoric* (New York: Oxford University Press, 1965), *Principles of Literary Criticism* (New York: Harcourt Brace, 1950), pp. 298ff.; William Empson, *Seven Types of Ambiguity* (New York: Meridian Books, 1955): Cleanth Brooks, *The Well Wrought Urn* (New York: Harcourt Brace, 1947); and Rene Welleck and Austin Warren, *The Theory of Literature* (New York: Harcourt Brace, 1949).

2. Jerome Stolnitz, *Aesthetics and the Philosophy of Art Criticism* (Boston: Houghton Mifflin, 1960).

3. Monroe Beardsley, *Aesthetics: Problems in the Philosophy of Criticism* (New York: Harcourt Brace, 1958).

4. See Joseph Margolis, "Aesthetic Perception," *The Journal of Aesthetics and Art Criticism* (1960), pp. 209–13, reprinted in Margolis, *The Language of Art and Art Criticism* (Detroit, Wayne State University Press, 1965), pp. 23–33; and George Dickie, "The Myth of the Aesthetic Attitude," *American Philosophical Quarterly* (1964), pp. 56–65, reprinted in John Hospers, ed., *Introductory Readings in Aesthetics* (New York: Free Press, 1969), pp. 28–44.

5. Monroe Beardsley, *Aesthetics from Classical Greece to the Present* (New York: Macmillan, 1966).

6. Jerome Stolnitz, "On the Significance of Lord Shaftesbury in Modern Aesthetic Theory," *The Philosophical Quarterly* (1961), pp. 97.

7. Stolnitz, "Beauty: Some Stages in the History of an Idea," *Journal of the History of Ideas* (1961), pp. 185–204.

8. Stolnitz, "On the Origins of 'Aesthetic Disinterestedness,'" *The Journal of Aesthetics and Art Criticism* (1961), pp. 131–143.

9. Walter J. Hipple, Jr., *The Beautiful, the Sublime, and the Picturesque in Eighteenth-Century British Aesthetic Theory* (Carbondale: Southern Illinois Univeristy Press, 1957).

10. George Dickie, *The Century of Taste: The Philosophical Odessey of Taste in the Eighteenth Century* (New York: Oxford University Press, 1996). See also my "Taste and Attitude: The Origin of the Aesthetic," *Theoria* (1973), pp. 153–170; Chapter 2 of *Art and the Aesthetic*, (Ithaca, N.Y.: Cornell University Press, 1974), pp. 53–77; "Hume's Way: The Path Not Taken," in *The Reasons of Art* (1985), (ed.) Peter J. McCormick, (Ottawa: University of Ottowa Press), pp. 309–314; and "Kant, Mothersill, and Principles of Taste," *The Journal of Aesthetics and Art Criticism* (1989), pp. 375–376.

Chapter 2

1. Plato, *Symposium*, trans. W. Hamilton (Baltimore: Penguin Books, 1951).

2. Plato, *Philibus and Epinomis*, trans. A. E. Taylor (London: Nelson, 1956).

3. Thomas Aquinas, *Basic Writing of St. Thomas Aquinas*, vol. I, ed. Anton C. Pegis (New York: Random House, 1945), p. 46 and elsewhere.

4. Alexander Baumgarten, *Reflections of Poetry* (1735).

5. Shaftesbury, *Characteristics of Men, Manners, Opinions, Times*, vol. II, J. M. Robertson, ed. (Indianapolis: Bobbs-Merrill, 1964), p. 126.

6. Shaftesbury, *op. cit,*, pp. 127–28.

7. Francis Hutcheson, *An Inquiry into to Original of Our Ideas of Beauty and Virtue*, 2nd ed. (London: 1726), p. 7.

8. *Ibid.*, p. 11.

9. Edmund Burke, *A Philosophical Enquiry into the Origins of Our Ideas of the Sublime and Beautiful*, 6th ed. (London: 1770).

10. *Ibid.*, p. 162.

11. *Loc. cit.*

12. Burke, *op. cit.* p. 163.

13. David Hume, "Of the Standard of Taste," in *Essays, Literary, Moral, and Political* (London: 1870), pp. 134–49.

14. *Ibid.*, p. 136.

15. *Ibid.*, p. 137.

16. *Ibid.*, p, 138.

17. *Ibid.*, p. 139.

18. *Ibid.*, p. 146.

19. Archibald Alison, *Essays on the Nature and Principles of Taste* selections reprinted in Alexander Sesonske, ed., *What is Art?* (New York: Oxford U. P., 1965), pp. 182–195.

20. *Ibid.*, p. 182.

21. *Ibid.*, p. 185.

22. Kant's most complete statement of his philosophy of taste is set forth in his *Critique of*

Judgment trans. Werner S. Pluhar, (Indianapolis: Hackett Publishers Company: 1987). This work is the basis of my account of Kant's aesthetics.

23. Immanuel Kant, *Critique of Pure Reason,* trans. N. K. Smith (New York: St. Martin's, 1965).

24. *Critique of Judgment, op. cit.,* p. 334.

25. Arthur Schopenhauer, *The World as Will and Idea* (London: Routledge and Kegan Paul, 1883), pp. 270–71.

26. Arthur Schopenhauer, *The World as Will and Representation,* trans. E. F. J. Payne (New York: Dover 1966), vol. I, p. 176.

27. *Ibid.,* p. 178.

28. *Ibid.,* p. 178.

29. *Ibid.,* vol. II, p. 369.

30. *Loc. cit.*

31. *Ibid.,* p. 370.

32. *Ibid.*

Chapter 3

1. Edward Bullough, "'Psychical Distance' as a Factor in Art and an Aesthetic Principle," reprinted in M. Levich, ed., *Aesthetics and the Philosophy of Criticism* (New York: Random House, 1963), pp. 233–254.

2. Jerome Stolnitz, *Aesthetics and Philosophy of Art Criticism* (Boston: Houghton Mifflin, 1960).

3. Eliseo Vivas, "A Definition of Esthetic Experience," *Journal of Philosophy* (1937), pp. 628–634, reprinted in E. Vivas and M. Krieger, eds., *The Problems of Aesthetics* (New York: Rinehart, 1953), pp. 406–411; Vivas, "Contextualism Reconsidered," *The Journal of Aesthetics and Art Criticism* (1959), pp. 222–240.

4. Virgil Aldrich, *Philosophy of Art* (Englewood Cliffs, N.J.: Prentice Hall, 1963), pp. 19–27.

5. For examples of theories similar to the attitude theories, see J. O. Urmson, "What Makes a Situation Aesthetic?" *Proc. of the Aristotelian Society,* sup. vol. (1957), pp. 75–92, reprinted in J. Margolis, ed., *Philosophy Looks at the Arts* (New York: Scribner's, 1962), pp. 13–27; and V. Tomas, "Aesthetic Vision," *The Philosophical Review* (1959), pp. 52–67.

6. Monroe Beardsley, *Aesthetics* (New York: Harcourt Brace, 1958), pp. 15–65.

7. Bullough, in Levich, *op. cit.,* p. 235.

8. Sheila Dawson, "'Distancing' as an Aesthetic Principle," *Australasian Journal of Philosophy* (1961), pp. 155–74.

9. Suzanne Langer, *Feeling and Form* (New York: Scribner's, 1953).

10. Dawson, *op. cit.,* p. 168.

11. Langer, *op. cit.,* p. 318.

12. Stolnitz, *op. cit.,* pp. 34–35.

13. Vivas, "Contextualism Reconsidered," *op. cit.,* p. 237.

14. Aldrich, *op. cit.,* p. 22.

15. *Loc. cit.*

16. Virgil Aldrich, "Back to Aesthetic Experience," *The Journal of Aesthetics and Art Criticism* (1966), pp. 368–69.

Chapter 4

1. For a similar argument see Joseph Margolis's review of Beardsley's *Aesthetics* in *The Journal of Aesthetics and Art Criticism* (1959), p. 267.
2. For a more detailed account of the notion of aesthetic object, see my "Art Narrowly and Broadly Speaking," *American Philosophical Quarterly* (1968), pp. 71–77; See also my *Art and the Aesthetic* (Ithaca, N.Y.: Cornell University Press, 1974), pp. 147–81.

Chapter 5

1. Plato, *The Republic of Plato*, trans. F. M. Cornford (New York: Oxford Univeristy Press, 1945), pp. 325ff.
2. Plato, *Ion,* trans. W. R. M. Lamb (London: Loeb Library, 1925).
3. Plato, *Phaedrus*, trans. R. Hackforth (Cambridge: Cambridge University Press, 1952), p. 172.
4. Aristotle, *On Poetry and Style*, trans. G. M. A. Grube (Indianapolis: Bobbs-Merrill, 1958).
5. *Ibid.*, p. 12.
6. See Grube's discussion of catharsis, *ibid.*, pp. xiv–xvii.
7. Friedrich Nietzsche, *The Will to Power*, vol. 11, trans. O. Levy (London: 1910), p. 256.
8. Eugène Véron, *Aesthetics*, trans. W. H. Armstrong (London: 1879), p. 89.
9. Alexander Smith, "The Philosophy of Poetry," reprinted in Sesonske, *op. cit.*, p. 366.
10. Leo Tolstoy, *What Is Art* (Indianapolis: Bobbs-Merrill, 1960), p. 51.

Chapter 6

1. Clive Bell, *Art* (New York: Capricorn Books, 1958).
2. G. E. Moore, *Principia Ethica* (Cambridge: Cambridge University Press, 1903), Chapter I.
3. *Ibid.*, p. xiii.
4. Bell, *op. cit.*, pp. 16–17.
5. *Ibid.*, p. 17.
6. *Ibid.*, pp. 17–18.
7. *Ibid.*, p. 147.
8. *Ibid.*, p. 20.
9. *Ibid.*, p. 27.
10. Susanne Langer, *Philosophy in a New Key* (New York: New American Library, 1948).
11. Langer, *Feeling and Form* (New York: Scribner's, 1953).
12 Langer, *Problems of Art* (New York: Scribner's, 1957).
13. Langer, *Feeling and Form*, p. 40.
14. Langer, *Problems of Art*, pp. 124–39.
15. Langer, *Feeling and Form*, p. 27.
16. *Ibid.*, pp. 94–95.
17. *Ibid.*, p. xi.
18. *Ibid.*, p. 49.
19. Langer, *Problems of Art*, p. 125.
20. *Ibid.* p. 133.
21. See especially Ernest Nagel's review of *Philosophy in a New Key, Journal of Philosophy* (1943), pp. 323–29.

22. Langer, *Problems of Art*, p. 126.

23. Monroe Beardsley, *Aesthetics* (New York: Harcourt Brace, 1958), p. 336.

24. Langer, *Feeling and Form*, p. 72.

25. *Webster's New Collegiate Dictionary*, 2nd ed. (Springfield, Mass.: 1953).

26. Langer, *Problems of Art*, p. 133.

27. R. G. Collingwood, *The Principles of Art* (New York: Oxford University Press, 1958).

28. *Ibid.*, p. 78.

29. *Ibid.*, p. 278.

30. *Ibid.*, p. 72.

31. *Ibid.*, p. 79.

32. *Ibid.*, p. 108.

33. *Ibid.*, p. 109.

34. *Ibid.*, p. 235.

35. *Ibid.*, p. 229.

36. *Ibid.*, p. 235.

37. *Ibid.*, p. 273.

38. *Ibid.*, pp. 109–110.

39. *Ibid.*, p. 116.

40. *Ibid.*, p. 103.

41. *Ibid.*, p. 118.

42. *Ibid.*, p. 273.

43. Alan Donagan, *The Later Philosophy of R. G. Collingwood* (Oxford: Clarendon, 1962), pp. 116ff.

44. This point about the expression in the expression of emotion not being in the mind is due to Syed Salman Lateef who was a member of my introductory aesthetic class in the fall semester of 1994.

45. Collingwood, *op. cit.*, p. 280.

46. *Webster's New Collegiate Dictionary*.

47. Collingwood, *op. cit.*, p. 282.

48. *Ibid.*, p. 264.

49. *Ibid.*, p. 336.

50. Morris Weitz, "The Role of Theory in Aesthetics," reprinted in Francis Coleman, ed., *Contemporary Studies in Aesthetics* (New York: McGraw-Hill, 1968), pp. 84–94.

51. *Ibid.*, p. 90.

52. *Loc. cit.*

Chapter 7

1. Marshall Cohen, "Aesthetic Essence," *Philosophy in America*, M. Black, ed., (Ithaca: Cornell University Press, 1965), pp.115–133; George Dickie, "Is Psychology Relevant to Aesthetics?" *The Philosophical Review*, (1962), pp. 285–302; George Dickie, "The Myth of the Aesthetic Attitude," *American Philosophical Quarterly* (1964), pp. 56–65.

2. Arthur Danto, "The Artworld," *Journal of Philosophy* (1964), pp. 571–84; Maurice Mandelbaum, "Family Resemblances and Generalization Concerning the Arts," *American Philosophical Quarterly* (1965), pp. 219–28.

3. Maurice Mandelbaum, *op. cit.* (1965), p. 221.

4. *Ibid.*, p. 222.

5. Arthur Danto, "The Artworld," *Journal of Philosophy* (1964), pp. 571–84; "Artworks and Real Things," *Theoria* (1973), pp. 1–17; "The Transfiguration of the Commonplace, *The Journal of Aesthetics and Art Criticism* (1974), pp.139–48.

6. Arthur Danto, *The Transfiguration of the Commonplace* (Cambridge, Mass.: Harvard University Press, 1981), p. 212.

7. "The Artworld," p. 580.

Chapter 8

1. George Dickie, "Defining Art," *The American Philosophical Quarterly* (1969), pp. 253–56.

2. George Dickie, *Art and the Aesthetic* (Ithaca, N.Y.: Cornell University Press, 1974), p.204.

3. George Dickie, *The Art Circle* (New York: Haven Publications,1984), p. 116.

4. *Art and the Aesthetic*, p. 34.

5. "Is Art Essentially Institutional?," in: *Culture and Art*, Lars Aagaard-Mogensen, ed. (Atlantic Highlands, N. J.: Humanities Press, 1976), p. 202.

6. *The Art Circle*, pp. 80–82.

7. Jerrold Levinson, "Defining Art Historically," *The British Journal of Aesthetics*, 19 (1979), pp. 232–50; and "Extending Art Historically," *The Journal of Aesthetics and Art Criticism*, 51 (1993), pp. 421–22.

8. Noel Carroll, "Art, Practice, and Narrative," *The Monist*, 71 (1988), pp. 140–56; "Historical Narratives and the Philosophy of Art," *The Journal of Aesthetics and Art Criticism*, 51 (1993), pp. 313–26; and "Identifying Art" in *Institutions of Art* ed. Robert J. Yanal, (University Park, Pa.: The Pennsylvania State University Press, 1994), pp. 3–38.

9. Stephen Davies, *Definitions of Art* (Ithaca, N.Y.: Cornell University Press, 1991), p. 243.

Chapter 9

1. For specific examples of intentionalist criticism, see W. K. Wimsatt and Monroe Beardsley, "The Intentional Fallacy," *Sewanee Review* (1946), pp. 468–488 and widely reprinted; and Monroe Beardsley, *Aesthetics* (New York: Harcourt Brace, 1958), pp. 17–29. See also Beardsley, "Textual Meaning and Authorial Meaning," *Genre* (1968), pp. 169–81. For an earlier version of the account presented in this section see my "Meaning and Intention," *Genre* (1968), pp. 182–89. For a defense of intentionalist criticism see E. D. Hirsch, Jr., *Validity in Interpretation* (New Haven: Yale University Press, 1967).

2. Beardsley, *Aesthetics*, p. 458.

3. E. D. Hirsch, *Validity in Interpretation* (New Haven: Yale University Press, 1967), p. 99.

4. Paul Grice has over a period of years presented a sophisticated, intentionalist theory of meaning. For an attempted refutation of Grice's view see George Dickie and W. Kent Wilson, "Defending Beardsley," *The Journal of Aesthetics and Art Criticism* (1995), pp. 233–50.

Chapter 10

1. My account of symbolism in art draws on Beardsley, *Aesthetics*, pp. 288–293; Isabel Hungerland, "Symbols in Poetry," reprinted in W. E. Kennick, ed., *Art and Philosophy* (New York: St. Martin's, 1964), pp. 425–48; and Gören Hermerén, *Representation and Meaning in the Visual Arts* (Lund: Berlingska, Boktryckeriet, 1969).
2. Hermerén, *op. cit.*, p. 98.
3. Hungerland, *op. cit.*, p. 427.
4. Hungerland, *op. cit.,* p. 426.
5. Beardsley, *Aesthetics*, p. 408.

Chapter 11

1. My account of metaphor draws on Monroe Beardsley, "The Metaphorical Twist," *Philosophy and Phenomenological Research* (1962), pp. 293–307; and Max Black, "Metaphor," *Proc. of the Aristotelian Society* (1954–55), pp. 273–94. Black's article has been reprinted in J. Margolis, ed., *Philosophy Looks at the Arts* (New York: Scribner's, 1962), pp. 218–35.
2. The first three on the list are used as examples by Black, in Margolis, *op. cit.*, p. 219.
3. The fourth example of metaphor is used by Beardsley, in "The Metaphorical Twist," p. 294.
4. For a discussion of these theories see Beardsley, *Aesthetics*, pp. 134–36.
5. Black, in Margolis, *op. cit.*, p. 226.
6. Beardsley, "The Metaphorical Twist," p. 293.
7. *Ibid.*, p. 294.
8. *Ibid.*, pp. 298ff. I have altered Beardsley's argument somewhat by making the significance of the referential aspect of language more explicit and by relating literalness to dictionary senses.
9. Black, in Margolis, *op. cit.*, pp. 229ff.

Chapter 12

1. The analysis of expression given here leans heavily on the following: Vincent Tomas, "The Concept of Expression in Art," reprinted in Margolis, *op. cit.*, pp. 30–45; John Hospers, "The Concept of Aesthetic Expression," *Proc. of the Aristotelian Society* (1954 55), pp. 313–44; and Monroe Beardsley, *Aesthetics*, pp. 325–32. See also Alan Tormey, *The Concept of Expression* (Princeton, N.J.: Princeton University Press, 1971).

Chapter 13

1. For examples, see C. J. Ducasse, *The Philosophy of Art* (New York: Dial, 1929), Chapters 14 and 15; and George Boas, *A Primer of Critics* (Baltimore: Johns Hopkins University Press, 1937), Chapters I and 3.
2. G. E. Moore, *Principia Ethica* (Cambridge: Cambridge University Press, 1903), Chapter 1.
3. For examples of intuitionist theories, see C. E. M. Joad, *Matter, Life and Value* (London: Oxford University Press, 1929), pp. 266–83, in part reprinted in E. Vivas and M.

Krieger, eds., *Problems of Aesthetics* (New York: Rinehart, 1953), pp. 463–79; Harold Osborne, *Theory of Beauty* (London: Routledge and Kegan Paul, 1952) and T. E. Jessop, "The Definition 0f Beauty," *Prof. of the Aristotelian Society* (1933), pp. 159–72.

4. A. J. Ayer, *Language, Truth, and Logic* (New York: Dover, 1946), pp. 102–14.

5. C. L. Stevenson, *Ethics and Language* (New Haven: Yale University Press, 1944).

6. R. M. Hare, *The Language of Morals* (New York: Oxford University Press, 1964), and *Freedom and Reason* (Oxford: Clarendon, 1963).

7. Bernard Heyl, *New Bearings in Esthetics and Art Criticism* (New Haven: Yale University Press, 1943).

8. For examples, see Arnold Isenberg, "Critical Communication," reprinted in W. Elton, ed., *Aesthetics and Language* (New York: Philosophical Library, 1954), pp. 131–46; and Stuart Hampshire, "Logic and Appreciation," reprinted in Elton, pp. 161–69.

Chapter 14

1. The view set forth here as Beardsley's is actually a composite of the position developed in his book, *Aesthetics* (New York: Harcourt Brace, 1958), pp. 454–89, and the position developed in his later article, "On the Generality of Critical Reasons," *Journal of Philosophy* (1962), pp. 477–486, also in the Bobbs-Merrill Reprint Series in Philosophy. Where the two positions differ, the later article's line is followed.

2. In private correspondence, Beardsley expressed misgivings about a strict deductive interpretation of his view. In this correspondence he was inclined to think that the relationship between reasons and evaluations is somewhat looser than a deductive one. The reader is thus warned that Beardsley did not endorse all aspects of the view that I am here calling "Beardsley's theory." The deductive interpretation of Beardsley's theory is based on his article, "On the Generality of Critical Reasons"; the earlier account of evaluation he gave in his book was not deductive in nature.

3. Beardsley, "On the Generality of Critical Reasons," p. 485.

4. Obviously the critic's remarks at this point could and ought to be greatly expanded. For a detailed discussion of this and many other of Cezanne's paintings, see Erle Loran, *Cezanne's Composition* (Berkeley: University of California Press, 1963).

5. The account of Beardsley's theory of aesthetic experience given here is the one he set forth in his 1958 book. He altered his account in various ways in his later writings but not in any way important to my treatment of his views. In my account of Beardsley's theory of evaluation, I sometimes make explicit aspects implied by his theory of which he was not aware.

6. Beardsley, *Aesthetics*, p. 528.

7. *Loc. cit.*

8. Beardsley, *Aesthetics*, p. 529.

9. See my "Beardsley's Phantom Aesthetic Experience," *Journal of Philosophy* (1965), pp.129–36, for a criticism of Beardsley's notion of a unity of experience. See Beardsley's reply, "Aesthetic Experience Regained," *The Journal of Aesthetics and Art Criticism* (1969), pp. 3–11.

10. Beardsley, *Aesthetics*, p. 530.

11. From time to time attempts are made to ban this great novel in some way because some of its language is deemed offensive. Such attempts, I believe, are based on a misunderstanding.

Chapter 15

1. Nelson Goodman, *Languages of Art* (Bobbs-Merrill, 1968), pp. 255–65. See also Nelson Goodman, "When Is Art?" in *Ways of Worldmaking* (Hacket Publishing Company, 1978), pp. 57–70.

2. *Op. Cit.*, *Languages of Art*, pp. 255–65.

Chapter 16

1. The formulation of this principle and other principles with an isolation clause is in part due to Frank Sibley's "General Criteria and Reasons in Aesthetic." in *Essays on Aesthetics: Perspectives on the Work of Monroe Beardsley,* ed. John Fisher, (Philadephia: Temple University Press, 1983), pp. 3–20.

2. The wording of the principles involving cognitive properties is in large part due to Nicholas Wolterstorff's *Art in Action* (Grand Rapids, Mich.: William B. Eerdmans Publishing Co., 1980), p. 159.

3. David Hume, "Of the Standard of Taste," reprinted in *Aesthetics: A Critical Anthology*, eds. George Dickie and Richard Sclafani (New York: St. Martin's Press, 1977), pp. 592–606.

4. Many of the ideas involved in my discussion of the overall evaluational of works of art derive from Bruce Vermazen's "Comparing Evaluations of Works of Art," reprinted in *Art and Philosphy*, 2nd ed; ed. W. E. Kennick (New York: St. Martin's Press, 1979), pp. 707–18.

5. For a more extensive account of my views on the evaluation of art, see my *Evaluating Art* (Philadelphia: Temple University Press, 1988).

Bibliography

Primary Sources

Aldrich, Virgil. *Philosophy of Art*. Englewood Cliffs, N. J.: Prentice Hall, 1963.

Beardsley, Monroe. *Aesthetics*. New York: Harcourt Brace, 1958. See the magnificent anno-
tated bibliography in this book.

———. *Aesthetics from Classical Greece to the Present*. New York: Macmillan, 1966.

———. *The Possibility of Criticism*. Detroit: Wayne State University Press, 1970.

Bell, Clive. *Art*. New York: Capricorn Books, 1958.

Collingwood, R. G. *The Principles of Art*. New York: Oxford University Press, 1958.

Cooper, David (ed.). *A Companion to Aesthetics*. Oxford: Blackwell, 1992.

Croce, Benedetto. *Aesthetic*. Trans. Douglas Ainslie, 2nd ed. New York: Macmillan, 1922.

Davies, Stephen. *Definitions of Art*. Ithaca, N.Y.: Cornell University Press, 1991.

Danto, Arthur. *The Transfiguration of the Commonplace*. Cambridge, Mass.: Harvard University Press, 1981.

Dickie, George. *Art and the Aesthetic*. Ithaca, N.Y.: Cornell University Press, 1974.

———. *The Art Circle: A Theory of Art*. New York: Haven, 1984.

———. *The Century of Taste*. New York: Oxford University Press, 1996.

———. *Evaluating Art*. Philadelphia: Temple University Press, 1988.

Dewey, John. *Art as Experience*. New York: Minton, Balch, 1934.

Eaton, Marcia. *Aesthetics and the Good Life*. Rutherford, N. J.: Fairleigh Dickinson University Press, 1989.

———. *Art and Nonart*. Rutherford, N.J.: Fairleigh Dickinson University Press, 1983.

Guyer, Paul. *Kant and the Claims of Taste*. Cambridge, Mass.: Harvard University Press, 1979.

Hermerén, Gören. *Representation and Meaning in the Visual Arts*. Lund: Berlingska, Boktryckeriet, 1969.

Heyl, Bernard. *New Bearings in Esthetics and Art Criticism*. New Haven: Yale University Press, 1943.

Hipple, Jr., Walter J. *The Beautiful, the Sublime, and the Picturesque in Eighteenth-Century British Aesthetic Theory*. Carbondale.: Southern Illinois University Press, 1957.

Hirsch, E. D., Jr. *Validity in Interpretation*. New Haven: Yale University Press, 1967.

Hospers, John. *Meaning and Truth in the Arts*. Chapel Hill, N.C.: University of North Carolina Press, 1946.

Kant, Immanuel. *The Critique of Judgment*. Werner S. Pluhar (trans), Indianapolis: Hackett Publishing Co., 1987.

Langer, Suzanne. *Feeling and Form*. New York: Scribner's, 1953.

———. *Philosophy in a New Key*. New York: New American Library, 1948.

———. *Problems of Art*. New York: Scribner's, 1957.

Langfeld, Herbert S. *The Aesthetic Attitude*. New York: Harcourt Brace, 1920.

Margolis, Joseph. *Art and Philosophy*. Atlantic Highlands, N. J.: Humanities Press, 1980.

———. *The Language of Art and Art Criticism*. Detroit: Wayne State University Press, 1965.

Moore, G. E. *Principia Ethica*. Cambridge: Cambridge University Press, 1903.

Mothersill, Mary. *Beauty Restored*. Oxford: Oxford University Press, 1984.

Osborne, Harold. *Aesthetics and Criticism*. London: Routledge and Kegan Paul, 1955.

———. *Theory of Beauty*. London: Routledge and Kegan Paul, 1952.

Parker, DeWitt. *The Principles of Aesthetics*. 2nd ed. New York: Appleton-Century-Crofts, 1920.

———. *The Analysis of Art*. New Haven: Yale University Press, 1926.

Pepper, Stephen. *The Basis of Criticism in the Arts*. Cambridge, Mass.: Harvard University Press, 1949.

———. *The Work of Art*. Bloomington: Indiana University Press, 1955.

Prall, David W. *Aesthetic Analysis*. New York: Crowell, 1936.

———. *Aesthetic Judgment*. New York: Crowell, 1929.

Rollins, Mark (ed.). *Danto and his Critics*. Oxford: Blackwell, 1993.

Santayana, George. *The Sense of Beauty*. New York: Modern Library, 1955.

Stolnitz, Jerome. *Aesthetics and Philosophy of Art Criticism*. Boston: Houghton Mifflin, 1960.

Tilghman, Ben. *But Is It Art*. New York: Blackwell, 1984.

Tormey, Alan. *The Concept of Expression*. Princeton, N.J.: Princeton University Press, 1971.

Walton, Kendall, *Mimesis as Make-Believe*. Cambridge, Mass.: Harvard University Press, 1990.

Weitz, Morris. *Philosophy of the Arts*. Cambridge, Mass.: Harvard University Press, 1950.

Wittgenstein, Ludwig. *Philosophical Investigations*. Trans. C. E. M. Anscombe. New York: Macmillan, 1953.

Wolterstorff, Nicholas. *Art in Action*. Grand Rapids, Mich.: William B. Eerdmans Publishing Co., 1980.

———. *Works and Worlds of Art*. New York: Oxford University Press, 1980.

Yanal, Robert (ed.). *Institutions of Art: Reconsiderations of George Dickie's Philosophy*. University Park: Pennsylvania State University Press, 1994.

Anthologies

Aagaard–Mogensen, Lars, *Culture and Art.* Atlantic Highlands, N.J.: Humanities Press, 1976.

Alperson, Philip (ed.). *The Philosophy of the Visual Arts.* New York: Oxford University Press, 1992.

Aschenbrenner, K. and A. Isenberg (eds.). *Aesthetic Theories: Studies in the Philosophy of Art.* Englewood Cliffs, N.J.: Prentice-Hall, 1965.

Beardsley, M. and H. Schueller, eds. *Aesthetic Inquiry: Essays on Art Criticism and the Philosophy of Art.* Belmont, Calif.: Dickerson, 1967.

Blocker, Gene and Bender, John (eds.). *Contemporary Philosophy of Art.* Englewoods Cliffs, N.J.: Prentice Hall, 1993.

Brand, Peggy and Korsmeyer, Carolyn (eds.). *Feminism and Tradition in Aesthetics.* University Park: Pennsylvania State University Press, 1995.

Coleman, Francis (ed.). *Contemporary Studies in Aesthetics.* New York: McGraw-Hill, 1968.

Dickie, G., Sclafani, R., and Ronald Roblin (eds.). *Aesthetics: A Critical Anthology,* 2nd ed., New York: St. Martin's Press, 1989.

Elton, William (ed.). *Aesthetics and Language.* New York: Philosophical Library, 1954.

Hofstadter, A. and Richard Kuhns (eds.). *Philosophies of Art and Beauty.* New York: Modern Library, 1964.

Hospers, John (ed.). *Introductory Readings in Aesthetics.* New York: Free Press, 1969.

Kennick, W. E. (eds.). *Art and Philosophy.* 2nd ed. New York: St. Martin's, 1979.

Levich, Marvin (ed.). *Aesthetics and the Philosophy of Criticism.* New York: Random House, 1963.

Margolis, Joseph (ed.). *Philosophy Looks at the Arts.* 3rd ed. Philadephia: Temple University Press, 1987.

Philipson, Morris (ed.). *Aesthetics Today.* New York: Meridian Books, 1961.

Rader, Melvin (ed.). *A Modern Book of Esthetics,* 5th ed. New York: Holt, 1979.

Richter, Peyton (ed.). *Perspectives in Aesthetics.* New York: Odyssey, 1967.

Sesonske, Alexander, ed. *What Is Art? Aesthetic Theory from Plato to Tolstoy.* New York: Oxford University Press, 1965.

Shusterman, Richard (ed.). *Analytic Aesthetics.* New York: Blackwell, 1989.

Tillman, F. and S. Cahn (eds.). *Philosophy of Art and Aesthetics.* New York: Harper and Row, 1969.

Weitz, Morris (ed.). *Problems in Aesthetics.* New York: Macmillan, 1959.

Werhane, Patricia (ed.). *Philosophical Issues in Art.* Englewood Cliffs, N.J.: Prentice-Hall, 1984.

Index